Land's End

LAND'S END

Capitalist Relations on an Indigenous Frontier

TANIA MURRAY LI

Duke University Press Durham and London 2014

Printed in the United States of America
on acid-free paper ∞
Designed by Amy Ruth Buchanan
Typeset in Quadraat by Graphic Composition, Inc.
Cover photograph courtesy of the author.

Library of Congress Cataloging-in-Publication Data
Li, Tania, 1959–
Land's end : capitalist relations on an indigenous frontier /
Tania Murray Li.
pages cm
Includes bibliographical references and index.
ISBN 978-0-8223-5694-3 (cloth : alk. paper)
ISBN 978-0-8223-5705-6 (pbk. : alk. paper)
1. Land use, Rural—Indonesia. 2. Lauje (Indonesian
people). 3. Capitalism—Indonesia. I. Title.
HD893.L5 2014
330.9598'44—dc23
2014000757

For my mother, Anita, whose
adventurous and trusting spirit
enables and inspires.

Contents

Acknowledgments

The goal I had for this book, when I started writing it in 2006, was to help renew ethnographic engagement with the rural places that continue to be home to half the world's population. Twenty years of repeat visits to one rural place gave me intimate insights into people's lives and the dilemmas they faced during a period of far-reaching change, but finding a way to tell their story was harder than I anticipated. I relied on the help of many colleagues and students who read drafts of the manuscript as it evolved, listened to me present parts of it in lectures and seminars, and gave me copious comments and excellent advice. I haven't footnoted every idea or correction I took on board from my interlocutors, but I trust they will recognize their input. Some of them were conscripts (students from my Core Concepts in Anthropology undergraduate class in 2011), but most of them were volunteers, and I'm hugely grateful for their generosity.

Donald Moore, Gavin Smith, and Ben White helped me conceptualize the project at the outset, read several drafts, discussed it at length in person and on the phone, and gently guided me away from some serious errors. I received written comments on a complete draft from Junko Asano, Henry Bernstein, Michael Eilenberg, Gaston Gordillo, Derek Hall, Kregg Hetherington, Holly High, Esther Kuhn, Christian Lund, Jerome Rousseau, Alpa Shah, Ken Wissoker, Jeremy Withers, and graduate students who organized group discussions on the manuscript: in Zurich Irina Wenk, Esther Leeman, Eva Keller, and Danilo Geiger; in Toronto Zach Anderson, Lukas Ley, and Elizabeth Lord. Henke Schulte Nordholte and Gerry Van Klinken organized a day-long book workshop at KITLV in Leiden to give me the benefit of input from Indonesia specialists Suraya Afiff, David Henley, John McCarthy, Gerben Nooteboom, Jacqueline Vel, Adriaan Bedner, and (again) Ben White.

Paige West invited me to discuss selected chapters with an interdisciplinary group convened at Columbia around the topic of "Culture and Ecology": Richard Schroeder, David Hughes, Joshua Drew, Jenny Newell, Cindy Katz, Anne Rademacher, Ben Orlove, Charles Zerner, Katharine Pistor, Sarah Vaughn, Helene Artaud, and Ariela Zycherman. Toronto-based colleagues and students who gave me feedback on selected chapters include Joshua Barker, Ritu Birla, Frank Cody, Saul Cohen, Olga Fedorenko, Andrew Gilbert, Shubhra Gururani, Ken Kawashima, Chris Krupa, Michael Lambek, Ashley Lebner, Hy Van Luong, Carlotta McAlister, Bonnie McElhinny, Suichi Nagata, Valentina Napolitano, Jacob Nerenberg, Katharine Rankin, Shiho Satsuka, Rachel Silvey, Jesook Song, Jessica Taylor, and Zoe Wool.

Colleagues in the Challenges of Agrarian Transition in Southeast Asia research program directed by Rodolphe De Koninck shaped my thinking about re-studies and long-term field research, notably Rob Cramb, Phil Hirsch, Phil Kelly, Nancy Peluso, Jonathan Rigg, Pujo Semedi, Peter Vandergeest, Ben White, Mary Young, and the late Frans Husken. I received useful input when I presented parts of this work in lectures at the Universities of McGill, Michigan, Cambridge, Oxford, and at CIRAD in Montpellier. Louisa Jones and Bernard Dupont read the manuscript and hosted Victor and me for extended writing visits at their home in France. Louisa's commitment to writing in ways that open a text to nonacademic readers was an inspiration and a challenge.

It is a privilege to have been able to write in this dialogic way, with time to revisit, write, seek input, reflect, rethink, and revise. For extending me this opportunity, I thank my department chairs at Dalhousie and Toronto, the Canadian Social Science and Humanities Research Council, and the Canada Research Chairs Program. Colleagues who offered encouragement and provided crucial support over the years include John Clarke, Michael Dove, Gillian Hart, Robert Hefner, Nancy Peluso, James Scott, Anna Tsing, and Michael Watts. Thanks also to unnamed referees who evaluated grant proposals and gave me astute critical feedback on the early articles in which I began to develop my ideas. Thanks to the fantastically professional and supportive team at Duke University Press for putting the book together so beautifully.

The research and writing that went into this book have been part of my family life for a very long time, and I thank Victor; our children Nicholas, Simon, and Allanah; and my mother Anita for their generosity and tolerance.

Tim Babcock got me started on this project in 1990, hosted me in Jakarta, and provided sage advice. Jennifer Nourse shared her unpublished dissertation with me in 1989, giving me an early orientation to the research area. Sulaiman Mamar of Tadulako University accompanied me during my preliminary field visit and facilitated in practical ways. Lise Tonelli and Bill Duggan shared insights and provided companionship in 1991 and 1992. My late friend and Lauje interpreter, whom I call "Rina," accompanied me on long hot hikes far from her comfort zone. Sahnun, Yan, Om Dullah, and Ibrahim saved the day on numerous occasions. The willingness of Lauje villagers to open their homes and their hearts to a stranger was the foundation for everything else. Even with all this help, shortcoming and errors remain, and I take responsibility for them.

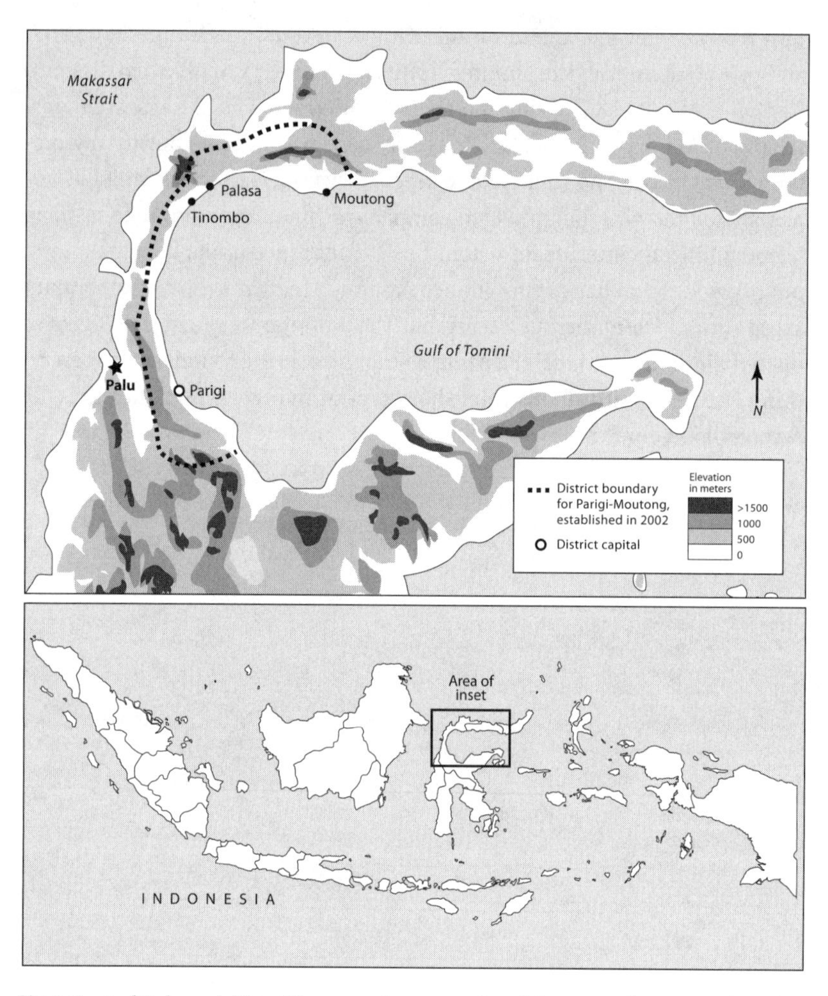

Map 1. Central Sulawesi. *Note*: The rugged topography of the research area can best be viewed on Google Earth, using the search term "Tinombo."

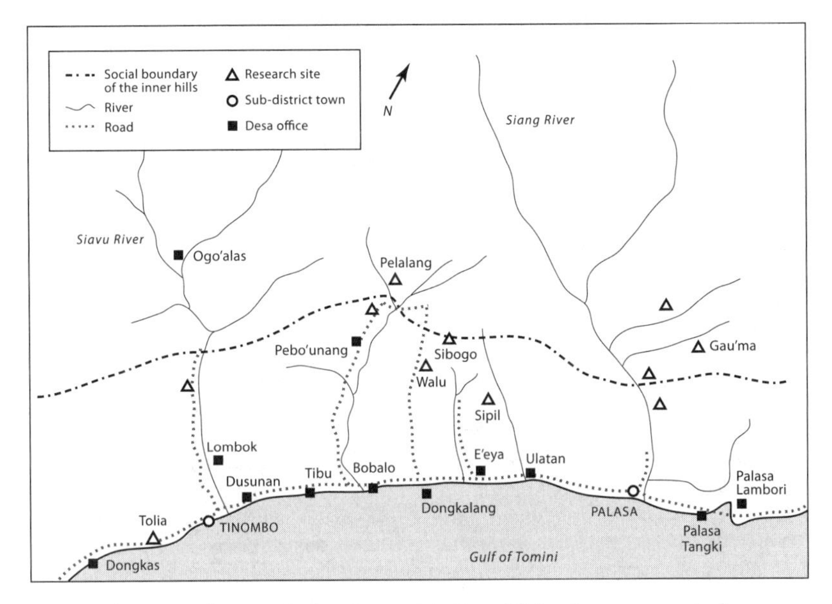

Map 2. Lauje area and research sites (ca. 2009). *Note:* Of the eleven research sites shown on the map, the six that are discussed in detail in the text have been given pseudonyms. The social boundary marks the approximate divide between the Muslim Lauje of the middle hills and Christian or animist Lauje of the inner hills.

Introduction

Kasar was the last person I stopped to visit as I hiked down from the Sulawesi highlands in 2006. He was in terrible shape. His bamboo house was rickety and in danger of collapse. The condition of his son, aged about twelve, was even more alarming. Terribly thin and visibly exhausted, the boy was moving heavy sacks of kapok, the tree crop his father had planted on the hot, dry land he previously used for tobacco. "I tried to plant cacao," Kasar said, "but this land is not good for cacao and it is the only land I have. Kapok grows OK, but the price is too low." Even if he cut down his kapok trees, he didn't have enough land to revert to food production and he couldn't borrow land for food, as he had in the past, as everyone's land was full of trees. He planted new crops with the hope of improving his family's situation, but ended up with this one barren plot.

Kasar was painfully aware that he had no way out, no way back, and no future for his children. He was also embarrassed by my visit. He knew that I had already visited some of his neighbors who had attained wealth and security in the two decades since we first met. He was in his midforties but looked much older. He was so physically worn out that he could no longer do the strenuous work of hauling rattan vines out from the forest on piece rate, his occasional source of income in previous years. Wage work locally was scarce, as the new tree crops needed little labor. I feared that the boy lifting the sacks might not survive.[1] Their house was in the foothills only about a one-hour hike from the nearest school on the coast, but unlike his father who hiked up and down to school in the 1970s the boy was so ashamed of his ragged clothing he dropped out at grade three. He spoke only the local language, Lauje (pronounced Laujay), hardly a word of Indonesian.

Land's End is about the attempt made by indigenous highlanders to join the march of progress promised in modernization narratives, only to encounter the polarizing effect of the capitalist relations that soon emerged among them. Farmers able to accumulate land and capital prospered, and those who could not compete were squeezed out. My title plays on several meanings of land's end: the changed use of land, the end of a customary system of land sharing, and the end of the primary forest that had served as highlanders' land frontier, the place in which they could expand when need or opportunity presented. It also flags their sense of bewilderment—coming to a dead end, the end of a peninsula surrounded by sea, without a raft or a sense of direction. This was the predicament of Kasar and others like him, who could no longer sustain their families on the old terms, but had no viable alternative.

Modernization theories recognize that some people lose out when agriculture intensifies and becomes more competitive, but they assume that ex-farmers will become workers who survive by selling their labor.[2] Yet jobs in the province of Central Sulawesi are hard to find. The commercial tree crops that increasingly blanket the countryside—cacao, oil palm, clove, coconut—need few workers. Alternatives are scarce: in 2009 only 5 percent of the labor force found work in mining and manufacture combined.[3] None of the highlanders in my study received remittances from family members working elsewhere. Nor did they receive regular state transfers such as pensions or child allowances.[4] In contrast to rural people in many parts of the world whose livelihoods appear to be farm-based, but are actually supported by subsidies and remittances, these highlanders were highly dependent on their own farms or wage work in the local area.[5] They had not successfully inserted themselves into migrant labor streams headed for other provinces or countries, which tend to require Indonesian-language skills and connections they didn't possess. Nor, finally, could they move off to find land somewhere else in the province because the land frontier outside their immediate area had effectively closed down as well.

The problem isn't unique. If we take a global perspective, most of the manufacturing jobs created in the 1990s were concentrated in China, which isn't much help to Kasar or the billion or so un- or underemployed people around the world who desperately need work. Even in China, where jobs are surely needed, factory owners are installing robotics.[6] Well-educated young people who aspire to urban lives and stable jobs also find themselves without work or in precarious employment. The protagonists of the Arab Spring of 2009 and Occupy Wall Street, the Spanish Indignados, and my undergraduate students in Toronto are among them. Like Kasar, they are in uncharted territory, lacking not just a means of livelihood but a sense of a future in which they will have a part.

Indonesia's impressive growth in the past few decades has been virtually jobless, a pattern repeated in India, South Africa, and elsewhere.[7] According to demographer Graeme Hugo, Indonesia is a classic "labor surplus nation" with about 20 percent of the workforce, forty-five million people, un- or underemployed.[8] Some people migrate. About four million Indonesians work abroad, but migration hardly makes a dent in the employment problem. Indeed, the attention paid to migration in recent years, in Indonesia and globally, sometimes occludes an important fact: although UN agencies announced that in 2008, half the world's population was living in cities, more than half the population of Asia and Africa continued to live and work in rural areas, and gained their livelihoods mainly from agriculture.

Even as economic growth has drawn some people out from rural areas to brighter prospects in the city, and many are pushed out from the countryside into urban slums, the total number of people living in rural areas is bigger than ever, and they will be there for decades to come. For billions of rural people, the promise that modernization would provide a pathway from country to city, and from farm to factory, has proven to be a mirage. Lacking an exit path, they stay where they are, but all too often the old set of relations that enabled them to live and work in the countryside has disappeared, and the new ones—increasingly capitalist in form—do not provide a viable livelihood.

The surprising finding of this book is that indigenous highlanders, people who are imagined by activists of the global indigenous and peasant movements to be securely attached to their land and communities, joined the ranks of people unable to sustain themselves. Surely, if anyone could continue to live in the countryside on the old terms, it should be them. More surprising still, the process that dislodged them from their land wasn't initiated by land-grabbing corporations or state agencies. There was no "primitive accumulation" of the kind Marx described, "written in the annals of mankind in letters of blood and fire."[9] The process through which they lost control over their collectively owned land was far less dramatic, even mundane. It was the highlanders themselves who took the initiative to plant tree crops, which had the effect of individualizing their land rights and led to the formation of capitalist relations in which their capacity to survive was governed by rules of competition and profit. So long as social movements don't recognize the insidious ways in which capitalist relations take hold even in unlikely places, they can't be effective in promoting alternatives that will actually work.[10] My goal in writing this book is to examine closely just what happened in these highlands and draw out the implications for politics.

For too long, important political debates have been foreclosed by transition narratives that posit an apparently natural evolution in which farming becomes more efficient and exclusive, and people whose labor is not needed on the land move into other sectors of the economy. My findings challenge notions of agrarian transition as a teleological unfolding. They also counter understandings of capitalism as a totalizing system in which—for better or worse—everyone will eventually be incorporated. While I agree that all the land and natural resources of the globe may one day be incorporated, I argue that a great many people have and will have no part to play in production organized on the basis of profit. They are not heading toward the proletarian futures transition thinking maps out for them, because no such futures are in place, nor are they on the horizon. But they can't stay as they are, or turn back to a past condition imagined to be more wholesome, as social movements promoting development "alternatives" propose. There were good reasons for the steps Kasar and his highland neighbors took to try to improve their situation, even though for many of them the result was not as they hoped. The dead end reached by Lauje highlanders circa 2000 also exposes the limits of the current repertoire of "alternatives" promoted by social movements (local, community-based, food-first, small-scale), to highlight the need for a different political response.

The analytical framework I adopt in this book focuses on the specificity of this conjuncture: the set of elements, processes, and relations that shaped people's lives at this time and place, and the political challenges that arise from that location. My analysis draws on ethnographic research that I conducted through repeated visits over a period of twenty years (1990–2009). An ethnographic approach enabled me to pay close attention to the perspectives of the highlanders themselves and follow struggles and debates as they unfolded. Revisiting offered insights that are hard to glean from one-shot research designs, whether based on surveys or ethnographic research.[11] It enabled me to track subtle shifts in everyday ways of thinking and acting before they had settled into a "new normal" that no longer seemed strange.

In 2009, the fact that some highlanders had no land at all was not something they noted with surprise, but rereading my field notes reminded me that this situation was not anticipated and indeed was unthinkable two decades before. Knowledge gained from previous visits enabled me to have searching conversations with highlanders that would not have been possible if I had arrived for the first time in 2009, asking about the past. It was not just that memories became dulled with the passage of time. Selective forgetting and remembering was integral to how the new relations were experienced, and how they were shaped.[12] Each visit also brought surprises, reminders that my study did not enable me to predict the future. By 2009 much of the cacao—the crop that stimulated the enclosure of land and many other changes I will describe—was dead, hit by an incurable virus. How highland lives and livelihoods will re-form minus cacao isn't a future I can foretell, although in chapter 5 I reflect on elements that were shaping the new conjuncture.

Ethnographic research obliges the ethnographer to confront the gap between the chaotic "common sense" of lived realities and the schemes he or she must apply in seeking to make sense of them. It disrupts the ethnographer's prior categories and assumptions, exposing uncharted territory where familiar categories don't hold. As it disrupts, it opens up the possibility of generating new knowledge and connections. This kind of intellectual work is intrinsically political in the definition proposed by the Italian scholar Antonio Gramsci.[13] With this book, I would like to do some more specific, political work, by challenging policies that promote the intensification of capitalist relations as a recipe for poverty reduction, and social movement agendas that render people like Kasar invisible or unrecognizable because they fail to fit the "alternative-development" niche. If these disruptions are productive, they can help build a future in which Kasar and his children will have a part.

Capitalist Relations

Livelihoods in much of the world are shaped by capitalist relations, yet we seldom stop to examine precisely what is distinctive about these relations, nor to consider how they are formed. This book brings capitalist relations sharply into focus. It offers a close-up account of the processes through which capitalist relations emerged among highland farmers, reconfiguring the ways in which they were able to reproduce themselves both socially and materially.

The formation of capitalist relations has been a core theme of "agrarian studies" where debates have centered on whether noncapitalist relations are displaced by capitalist ones, persist alongside them, or are combined in uneven but enduring configurations. These are questions with important political stakes. Many scholars have argued that the persistence of noncapitalist, "peasant" forms of production impedes the full development of capitalism. Some scholars see this impediment as a progressive outcome, since less capitalism means less inequality. Other scholars see the impediment as regressive, because they consider that capitalism must develop fully before we can have a socialist future. Still others argue that peasants, especially "middle peasants" whose control over their own land gives them some autonomy, can themselves be a progressive or perhaps revolutionary force.[14] These are important debates, but the figures that populate them tend to be rather static: they are smallholders, landlords, tenants, laborers, moneylenders, or tax collectors. I build on the agrarian studies tradition while using an ethnographic approach to delve more deeply into rural peoples' understanding of their own lives, their hopes and fears, and the social and political projects that engage them.

Empirical questions derived from Marx, neatly summarized by Henry Bernstein—who owns what, who does what, who gets what, and what do they do with it—are indispensable tools for making sense of rural livelihoods.[15] They also help to sort out whether or not capitalist relations, with their uniquely dynamic character, have actually taken hold. A distinguishing feature of capitalist relations, which Marx identified, is the ironic combination of an ideology that stresses freedom with material relations that restrict it. Building on his work, theorists Robert Brenner and Ellen Wood make the shift from market-as-opportunity to market-as-compulsion the critical diagnostic of capitalist relations.[16] As I will show in chapter 1, Lauje highlanders had long been familiar with markets, and they sold food and cash crops as well as their labor, on occasion. They had a solid understanding of profit and loss, and were alert to the value of the labor they invested in producing crops for use or sale. It made no difference to them whether the market for their products was local or global, so long as they made a reasonable return on their hard work. They took advantage of market opportunities when they found them attractive but—crucially—they were not compelled to sell food or labor if the terms didn't suit them.

Highlanders' autonomy was grounded in their system of shared access to common land, and an open land frontier. All highlanders who wanted to farm had free access to land, and they could survive on the food they grew for themselves. Their autonomy was only slightly modified by state rule and taxation, which were light and incomplete in this rather remote region. The big shift occurred when they started to plant tree crops, which had the effect of making their land into individual property. Initial landownership was unequal and over time, efficient farmers were able to accumulate land and capital, and pay workers to expand their farms and profits. Farmers who failed to compete lost control of their land and were compelled to sell their labor—if they could find someone who wanted to buy it.

The emergence of capitalist relations governed by competition isn't an inevitable progression. Land in many rural societies is individually owned, and land and labor may be bought and sold, but they aren't necessarily treated as fully fledged commodities that circulate "freely" in response to competitive pressures. Similarly, production of crops for the market isn't by itself an indicator that capitalist relations have taken hold. Farmers often produce for markets while retaining control of their means of production—their land, their labor, and enough capital to keep their farms going from year to year, and one generation to the next.[17] Under these conditions, they may make a profit, but they don't need to farm efficiently or maximize profit as a condition of sustaining themselves and holding on to their land. Yet the stable "middle-peasant" households that reach such an equilibrium should not be treated as "natural" units. As anthropologist William Roseberry points out, the emergence of capitalist relations governed by competition and profit, and the absence or blocking of such relations, are both phenomena that need to be explained. They arise at some conjunctures, but not at others, with far-reaching consequences for people whose livelihoods depend on their farms.[18]

The structure of capitalist relations, and the way they produce new forms of poverty, is invisible in liberal accounts that advocate the expansion of "the market" as the route to increased productivity and wealth. For Kasar in 2006 "the market" was already well developed. Indeed, it pressed in on him from all sides. Everything he needed to engage in production—land, labor, seed, fertilizers—had become a commodity, and so had the food he consumed.[19] Nor was he making wrong choices, another assumption of liberal thought. As Marx observed, landless workers are not free to choose how to spend their time. Their lives are governed by a "dull compulsion" as they must sell their labor every day in order to survive.[20] For farmers with inadequate plots of land the constraints are almost as severe. If Kasar could not access credit to buy seed and fertilizer, he could not farm; if the market value of his crops didn't equal the cost of food, he couldn't survive; and if no one needed his labor, he could not earn a wage. Choice didn't enter into it.

Roni, a merchant who supplied credit and bought highlanders' crops, also encountered a form of compulsion. Unlike his father and grandfather, merchants of the old school who had inherited their capital and could earn enough to support their families just by keeping their capital in circulation from year to year, Roni had borrowed his capital from a bank. He could use this capital to make loans to farmers, or he could use it to buy land and labor to engage in production. What he could not afford to do was to make loans to losing ventures like Kasar's. If he did this, he would lose his capacity to borrow from the bank, and he would also be outcompeted by merchants with more capital to invest and to lend out at interest. So he too lacked choice: he had to keep his money moving to generate a profit, or go bankrupt.

Kasar's slide into destitution occurred during the same period of time, and through the same set of processes, that enabled his neighbors to prosper. His poverty wasn't residual, a matter of being left behind. Nor did he simply live alongside neighbors who happened to prosper. Rather, the capacity of some highlanders to prosper depended upon the failure of their neighbors who fell into debt and were forced to sell their land. Like Kasar and Roni, the practices of these prosperous farmers were channeled and their "choices" increasingly constrained by capitalist imperatives of efficiency and profit. They helped their neighbors and kin on occasion, as they sought to balance their own accumulation with care for others.[21] But they too were obliged to run their farms as profitable enterprises, or risk losing their land.

To summarize, my shorthand "capitalist relations" refers to the ensemble of relations characterized by private and unequal ownership of the means of production (land, capital), a group of nonowners compelled to sell their labor, and the use of capital to generate profit under competitive conditions. Competition means that the owners of capital must seek profit to generate more capital to invest simply to reproduce themselves as they are, that is, as owners. To the extent they succeed, their accumulation squeezes others out, entrenching and sometimes deepening the unequal ownership with which the cycle began.

The emergence of capitalist relations in their routine but insidious form is a topic that has received limited scholarly attention in recent years. Since the threat of communism abated, and with it the Cold War fear that dispossessed rural people could become "dangerous classes," national governments and transnational development agencies no longer worry so much about the political implications of rural inequality. They promote optimistic, win-win scenarios based on the assumption that economic growth will benefit everyone in the end.[22] They talk of the need for social protection and safety nets, but so long as people like Kasar pose no threat to economic growth or political stability, governments and transnational agencies can abandon them with impunity. For highlanders to become a threat, or less dramatically, to have traction as a political force, they would need to be organized and to have allies.

The mundane way in which capitalist relations emerged among highlanders helps to account for why no allies rallied to help the people who lost out in the process. Contemporary social movements focused on rural livelihoods tend to highlight spectacular episodes of dispossession by corporations (land grabbing), the monopolistic practices of transnational agribusiness corporations, or attempts by rural people to defend culturally rich and environmentally sustainable ways of life from external threats. In these highlands, in contrast, capitalist relations emerged by stealth. No rapacious agribusiness corporation grabbed land from highlanders or obliged them to plant cacao. No government department evicted them. Nor was there a misguided development scheme that disrupted their old way of life. The noncommoditized social relations through which they previously accessed land, labor, and food were not destroyed by "capitalism," envisaged as a force that arrives from the outside. They eroded piecemeal, in a manner that was unexpected and unplanned.

Why highlanders didn't mobilize to prevent the commoditization of their land and labor, engaging in a "countermovement" of the kind Karl Polanyi describes;[23] why they permitted the emergence of steep and enduring inequalities among them; and why they didn't seek to limit their exposure to market risk are questions I will address in the pages to follow. These absences—institutions highlanders didn't have, steps they didn't take, combined with the initiatives they did take (to plant cacao and seek access to a modern life)—make them unrecognizable as "indigenous people" or even as "peasants" from the perspective of contemporary social movements. I take the gap between the relations social movement advocates expect to find among indigenous highlanders, and the ones that emerged at this conjuncture, as a productive disruption. It obliges us to look critically at conjunctures that aren't shaped by dramatic events. More specifically, the gap indicates that we need to probe more deeply into what it means to be indigenous on a land frontier.

An Indigenous Frontier

The image of indigenous people that has become familiar through the social movement literature emphasizes their attachment to their lands, forests, and communities, and their capacities for self-government. The realities are of course very diverse. Here I provide a brief orientation to some of the distinctive features of the indigenous frontier at the center of my account. First the name: Lauje highlanders call themselves highlanders, farmers, or Lauje, depending on the context. They don't see themselves, nor are they treated by others, as ethnically distinct from the coastal population, with whom they share common ancestors. The main difference is that they live in the highlands, and until the 1990s they farmed by the shifting-cultivation technique, which meant opening new farm plots from forestland and leaving old plots to fallow. They didn't live in concentrated hamlets but scattered in their fields, guarding their main food crop, corn, from attack by wild pigs. They did not congratulate themselves on their "genius for managing without states," as James Scott has argued for highlanders in the Southeast Asian mainland.[24] They welcomed their inclusion in the system of rule through headmen situated on the coast that had been in place since Dutch colonial times because they found it helpful in keeping the peace, and resolving disputes.[25] It was the Dutch rulers, they claimed, who gave them their *adat*, usually translated as "customary law," by which they meant their lightly institutionalized system for convening disputing parties and reaching settlements paid in fines. Highlanders' sense of what was "customary" was unwritten, and largely implicit: I didn't meet anyone who was willing to pontificate on Lauje custom or to generalize his or her sense of "how we do things" to something like "Lauje culture" overall. Although many Indonesians associate adat with autochthony and authentic indigeneity, other isolated people such as the Wana of highland Sulawesi and Meratus Dayak in Kalimantan are similarly coy about custom, and claim that their adat was given to them by external authorities.[26]

Lauje elders I met deep in the highland interior in the 1990s described the period of their youth as one characterized by conflict, violence, feuding, and flight because the presence of "the government" was not strong. They were afraid to travel from one watershed to the next because they did not trust strangers, and relations with kin could also be tense. Serious disputes could arise over women (adultery, failed marriage proposals), over forest resources (e.g., tapping another person's resin trees without permission), and over threats or insults. One highlander, Gilanan, described a terrifying time in the 1970s when conflict with kin forced his family to run off to live in isolation in the forest, surviving on wild sago and hiking long distances to barter for food. The family's attempt to plant rice and corn failed because their lone farm in the middle of the forest was devastated by monkeys, birds, and wild pigs. They were relieved when another group of kin took them in and supplied them with food while they developed new gardens and re-established a more settled life.[27]

Even in the 1990s many highlanders preferred to build their houses at some distance from neighbors so they could avoid excessive interaction with all the small sources of friction that can arise from quarrels among children, or fights between dogs. They thought that living close to other households was good for cooperation. Coordination among neighbors was especially important for growing rice, which worked best when a group of people cleared adjacent patches of forest and then planted their fields in a short period of time. Doing so minimized attack by pests and "shared the birds," as they put it. But too much closeness was problematic, and the clustering of many households in proximity was difficult to sustain.

Larger neighborhoods were sometimes drawn together by charismatic leaders, until they fractured and dispersed. In 1992 I visited Gau'ma, a close, cooperative neighborhood of about twenty households about six hours' hike from the coast. The households were gathered around Mopu, a strong leader to whom most of them were related. During my visit they planted a whole hillside with rice in massive collective work-parties. When I revisited in 1993, Mopu had died, his kin had scattered, and no one planted rice. Two men, one of Mopu's brothers and one of his sons, were competing for the leadership role. In 1996 the households had not regrouped. By 2006 Mopu's kin had become Christian and some of them had again built houses close together, this time not clustered around a person but around a church. No obvious leader had emerged. There were still tensions as I sensed quite acutely when a dispute erupted over allegations of adultery. The whole neighborhood seemed to be on edge, afraid that the protagonists would take up their knives and attack each other. In the end some wise talkers succeeded in calming everyone down, but as I sat with a group of frightened people in a hut near where the parties had gathered for the "customary" process of dispute resolution, they were not confident violence would be avoided.

If Mopu had still been around I suspect his words would have been enough. He was feared as well as respected. Arguing against his judgment or taking up knives would have been out of the question. He concentrated in his person powers of several kinds. He was a *pasori*, the person responsible for placating the spirits when clearing primary forest for new gardens, and ensuring the safety of hunters and rattan collectors when they were in the forest. He was also a *pasobo*, the person who conducted the ritual offering when planting the first rice seeds of the season, initiating the cycle of labor exchanges between all the households in his neighborhood. Further, he was the officially recognized chief of custom appointed by the headman on the coast to take care of negotiating marriages and settling disputes.

In view of the list of roles Mopu occupied it was not surprising that his kin found it difficult to replace him. However, his rather autocratic style was unusual. In most of the highland neighborhoods I came to know, leadership roles were dispersed or disputed and often there was no incumbent, or the incumbent was ineffective. Many competent men were diffident about leadership and reluctant to assert authority. They were also reluctant to accept direction from people they regarded as their peers. This made it difficult for highlanders to organize collective projects like holding a neighborhood ritual. Yet highlanders in the 1990s did not read the difficulties of pulling neighborhoods together as a symptom of decline in which a previous state of unity had given way to fragmentation. Rather, their stories about the past indicated that conflict was an ever-present possibility.

The highlanders' dispersed settlement and the flux of who was farming in which place was a huge source of irritation for government officials, especially the headmen who lived on the coast but were responsible for governing sections of the interior. These men were also Lauje, but they had little sympathy for the highlanders, whom they viewed as unruly and primitive.[28] This is a common stance among officials, as James Scott has argued. Ruling regimes seek to incorporate frontier places and people into "state-space" by drawing maps, conducting a census, and issuing identity cards. Often, they extend road networks to secure access for bureaucratic supervision and build primary schools to teach children to speak the national language and identify with the nation and its symbols.[29] In Africa and Latin America as well as Asia, the wildness of frontiers also figures in culturally coded, sometimes racialized hierarchies in which people who live in cities, in the lowlands, or on the coast see themselves as civilized in contrast to people of the highlands and hinterlands, whom they see as wild and backward.[30]

An evolutionary scheme mapped onto a social hierarchy and topographical arrangement of space was central in the Lauje area, and I explain its features in chapter 1. The important point for the moment is to note that Lauje highlanders generally concurred with the headmen's assessment that their lives were lacking in key elements which they associate with a modern life: decent housing, clothing, roads, and schools.[31] Their desire to access these things set in motion the profound economic and cultural shifts I trace in this book and had important political implications as well. Far from rejecting "state-space" in favor of sustaining their autonomy, they welcomed incorporation. But decades of neglect had made them skeptical that the roads, schools, and other benefits promised to them by government officials would actually be delivered.

DESIRE AND POTENTIAL

Frontiers are not only characterized by lack. They are simultaneously coveted places, envisaged by various actors as sites of potential. Scholars have shown how colonial regimes interpreted sparse indigenous populations and forested landscapes as signs that land was neither used nor owned, and proceeded to lay claim to forests, develop plantation agriculture, and install migrant populations.[32] Notions of wildness are still deployed by contemporary development planners, who see frontier spaces as "underutilized" resources that should be put to efficient and productive use, and devise schemes to attract corporate investors.[33] Frontiers also attract spontaneous migrants in search of land, often people who hope to prosper from a boom in the price and demand for commodities such as gold, timber, coffee, cacao, rubber, and palm oil.[34] More often than has been recognized, the indigenous people who are the original inhabitants of these lightly incorporated but economically promising "frontiers" also see their land as a zone of potential.[35] The cacao boom that swept Central Sulawesi in the 1980s and '90s was led by migrants who moved into forested areas and bought land cheaply from the indigenous inhabitants, but indigenous farmers also took the initiative to plant the lucrative new crop in the hope that they too could prosper. Both migrant and indigenous smallholders were remarkably dynamic. Together, they expanded the total area of cacao from 13,000 hectares in 1990 to 225,000 hectares in 2009.[36]

The dynamism of what I'm calling an "indigenous frontier" isn't a new phenomenon. For centuries indigenous people across Southeast Asia have joined crop booms and extracted minerals, timber, and forest products to supply regional and global markets. Cloves were a boom crop in the "Spice Islands" in the fifteenth century.[37] Colonial officials in the nineteenth century expressed alarm at the willingness of indigenous farmers to abandon food production in favor of the latest cash crop.[38] These officials expected "native" populations to be risk-averse, and to emphasize subsistence security over profit. This was especially the case for highlanders whom they often classified as "tribes" and placed at the backward end of evolutionary schemes.[39] But this expectation was misplaced. As Clifford Geertz observed, the cautious model fits better among farmers in rice-producing areas who "involute" by intensifying production on their generally fertile, irrigated land.[40] It is less common among farmers in frontier areas where there is room to experiment. The ecology matters too. Frontier areas often have poor soils that don't respond to intensive techniques like terracing and irrigation. In these places, expanding farms onto new land at the expense of forest usually makes more sense.[41]

Counterintuitively, relative isolation is central to the dynamism of an indigenous frontier. All farmers need cash, and more so as their needs expand and they aspire to send their children to school. But there are limited ways to earn cash in areas located far from towns or cities where they might sell fruit and vegetables, engage in petty trade, or commute to jobs. In isolated locations, local markets are quickly saturated: only so many tomatoes will sell on market day. Alternative sources of income are hard to find. There is little scope for craft production since many people have the skills to weave mats and baskets, carve wooden handles for their knives, and build their own bamboo and timber houses. Hence the best option to make money is often to grow industrial crops for sale on national or global markets, which are harder to saturate. Prices on these markets are notoriously volatile, however, and prone to cycles of boom and bust. Adverse prices are seldom mitigated by state-supported buffers, because of the marginal status of small-scale farmers in frontier areas, and because their crises don't affect the price of rice, the staple food that impacts directly on political stability in urban areas.

The configuration of powers on Indonesia's frontiers further increases their dynamism. Indonesia lacks an entrenched landlord class of the feudal type found in parts of the Philippines, where private citizens have held vast estates for multiple generations, and dominate both local and national politics. In Indonesia's frontier zones, it isn't landownership that begets political power, but the reverse. Powerful people—government officials, village heads, army officers, customary chiefs, prominent villagers—grab land and claim ownership.[42] They take advantage of a legal vacuum created by overlapping laws and weak enforcement. Brute force often shapes outcomes, and money can buy land, even when it should not be for sale. The Lauje highlands are a case in point. The highlands are officially designated state forest land, under the control of the Department of Forestry. According to the Forest Law, no one should be living in the highlands, although indigenous highlanders have lived and farmed there for countless generations. Certainly, land in the highlands should not be for sale, but a vigorous land market developed there nonetheless, stimulated mainly by the highlanders' own initiatives as they responded to the opportunity presented by the boom in cacao.

Social movements supporting indigenous people often highlight their commitment to holding on to customary land and conserving forests, but the dynamics of frontier zones do not favor a conservative approach. Land is abundant there. It is labor that tends to be scarce. Hence indigenous tenure regimes seldom focus on protecting forests or allocating a scarce resource. They are designed, rather, to recognize the hard work it takes to bring forested land under cultivation, and to manage the conflicts that can erupt when one person tries to take advantage of another person's effort. In the Lauje highlands, loss of forest wasn't the blow that devastated Kasar. It was the end of access to land on which he could farm to produce family sustenance, and the dawning recognition that the frontier as a zone of desire and potential was closed to him. However hard he was willing to work, he had no means to improve his family's situation. This predicament is all too familiar in Asia's fertile agricultural heartlands, where land scarcity and outright landlessness have been entrenched for many generations. In the Lauje highlands, and in other places with hitherto open land frontiers, it is new.

The social movement model of indigenous people living tranquilly in harmony with nature and with each other, eager to pursue development "alternatives," fails to capture the frontier dynamics I have just outlined. It is especially ill-equipped to grasp how capitalist relations can emerge so quickly as indigenous concepts emphasizing the value of an individual's hard work combine with market opportunities that are enticing but volatile, and a land regime that enables private enclosure. Indeed capitalist relations on an indigenous frontier can take on a peculiarly stark and unmediated form, rather like the form outlined in economics textbooks in which competition reigns and market forces dominate, with little "distortion" from state subsidies, monopolies, or remittances.

The mismatch with social movement agendas is no trivial matter. In the Lauje highlands it was a formative absence, a nonrelation that left an emerging landless class abandoned, without allies. The initiatives highlanders took when they dismantled their system of shared land access and covered their land with industrial crops made them unrecognizable as indigenous people from the perspective of social movements that define indigeneity in terms of cultural authenticity, subsistence orientation, and a commitment to social and ecological balance. Nor did they fit the role of victim, a central figure in the campaigns of many social movements and humanitarian organizations. There was no apocalypse, no famine, no natural disaster, no eviction, no dramatic event, and no villain to blame. Nor was there an obvious way out.

An Analytic of Conjuncture

To analyze is to tease apart. I adopt an analytic of conjuncture to tease apart the set of elements that gave the lives of Lauje highlanders in 1990–2009 their particular form, and to explore how each element set the conditions of possibility for others, in changing configurations.[43] In addition to economic elements such as prices, market demand, profits, and the cost of credit, I explore the material qualities of the milieu (rainfall, pests, diseases, soils, distances, topography); the character of crops (longevity, storability, vulnerability to disease, labor requirements); social boundaries and the values people attributed to particular kinds of places and ways of living; institutional elements such as customary and official rules that regulated who could do what (build a road, use land, inherit, marry, consume family food, buy or sell property, organize a ritual, resolve disputes); meanings and desires; and unseen spirits that enabled or interfered with human plans.

Presented in this form the list of elements is a long and static one, and distinct categories are hard to sustain: material and social elements are clearly meaningful; the prevalence of crop diseases was part of the construction of space; it influenced the cost of credit, and so on. The elements come to life as they collide and align in particular constellations. A conjuncture is dynamic but it is not random. There is path dependence. It is not the case that anything goes. History is front and center because every element in a conjuncture has a history that actively shapes the present, while at every conjuncture a new history is produced, sometimes deliberately, more often as an unintended consequence of how various elements combine.[44] Together, the elements I have listed formed the terrain, the circuits, understandings, and practices within which capitalist relations emerged and left Kasar stranded on a tiny, barren plot of land.

Analyzing a conjuncture requires peeling back layers of meaning and practice, and tracking relations across different spans of space and time. It is usually the work of scholars who can access data and make connections that are not necessarily emphasized by actors on the ground. The actors' analysis is absolutely relevant, as it informs their actions, but like all analyses it offers a partial perspective on the situation. Scholars inevitably have a different perspective and can make use of the difference as a source of insight, so long as they don't lay claim to an omniscient, bird's-eye view. In the case at hand, many Lauje highlanders held fast to a teleological view of an ever-improving future that for analytical and political reasons I reject. But I don't dismiss their understanding as "false consciousness." Rather, I attempt to situate it in the conjuncture that formed it and attend to the work it does. I pay attention to the fact that shifts I identified as critical turning points, like the emergence of capitalist relations, were shifts highlanders treated as banal. The significance of the turning point they identified—the fact that land had come to an end—wasn't something I grasped at first. On reflection, I could see how central it was to their understanding of what had changed in their world, and I made it the title and organizing theme of the book.[45] The back-and-forth between highlanders' categories and the analyst's schemes is an integral part of ethnographic work. More generally, as I noted earlier, ethnographic attention to the specificities—who the people are, and what is important to them—provides a window on people's lives and the projects that engage them.

A conjunctural approach, which attends to "history at one point in time" and in space, is a form of analysis with an illustrious heritage.[46] It is consistent with Marx's method, which examines the multiple relations that constitute concrete, historical forms.[47] It is central to the work of scholars inspired by Marx who combine attention to processes of capital accumulation with an emphasis on emergence, contradiction, contestation, agency, and struggle—in short, the specific features of a conjuncture and the many relations that form it.[48] We find it in the work of feminist and postcolonial scholars who have broadened Marx's capital/labor framework to examine how relations between genders, generations, and social groups distinguished by ethnic identity or religion shape resource access and mechanisms of accumulation.[49] We find it in the work of scholars inspired by Gramsci, who explore the way in which power is lived and inequality is normalized at the nexus of force, consent, and the production of desires for particular ways of living.[50] It is especially prominent in the work of geographers who build on the work of Henri Lefebvre.[51] Thus Doreen Massey highlights situated, embodied practices and the way places are relationally produced.[52] Allan Pred and Michael Watts stress that "how things develop depends in part on where they develop, on what has been historically sedimented there, on the social and spatial structures that are already in place there."[53] For Gillian Hart it means refusing to "take as given discrete objects, identities, places and events," and attending to "how multiple forces come together in practice to produce particular dynamics or trajectories."[54]

Within my discipline, anthropology, a conjunctural approach was elaborated in the 1950s by some of the scholars associated with the Manchester School, who insisted on situating events and processes in historically constituted fields of force.[55] It was developed by anthropologists working in a broadly Marxist tradition.[56] It is an approach that works against a notion of "cultures" as isolates or bounded wholes, hard on their edges like billiard balls that spin off each other, in Eric Wolf's memorable image.[57] It moves away from notions of authenticity, or the attempt to figure out whether change is generated from the inside, or by the impact of processes arriving from the "outside," because it doesn't assume there is an "inside" or a prior condition of fixity before change started to occur.[58] Rejecting notions of functional equilibrium, a conjunctural approach treats practices that appear to hold constant for a period of time as a puzzle, as much in need of explanation as dramatic change.

A conjunctural approach has implications for how we understand human subjectivity and agency. In place of "the individual" understood as a universal figure, the focus is on historically situated "socially determinate" subjects, further differentiated along lines of class, gender, and generation, among others.[59] It means rejecting the liberal concept of the self-sovereign, strategizing subject who makes more or less rational "choices" between a set of "options." Instead it foregrounds practices, taken-for-granted habits, and material configurations. In this vein, anthropologist Pierre Bourdieu explored the formative effect of daily routines, embodied dispositions, and the layout of a house.[60] Calling attention to that which is not said, cultural critic Raymond Williams emphasized "structures of feeling" that are both social and material, the "experienced tensions, shifts, uncertainties, the intricate forms of unevenness and confusion" of life as it is lived at a particular period.[61] Picture Kasar, who embodied experiences of exhaustion and isolation, but wasn't inclined to talk about them.

Similarly, the philosopher and historian Michel Foucault explored how power works continuously to form our desires, practices, and identities in ways that we are often unaware. His concept of power rejects the binary in which power is situated on one side of an equation, while freedom, autonomy, and resistance are situated on the other.[62] Yet it doesn't remove agency, or portray people as automatons. A subject, for Foucault, is always capable of action and reflection. The challenge, neatly summarized by geographer John Allen, is to examine how power works to form subjects through "a variety of modes playing across one another. The erosion of choice, the closure of possibilities, the manipulation of outcomes, the threat of force, the assent of authority or the inviting gestures of a seductive presence."[63] My account in this book builds on these understandings of the subject as an agent whose desires don't stand outside a conjuncture but are formed within it, and are formative in turn.

Adopting a conjunctural approach has implications for method. It works against an understanding of spatial scope as a hierarchy in which relations often described as "broad" or "wide" or "large" or even "global" are implicitly flagged as more effective than "local" ones.[64] Instead of drawing a boundary around a field site, or fixing the span of time, space, and quantity to be investigated, these parameters can be selected flexibly according to their relevance to the matter under study. Both spatially and temporally, the research focus can be more or less fine-grained as the topic requires, but even when the grain is fine enough for an ethnographer to exercise the art of observing and listening closely, the conjuncture under study isn't bounded.[65] It is still composed of a set of elements that have varied spatial and temporal scope. It is also formed by elements that are weak or absent.

Some elements of the conjuncture I examine in this book were put in place centuries ago, while others were made or remade in recent years. Their spatial scope varied: some of them connected the highlands to faraway places, while others involved exchanges among people who met face-to-face. Many of them mixed spatial scope. For Kasar, the problem was the low price of kapok, the tree crop he had planted, in relation to the cost of the food he now had to purchase. Kapok is a fiber used locally for making mattresses and pillows, its price fixed by a relatively restricted market. The price of cacao, in contrast, was fixed on world markets, mediated by the exchange rate for the Indonesian rupiah in relation to the U.S. dollar. Cacao's cost of production was shaped by the price of agricultural chemicals, and by the interest local merchants charged on credit. Whether a particular highland neighborhood had a church in it or a mosque was the outcome of transnational networks of missionary activity, movements of specific groups of people up hill or down, and localized practices of social boundary marking. Some relations were shaped even more immediately by features of the landscape that determined which crops would grow where, or the prevalence of rainfall and disease.[66] The arrival of cacao as a boom crop in Sulawesi in the 1980s had a specific, relational trajectory. Sulawesi farmers filled a gap in the market that opened up when crop disease and civil war in the Ivory Coast disrupted production. Transnational corporations and government agencies were largely absent from the cacao boom, and twenty years on most of the cacao was still exported without processing.[67] Other elements that figure in my account as formative absences are roads, schools, and political parties or social movements with an interest in highlanders' struggles.

Comparison across conjunctures helps to identify the distinctive set of relations that form them.[68] In *The Will to Improve* I examined a different conjuncture in the same province that was also shaped by the cacao boom, but included an influx of migrants and a plethora of development schemes, elements that were absent from the Lauje highlands. If we compare on a historical axis, farmers in west Sumatra in the 1920s experienced a crop boom rather like the one I examine. They caught "coffee fever" and planted much of their land with this crop. As in Sulawesi, the customary land-sharing system was soon dismantled, some farmers lost their land to merchants and moneylenders, and some sold land to their more successful neighbors and kin.[69] In both Sulawesi and Sumatra, restricted land access was exacerbated by enclosures of large land areas as state officials granted leases to plantations or set land aside as forest reserves.[70] It was the pincer effect of the two processes together—state-orchestrated enclosure of large land areas, and a process of enclosure initiated by farmers—that aggravated inequality among farmers and left some of them short of land. A significant difference between the two conjunctures was that in Sumatra in the 1920s the Communist Party took up the farmers' cause, while circa 2000 Indonesia's social movements had little interest in Sulawesi's struggling cacao farmers or land-short highlanders, a point I take up in chapter 5.

Research Process

Anthropologists are part of the conjunctures they study, sometimes in an activist role, but more often in the minor role of people who ask questions, and launch topics that may—or may not—stimulate discussion and debate. My involvement with the Lauje area began in 1990, when I held a three-year postdoctoral research fellowship. My initial research was concerned with exploring landscapes, livelihoods, and identities in upland areas. I focused on the nine *desas* (administrative units) where the Lauje language is spoken, a zone that extends roughly forty kilometers along the northern shore of the Gulf of Tomini and twenty kilometers inland, ending at the rugged cliffs situated near the center of the peninsula. The area straddles two subdistricts, Tinombo with its capital in Tinombo town, and Tomini with its capital in Palasa. Of the total population of the Lauje area, around thirty thousand people in 1990, about two-thirds lived scattered in the highlands up to two days' hike from the coast. The balance was crammed onto the narrow coastal strip, which was at most one kilometer wide, and less than fifty meters in places where the mountains rose almost directly from the sea.

I chose the Lauje area because a Canadian project designed to bring development to this rather neglected corner of Indonesia was about to commence there. My hope was that the project planners would make use of my qualitative research in highland neighborhoods to guide their interventions and make them effective. This part of my plan worked well as the reports I volunteered about changing farm practices and some unintended effects of project inputs were taken seriously by the project managers. However, the project ended prematurely without having much impact, and my role as purveyor of information that might directly influence the course of development in the area ended with it. The feature that kept me going back for two decades was the opportunity to track the remarkable transformation I analyze here.

I visited the Lauje area nine times, in 1990 (twice), 1991, 1992, 1993, 1996, 1998, 2006, and 2009, and spent about a year there in total. My research design was conditioned by the organization of space in the area, which did not lend itself to a village study of the classic kind. The boundaries of the official administrative units (called desas) were perpendicular to the coast, so that each of the nine desas in the Lauje area included a portion of the coastal strip and a portion of the highland interior. In 1990, all the desas had their administrative center on the coast, where desa headmen and other desa officials were appointed from among the members of the local coastal elite, most of whom were Lauje or migrants from other parts of Sulawesi who had married into Lauje families. Some of the desas covered a huge area, with a range from twenty to one hundred square kilometers, although the numbers are approximate as the borders of the desas in the interior were not mapped or marked. Population counts were incomplete, but the official data given in table I.1 provides an approximation.

Table I.1. Lauje Desas in 1990 and 2010

1990		2010				
Desas	Population	Desas	Population	Area km²	Population per km²	Estimated population in highlands
Dongkas	1,086	Dongkas	1,350	35	39	1,215
Tinombo	2,999	Tinombo	3,523	20	170	2,642
Lombok	5,660	Lombok	5,497	60	91	4,672
		Ogo'alas	2,758	38	72	2,758
Dusunan	1,663	Dusunan	2,018	24	85	1,715
Tibu	963	Tibu	988	35	29	840
Bobalo	4,558	Bobalo	2,058	13	161	1,338
		Dongkalang	1,802	17	105	1,171
		Pebo'unang	3,092	12	258	3,092
E'eya	1,810	E'eya	2,420	83	29	1,815
Ulatan	2,984	Ulatan	4,608	86	53	2,995
Palasa	8,443	Palasa	5,039	100	50	2,771
		Palasa Tangki	3,231	82	39	1,777
		Palasa Lambori	2,958	82	36	1,627
Totals	30,166		41,342	687	1,217	30,455

Source: Tomini and Tinombo Kecamatan Dalam Angka and census data from 1990 and 2010.

Note: The number of desas increased due to splitting. The new desas are shown alongside the originals so that the total population per original desa can be compared. The population growth corresponds to the provincial average of 1.4 percent per annum (BPS 2010, 93). My estimates of the highland population are based on the percentage of the desa land area that is flat or hilly, as noted in the Kecamatan Dalam Angka statistics.

As I've already noted with the example of Gau'ma, highlanders did not live in concentrated hamlets, but in transient clusters ranging in size from two to twenty households. Each household, which was generally based on a nuclear family of parents and unmarried children, built a small bamboo house in its current farm plot and shifted its residence when the plot was fallowed after two to five years. The typical pattern was for a few households of close kin to build houses near one another, with some distance—up to a kilometer—between their cluster and the next. Some of these clusters were acknowledged by the desa authorities as official neighborhoods (*rukun tetangga*, or RT), under the leadership of an appointed neighborhood head, but the boundaries of these official neighborhoods, and the set of households supposed to belong to them, were not well defined. Nevertheless, the concept of being a neighbor was important in the highlands, and I track the changing substance of what that relationship implied. I use the term "neighborhood" to refer to households that recognized themselves as belonging to a place and carried on neighborly relations with the people around them.

Following the standard procedure for rural research in Indonesia, I visited each of the desa headmen in their homes or offices on the coast and sought their permission before hiking up to visit the neighborhoods located in the desa interior. Initially, they were reluctant to grant access. Their standard reply was that the forests were dense, and the highland population was sparse, semi-clothed, residing in trees or under rocks, and prone to use poisoned blowpipes against strangers. Several headmen attempted to dissuade me. They may actually have believed their characterization of the highlands, since some of them had never hiked into their own desa interior. The hills were indeed rugged, the valleys steep and narrow, and there were no navigable rivers or plateaus. Access required fording rivers and climbing steep, winding, unmarked foot trails. The headmen were perhaps concerned that I would fall on a trail or drown in a flash flood. Or they may have preferred to maintain their monopoly over the data supplied to visiting officials, development planners, and anthropologists. I was polite but stubborn, and eventually they agreed to allow me to hike inland. They insisted that I must be accompanied by desa officials in my first forays and worried that I would complain about the highland diet, or about bathing in streams, or sleeping on the bamboo floors of highland homes. After a while the headmen relaxed and left me to hike as I pleased, accompanied by a Lauje-language interpreter and a guide of my choosing, usually someone from the highland neighborhood I planned to visit.

In the early 1990s, I visited about twenty neighborhoods located along the coast and in the highlands and came to an initial understanding of the landscapes, livelihoods, and identities of the people in each of three zones which I label coast, middle hills, and inner hills. I present these in summary form in table I.2, and explore them in detail in chapter 1. All the highlanders and almost all of the coastal dwellers were Lauje, and they acknowledged that they had common ancestors in ancient times, although sharp social and religious divisions had arisen among them. The people of the coast and the middle hills were Muslim. The inner hill people remained animist until the mid-1970s when the New Tribes Mission, a U.S.-based Christian evangelical group, set up a mission station in the highlands at Ogo'alas and began to convert them. For reasons I explain in chapter 1, the distinction between middle hill Muslims and inner hill animists was deeply formative of highland social dynamics. The two groups kept their distance and Muslims thought themselves superior. From a coastal perspective, however, all highlanders were wild and backward. These social distinctions coexisted with extensive trade relations between the three zones, relations in which highlanders' capacity for autonomous self-provisioning jostled with desires for inclusion and social advance.

During my visits to the highlands in the early 1990s, I observed that a major change was under way stimulated by the arrival of new tree crops, clove, and cacao. Each year, the farmers I visited were planting these crops in their farm plots alongside their staple foods, rice, corn, and cassava. Although they did not talk in terms of enclosing the land, the effect of planting these trees was to make previously common land into individual property, a process I describe in chapter 3. When they began planting trees, highlanders imagined they would still plant some food for their own use, but their supply of land quickly ran out. Polarization followed, as successful farmers bought up their neighbors' land.

To track the changes in land use and access I started to revisit ten hillside neighborhoods in the middle and inner hills of several Lauje desas. Each neighborhood had distinct features, the product of its distinct ecology, location, and the history of its population, making me realize how inappropriate it would have been to select one and make it stand in for an abstraction like "Lauje culture." But there were patterns to the changes taking place in all of them, and comparison across these sites helped me to clarify why a particular set of relations emerged in one place and not another; why at this time, and not before.

Table I.2. Timeline

Era	Coastal zone	Middle hills	Inner hills
1591 *Tomini Kingdom*	Settlement?	Food farms	Food farms
1600–1850	Slavers, raiders, merchants visit to buy forest products, tobacco. No permanent settlement	Food farms; collect forest products; grow tobacco for sale from 1820.	Food farms; sell forest products?
1850–1910	Permanent settlement of Lauje and migrants; coconuts planted; Islam established; trade in forest products and tobacco; fishing	Food farms; sell forest products, tobacco, Islam introduced?	Food farms; sell forest products?
1910 *Dutch rule imposed*	Highlanders forced down to coast; crowding; disease; famine	Highlanders return to hills; resume food and tobacco production	Avoid Dutch soldiers; hide
1910–70 *Colonial rule* 1910–42 *Japanese occupation* 1942–45 *Independence*, 1949– *Separatist movements* 1950s *New Order* 1965–	Coconut trees dominate landscape; land concentration; buy or barter for food in highlands; fishing; trade in highland products; pay taxes; limited administration, schools	Food farms; grow tobacco; wage work in ebony camps; pay taxes; Islam consolidated	Food farms; collect forest products regularly for sale
1970–90 *New Order consolidated*	Road opens 1975; rice imports become routine; coconut economy; fishing, trade in highland products; schools and basic health services	Tobacco collapses; some outmigration; some movement in land to grow food and shallots; rattan hauling as wage work	Food farms; collect forest products; rattan hauling as wage work; Christianity spreads
1990–2010 *End of New Order* 1998 *New district Parimo* 2002	Coconut economy declines; trade in cacao and cloves; supply goods to highlanders	Cacao and clove planted; land becomes scarce; food production much reduced; rattan hauling as wage work; some schools	Food farms; some shallots, garlic, cacao. Coastal people move in to buy land, plant clove and cacao; Christianity spreads, churches built; road building from 2005

On each revisit to these highland neighborhoods I stayed for a few days talking to farmers and informal leaders, and to the official neighborhood head if there was one. I asked them about the changes that had occurred there since my last visit, starting with an inventory of who had moved in or out, who had bought or sold land, and what they were growing in their fields. These were factual questions highlanders didn't find difficult to answer, and they didn't find them sensitive because I didn't try to probe the reasons for land sales in these inventory sessions, just whether or not they had occurred. The inventory exercise gave a helpful concreteness to my line of questioning, and from it I made a list of households for follow-up visits. But the inventory did not provide an indication of land areas, nor did it capture the set of land transactions that was taking place as ambitious farmers started to acquire land in different neighborhoods. There were no official documents covering landownership or sale, and the land tax system introduced in the mid-1990s recorded only a fraction of the land highlanders used and claimed as their own. So I tracked the quantitative element as best I could and focused my attention on the mechanisms driving these changes, the new sets of relations that were emerging, and the perspectives of the people directly involved.

From 1993 onward, I started to spend longer periods of two to ten weeks in three adjacent highland neighborhoods I have called Sibogo, Sipil, and Walu, with around 120 households in total.[71] These neighborhoods straddled the border between the Muslims of the middle hills and Christians/animists of the inner hills, making them apt sites for studying relations between these groups as struggles over land intensified throughout the 1990s. I also tracked changes in Pelalang, an inner hill neighborhood not far away, in which Lauje people from the coast arrived seeking land. Coastal peoples' mode of land acquisition involved the kind of bullying that would classify it as a "grab," and it became worse after 2005 as roads finally began to arrive in the highlands, increasing the pressure on inner hill folk who were nearing the end of their land frontier.

In the four sites where I spent the most time, I got to know the residents well enough to place them in their kinship networks, observe how they were living from day to day, and talk to them in some detail about the dilemmas they faced during this period of rapid change. "Individuals," as Lila Abu-Lughod observed, "are confronted with choices, struggle with others, make conflicting statements, argue about points of view on the same events, undergo ups and downs in various relationships and changes in their circumstances and desires, face new pressures, and fail to predict what will happen to them or to those around them."[72] In the chapters that follow I combine this insight, which enables me to "write against" a notion of culture that homogenizes experience, with the analytical task of exploring how highlanders formed new relations to each other and to the land. Hence I don't treat tensions as idiosyncratic, but attempt to situate them in the "structure of feeling" that characterized this particular milieu.

Revisiting as a method had one obvious advantage: it enabled me to track a set of processes as they took shape over time. It had the additional merit of enabling me to refine and reorient my research agenda as new questions arose and gave me time between visits to reflect on what I had learned and to write some articles in which I began to develop my analysis. It had disadvantages too. Most significantly, it limited my ability to learn the Lauje language as each time I began to make progress it was time to leave. Although I speak fluent Indonesian, the national language, and could use this language to talk to people like desa officials, merchants, coastal dwellers, and some highlanders, most highlanders couldn't speak Indonesian. This problem is rather rare in Indonesia, which prides itself on universal access to primary education which extends both literacy and the national language. In the Lauje highlands there were only two primary schools before 1990, and very few highlanders lived close enough to attend them. There is no dictionary or lexicon for the Lauje language so I could only learn it by listening. Over the years I came to understand a lot of what was said and learned about a hundred key words directly relevant to my research, but I continued to rely heavily on my interpreter, Rina, a woman trader from the coast of one of the Lauje desas I met in 1992.

Rina had only primary school education but she was intelligent, warm, and sociable; she put highlanders at ease; and she patiently transcribed a thousand pages of tape-recorded interviews, giving me access to rich details in highlanders' narratives that I wasn't able to pick up at the time. Highlanders agreed to the taping because they knew my Lauje-language skills were limited and I would need to go over the tapes with Rina to understand their stories in full. Rina also carried on her own conversations with highlanders, chatting about people and events, asking for clarification out of her own curiosity, and launching into topics that expanded my horizons. Highlanders enjoyed quizzing her about the rise and fall of members of the coastal elite, the cost of their weddings, their family dramas and goings-on. This was Rina's milieu, and she was happy to share the information. My social world was too strange and distant for this type of exchange. The most highlanders could do to situate me in my social milieu was to look at photos of my family, and learn the names of my children. At least they could address me correctly by the name of my oldest child, so "mother of Nick" was how I was known.

The written archive Rina and I created through our fieldwork process is extensive, but I don't treat people's statements recorded in transcripts and notes as "true" in any simple sense. Our archive was the product of a particular type of encounter, one shaped by the rugged terrain, the time and energy needed to hike from one place to another, my limited language skills, highlanders' tiny houses where we could only stay for a few days without outstaying our welcome, and many other elements. Most of the archive was generated by sitting and talking to people in their houses. The topics I raised stimulated highlanders to reflect on their practices and articulate perspectives that are usually left implicit. Sometimes they caught the line of reasoning guiding my questions, which they confirmed or rejected, setting me straight by proffering an alternative. Not surprisingly, they rationalized their actions and preferred to present themselves in a good light. The understanding I derived—situated and partial as it is—was built up gradually, by combining insights and observations from many sources, and cross-checking what was said with what was done wherever possible.

The people Rina and I visited frequently and got to know best took some pleasure in these conversations, or at least did not try to avoid them. Highlanders at Sibogo told us about the bush-telegraph system they used during our longer stays, sending children to find out which trail we had taken that morning (up- or downhill, east or west). They worked on tasks close to their homes if it seemed we were headed in their direction, and they had often made preparations like digging up cassava for our lunch. They were kind enough to welcome me back after long absences. When I was gone they kept in touch with Rina because they saw her at her market stall and invited her to their weddings and family events. Tragically Rina died in 2007 of diabetes, an illness that should not have been fatal if treatment was available. I didn't know of her death until I returned in 2009, and my visit to the highlands that year, accompanied by her cousin, was colored by my sadness and the sadness of many of our hosts who shared my affection for Rina, and a deep sense of loss.

Outline

Chapter 1 examines the processes that formed identities and drew highlanders, merchants, and government authorities into particular sets of relations over the two centuries before 1990. Chapter 2 takes a fine-grained view of some highland neighborhoods to explore relations of work and care among highlanders in the period when they had plenty of land, and they grew their own food. Chapter 3 explores the process of enclosure that began around 1990 when highlanders began to plant cacao on their common land. It tracks the emergence of a concept of land as a bounded unit of space that could be privately owned, bought, and sold. Chapter 4 explores how capitalist relations emerged in the highlands as land, labor, and capital started to move in circuits defined by competition and profit. Chapter 5 examines highlanders' responses to increasingly entrenched inequality, and the politics that emerge from this conjuncture.

1 Positions

The relations I explore in this chapter are those that positioned Lauje highlanders as poor and backward, and encouraged them to seek ways to improve their situation. These relations reach back in time to the eighteenth century, outward to colonial and national policies and distant markets, and inward to the very immediate and concrete: what crops would grow where, the pattern of rainfall, and encounters between highlanders and coastal folk when they met face-to-face. There was some coercion, but it was difficult to compel highlanders to do someone's bidding so long as they controlled their land and grew their own food. My title "positions" flags the way in which identities were formed relationally, as highlanders and coastal folk developed distinct habits and structures of feeling. Position also signals the spatial element of these relations, and the entanglement of topography with identities, practices, and powers.

Powers

In 1990, driving into the Lauje area from west to east along the road that hugs the coast on the north side of the Gulf of Tomini, it looked to me as though no one lived in the dry and barren hills that loomed to the left. For a casual observer who had no time or inclination to hike up into the hills, the barren appearance of the foothills was misleading. The slopes facing the coast were in a rain shadow for most of the year, and only good for one corn crop in the short season that brought rain from the east. No one lived on those slopes, although cattle roamed and poor people gathered fuel wood to sell. The twenty

1.1. Brick house on the coastal strip

thousand people who lived in the highlands were far inland, well out of sight. Along the narrow coastal strip there were substantial brick houses lining the road at the center of each of the desas, and shabby bamboo huts by the road at the desa peripheries, in the muddy lanes behind the brick houses, and on the shore alongside small wooden fishing boats. Coconut palms were the main vegetation, tall, skinny, and well past their prime. Access to the Lauje area was mainly by sea until 1975 when a rough road was completed along the coast. In 1990 the trip by road from the provincial capital Palu took about ten hours, reduced to six hours in 1993 when the coastal road was paved, longer if a flood had washed out one of the bridges.

On my first visit, the headman of one of the nine Lauje desas informed me that highlanders "don't grow anything," adding "they only grow rice and corn." We were standing in the desa administration office, a one-room wooden structure devoid of furniture except for an information board and a sketch map nailed to the wall. The spaces on the information board where desa officials were supposed to insert data on population, production, and so on were mainly blank. The map, like the desa maps shown to me by other headmen in the Lauje area, covered the neatly aligned houses, mosques, marketplace, schools, and other facilities of the coastal strip in some detail, but was vague about the highlands, representing them in spatially compressed form with a few strokes of the pen. It took me some hours sitting with the headman to fill in the blank spaces and establish that there were people living in the highlands, and the people, the hills, and the rivers had names.

The headman's derisive dismissal of highlanders' food production, together with highlanders' invisibility on the desa map and data board, were not idiosyncratic. They were an indication of how a characterization of highlanders as wild, backward, and unproductive worked to secure particular relations of power. The headman neglected to mention that coastal people had depended on food produced by "backward" highlanders during the centuries before improved transport enabled sacks of rice to be imported. He overlooked the role that highland food production still played in 1990 as the main source of cheap food—corn and tubers—for coastal people who could not afford to buy the prestige food, rice. He did not describe how highlanders had been "feeding" the coastal merchants for two centuries by supplying the forest products (timber, rattan, resin) and cash crops (tobacco, shallots) from which the merchants made their profits. Nor did he mention that highlanders had already begun their own small experiments with planting new tree crops, cacao, and cloves. Highlanders did not need official prodding to identify a new opportunity.

It isn't unusual for people in positions of power over others (employers, chiefs) to treat the people who "feed" them with disdain. The headman's perspective was echoed by other headmen in the Lauje desas and by merchants, whose disdain was colored by frustration. Merchants' livelihoods depended upon these "wild" people but it wasn't easy to bind them into extractive relations. So long as highlanders had abundant land to grow their own food, merchants had no reliable means to compel them to sell their labor or their products. Nor could the small chiefdoms that formed on the coast in the period before Dutch colonial rule compel highlanders to pay tribute. When the Dutch colonial administration attempted to impose its control in the Lauje area around 1910, it too lacked the capacity to force highlanders to pay taxes or obey commands. A century later, some highlanders were still not incorporated in the desa administrative system, and desa maps and neighborhood lists were incomplete. Underpaid census takers I encountered in 2009, reluctant to hike far inland, planned to complete the census of 2010 as they had completed previous ones: by copying outdated lists of names supplied by neighborhood heads and filling in the blanks with guesswork.

The limited reach of state administration in the Lauje highlands is unusual for Indonesia, and rare also in other parts of Southeast Asia where, as James Scott has argued, most highlanders were enmeshed in state-based administrative systems by the middle of the twentieth century.[1] The reason for limited administration was also different from the one Scott identified in other locales: Lauje highlanders did not resist rule, nor did they have a "genius" for managing their affairs without state interference. Desires for security and access to trade goods drew them into the orbit of coastal powers. Minimally they wanted salt, knife blades, cooking pots, cloth sarongs, shorts, shirts, and kerosene for the tiny wick lamps they made from discarded tin cans. These relations make little sense if we focus only on the coercive or "deductive" dimension of power emphasized by Scott in his discussion of how states or state-like entities subjugate people, impose fines and taxes, and extract goods and profits. It makes more sense if we examine how power works to produce subjects who desire particular ways of living. Desires come from somewhere, they have histories, but these are not histories of unilateral imposition. It was an array of powers—attraction, threat, coercion, the channeling of choice—that combined to position Lauje highlanders, and induced them to position themselves, in the spatially ordered hierarchy of an administrative regime and a set of extractive relations centered on the coast.

Historical Traces

Although the Austronesians who spread out from southern China to people the archipelago four thousand years ago must have arrived by sea, highlanders' origin myths do not recall this fact.[2] They assert that humanity began in the Lauje highlands, from where some people went down to the coast. According to highland elders I consulted, all the peoples of the world, including white folk like me, descended from the mythical ancestors who first emerged from a clump of bamboo. They headed to the east, the west, the north, and south, some uphill, some down, and some across the sea. The elders' emphasis on highland origins corresponds to the historical record that confirms much of the population of island Southeast Asia was concentrated in the highland interiors until the late nineteenth century.[3]

In centuries past, highlanders confined their visits to the coast to brief trips to fish, trade, or make salt. In many areas the coastal zone was swampy and difficult to cultivate. In the Lauje area it was simply very narrow, with hardly any distance separating the hills from the sea. It was easier to survive in the hills where rice could be grown in fields cleared annually from the forest and then left to fallow. This shifting cultivation method, also known as swidden, is well suited to conditions where land is abundant but labor scarce.[4] Highlanders also relied on the indigenous tubers taro (*colocasia*) and yam (*discorea*), on starch derived from the sago palm (*sagu*), and on the resilient and productive New World crops corn (maize, *Zea mays*), sweet potato (*pamoea batatas*), and cassava (*manihot esculenta*).[5] Disease was another reason to avoid the coast. Malaria was rampant there and cholera, smallpox, and typhoid were periodically imported by the merchants who visited along the shore.

Highlanders who ventured to the coast also risked attack by raiders seeking people to capture and sell as slaves, a practice that was widespread in the archipelago and especially vigorous in the Gulf of Tomini.[6] From 1750 to 1850 armed bands combined slave raiding with attempts to engage highlanders in trade. Their approach was to hand out prestige goods (brass trays, glass beads, textiles) as an advance, and return to collect deliveries of goods such as wax, bark cloth, or rice.[7] These merchant-raider bands presented highlanders with a dilemma. They could forgo access to prestige goods and keep a safe distance.[8] Or they could enter into exchanges with these bands, but be ready to retreat to the highlands if a deal turned sour. The advance payment system created debts that served both as a source of coercion and as a form of protection: a merchant who had handed out trade goods would lose his investment if another merchant band took his trading partners captive before they had delivered the promised goods. Hence the merchant-raiders meted out both violence and protection in unstable configurations.[9]

Dutch military might led to the end of slaving and raiding in the Gulf of Tomini by the middle of the nineteenth century, and trade in forest products increased to meet world demand for rattan and damar resin, the main exports of this period alongside tobacco.[10] Around this time, according to Lauje legend, one of their ancestors went down to settle permanently on the coast where she converted to Islam and married one of the non-Lauje merchants who was living there. It was from this mixed union and others that a multiethnic Muslim coastal merchant community emerged. Aspirant chiefs doubled as merchants, as they built their wealth and authority from their capacity to mediate trade between highlanders and the sea-borne trading network. The goods delivered to these merchant-chiefs were simultaneously a return on an advance, tribute, and labor service.[11] The merchant-chiefs often described highlanders as their subjects or slaves, while highlanders emphasized their autonomy, as they retained their capacity to keep their distance.[12] They could also launch attacks on merchants and chiefs who had wronged them, so they were feared as well as despised, and coastal trading settlements were often fortified. In 1892 a Dutch colonial official named Baron van Hoëvell visited Tinombo and left the only written record of a direct observation from this period: "There exists a tribe in the mountains that is looked upon as an under group. . . . They appear to be . . . peaceable . . . and do not hunt heads. . . . They number about 10,000. . . . They normally live spread out on their ladangs [fields]. They spend a lot of time cultivating padi [rice], millet and tobacco. A great deal is grown of this last, and the export of it makes Tinombo the largest trading place in Mooeton [Moutong]." He noted that the coastal people had already begun to plant coconuts, and their houses were spread out and not fortified, evidence that they "seldom fight with the inland tribes" with whom, he noted, they had intermarried.[13] Ten thousand was a huge concentration of people at that time, and especially unusual in a highland area, but must have been credible enough to Van Hoëvell that he took note of it. Whether or not it was accurate, it indicates that the coastal chiefs and merchants he consulted were aware of a very large population in the highlands.

ADMINISTRATION AND RULE, 1910–2000

Most Lauje continued to live in the highlands until around 1910 when the Dutch colonial government strengthened its hold on the region and sent soldiers to force highlanders down to the coast to plant coconut trees as a means to earn cash to pay the head tax. The government ordered highlanders to settle permanently on the coast, but many evaded these orders while those who obeyed them did not stay long. Their reason was that the tiny land base on the coast could not support the increased population, and famine, malaria, and other diseases killed many highlanders. Besides, the coastal strip was soon full of coconut trees that left no space for growing food. The survivors fled back to the hills but had to live in hiding for some time, experiencing hunger and hardship.[14]

Despite nominal Dutch rule, there are very few archival records for the Lauje area for the period of Dutch administration from 1900 to 1949. The nearest Dutch official, who arrived in 1899, was based in Parigi, which is 170 kilometers along the coast to the west.[15] The colonial authorities relied on indirect rule via non-Lauje merchants they appointed as *rajas* and set up in a palace in Tinombo town.[16] The *rajas* appointed headmen at intervals along the coast, drawing from among the members of the mixed Lauje-migrant merchant community already resident there. These headmen appointed Lauje highlanders as ward heads tasked with mediating between coast and hills, conveying government instructions, and maintaining order. During the brief period of Japanese occupation (1942–45), some highlanders from the middle hills were recruited into youth militias. In the 1990s older men remembered this time because they had to report to the coast daily for training exercises, learn to sing Japanese songs, and undertake forced labor.

With the declaration of Indonesia's independence in 1949, the new government resumed the colonial system of appointing headmen along the coast and relying on them to manage highland relations. The district head reappointed a non-Lauje merchant to the position of raja, much to the annoyance of members of a self-styled Lauje aristocracy that had emerged on the coast, and sought to reclaim authority from the in-marrying merchants they called "foreigners." But the aristocrats' authority was confined mainly to ritual matters focused on cleansing and curing, and drew on an esoteric form of Islam that enhanced their claims to spiritual power.[17] Although they aspired to draw Lauje highlanders and Lauje coastal dwellers together into a single ritual complex, their reach in the highlands was limited.[18] Highlanders were more likely to recognize the authority of the raja. Since the raja was not involved in the separatist struggles that rocked Sulawesi in the 1950s, the Lauje coast remained a peaceful backwater, and a safe haven for migrants who were fleeing strife in other parts of Sulawesi. Rule was light, with the government making few demands and offering few services. The colonial head tax was abolished and not replaced.

The New Order government (1965–98) replaced the position of raja with that of subdistrict head (*camat*), but maintained continuity by recruiting camats for Tinombo and Tomini from the ex-raja's family. The small settlements along the coast became the centers of new administrative units, desas, which followed the old system: each had a headman who lived on the coast, and was responsible for keeping the peace in a section of the highland interior. As I noted earlier, much of the highland population was not registered and desa boundaries were vague in the interior. Many highlanders in the 1990s defined their desa membership in terms of their loyalty to particular headmen, who continued to double as merchants as they had in centuries past. The headmen implemented the standard official system for desa administration based on subdividing spaces and appointing a head to each desa subdivision (*dusun*) and neighborhood (*rukun tetangga*, or RT). They maintained the colonial tradition of appointing a chief of custom (*kepala adat*) whose role was to help settle disputes. Highlanders thus appointed took pride in their mediating and oratorical skills and their capacity to resolve disputes without referring them to higher authorities—a capacity enhanced by the presence of that authority lurking in the background. As one of them explained, "If we cannot resolve the problem here, we go to the neighborhood head, then to the dusun head, then if that fails, straight down to the desa headman, then to the police and the jail. That is for the really hard-headed cases, those who don't want to listen."

The ward heads of old had many qualities: charisma, stamina, knowledge of the terrain, and wider-than-usual social networks. But most crucial of all was the backing of coastal authorities, the sense that they were the appointed vehicles for an external power. They brought the weight of "the government" to dispute settlement processes. They gained renown for their bravery, when they mediated between warring factions, or traveled deep into the hills to arrest men accused of murder (sometimes murder of close kin). Desa headmen in the New Order period looked for men with similar qualities to appoint as neighborhood heads and chiefs of custom, usually confirming the highlanders' preferred candidate, because a man who was not respected would not be able to do the job. Nevertheless, highlanders' practice of building their houses in their fields and moving them every few years made their social organization opaque to the desa headmen and contributed to the headmen's conviction that highlanders were hopelessly backward.

Social Hierarchies and Distinctions

During a visit in 1991 I encountered a planning official from the provincial capital Palu, who was scouting ideas for a Canadian-funded development project intended to relieve poverty in the Lauje area. "Those coconut trees are old," he commented, looking at the tall spindly trees that produced few fruit. "We can replace them with hybrid varieties, or plant cacao underneath." It did not occur to him to ask who actually owned the coconut trees, who was positioned to capture the benefit from increased productivity, or who would lose out. I explained to him what I had learned about the area thus far: that over the decades, ownership of the coconut trees had become concentrated in the hands of very few families as the owners had sold their trees to pay for weddings and cover debts. The people in the tiny huts under the trees were squatting on the land and had no right to cultivate long-term crops. Even if the old coconut trees were replaced by more productive ones, the poor would not benefit, and they might even be evicted if the landowners decided to plant more trees to maximize their profits. I also tried to explain that the poorest people were living in the highlands, out of sight, but he was not interested. "These people here are quite poor enough for our project," he said. "We don't need to look any further."

There were indeed many poor people on the coast. They were not quite as invisible as highlanders, but some of their houses were also out of sight from the coastal road, tucked along muddy paths. The men in these households supplied labor in the coconut sector. They climbed the trees to pluck the fruit, or made the coconut flesh into copra for export, neither task a steady source of employment in view of the large number of people who needed work. Men fished with whatever equipment they could afford and did odd jobs. The women made coconut oil for sale from "windfalls," fallen coconuts they treated as a common resource. These fallen coconuts also furnished an income for schoolchildren who went out to gather them early in the morning and sold them for cash to buy snacks from women vendors who waited near the school. Poor women did laundry in the homes of the rich. Some couples opened seasonal farms on the dry foothills and scratched out a crop of corn, but the poorest could not do this as they had no savings to sustain themselves while working on the land. They had to find paid work every day.

Before the coastal road was built, a significant number of men worked at the Tinombo dock loading copra onto the steamers that passed along the coast. Unionized in the 1960s, they suffered social stigma and official isolation when the dockworkers union was banned because of its affiliation with the Communist Party. Fortunately, none of the union members were killed in the dreadful anticommunist massacres that surrounded General Suharto's rise to power in 1965. Their brief experience of formal labor stood in sharp contrast to the longer term: one in which regular paid work has been scarce, and livelihoods must be improvised on a daily basis.

The more affluent coastal dwellers were desa officials, schoolteachers, and merchants. A few of them were major landowners who had bought up the aging coconut trees, together with the land on which they stood. Rina's uncle Haji Amir, for example, had accumulated thousands of trees in several desas. Some members of the coastal elite owned small areas of wet rice land in their home desas or in other desas along the coast.[19] In 1990 none of them owned land in the highlands, which wasn't yet a commodity available for sale, nor did they foresee the potential of this land for cacao or clove pro-

1.2. Lauje highlands with clove trees, grassy bald, and fields

duction. Some had small herds of cattle that they let loose to graze in the foothills, obliging the poorer people who made seasonal farms there to build fences to protect their crops. A bit farther inland, they burned some of the slopes repeatedly to encourage fresh grass shoots for the cattle to graze, producing a treeless grassy patch of land that was impossible to cultivate. Cattle were not very numerous, however, and they didn't loom large in status hierarchies or in strategies for capital accumulation.[20]

Members of the coastal elite often spoke disparagingly about the Lauje area as a whole, describing it as a "minus region" (*daerah minus*). This term didn't just flag the poor state of the infrastructure, but also the deficiencies of the people, whom they characterized as lazy, uneducated, and lacking in enterprise. With the exception of the self-styled Lauje aristocrats, most of them had little ethnic pride even though they spoke Lauje as their lingua franca and most of them had Lauje ancestry (often mixed with Chinese or Hadrami Arab, or one of Sulawesi's ethnic groups including Bugis, Mandar, Gorontalo, and Kaili). The economic and social networks of the elite spread laterally along the coasts of the archipelago and into the towns and cities. They were the first to hear about, and to take advantage of, investment opportunities, development handouts, or government schemes to build new roads and open land for settlement. Their children were educated to secondary school level, although few proceeded to university and access to government jobs required major bribes few families could afford. Hence young people were often at home, unemployed. The boys played soccer in inter-desa leagues, and some girls and young women, including my friend and Lauje-language interpreter Rina, played volleyball.

Rina belonged to the lower rung of the coastal elite. I lived at her parents' house when we were down on the coast between visits to the hills, so I had long conversations with members of her family over the decades we worked together. Her father, born in 1922, had been a clerk for a local merchant of Chinese descent. The merchant's main business in the period 1930–1960 was extracting ebony from the highland forests, and trading in forest products collected by highlanders: cinnamon bark, damar resin, and rattan pared into thin strips for binding house poles and fishing gear. Rina's mother and widowed sister sold cakes from a stall in the nearby market. One brother struggled as a fisherman. Lacking capital, his operation was limited to hook, line, and a wooden dugout canoe. Another brother was sponsored by the rich uncle, Haji Amir, to complete his education and become a schoolteacher. Another worked as a carpenter, building houses. Rina had limited education, but she was bright and enterprising and slowly built up her trading capital as she graduated from selling cakes near the school to selling clothing at the markets that rotated along the coast on a regular weekly schedule. She went to Palu periodically to take new stock on credit from her Chinese "boss." With the money she earned working for me for two months in 2006 she bought a secondhand van to transport her goods between markets and rented space in the van to other women traders.

BACKWARDNESS AND DEVELOPMENT

Rina and other coastal folk, rich and poor alike, subscribed to stereotypes about the backwardness of highlanders that are widespread in Southeast Asia and hinge on an evolutionary narrative in which highlanders remained primitive while their own ancestors became civilized.[21] They reserved their most extreme contempt for the pork-eating Christian or animist highlanders from the inner hills they called by the derogatory name *bela* L (I use L to distinguish Lauje words from Indonesian). They encountered "bela" on market days, when some of them hiked down to the coast wearing dirty and ragged clothing, clutching blowpipes, and carrying their belongings in cloth

1.3. Couple from the inner hills, hiking to the coastal market

bundles. Some "bela" had acquired gaudy items that made them look ridiculous, from a coastal perspective: false gold teeth, hair perms, brightly colored dresses and lipstick, cassette players or watches. Coastal folk claimed that "bela" could not count and were easily cheated.[22] Some poured water over their terraces to prevent uninvited highlanders from sleeping there, complaining about noise and dirt. A few brought out pots of food and permitted highlanders to sleep inside a storage shed, especially if it was raining.

Disparaging the Lauje highlanders was one of the ways in which Lauje on the coast established their distance from them and confirmed their own superiority. For desa headmen, highlanders' purported backwardness served a more specific purpose, which emerged during development planning meetings when officials from the provincial capital Palu arrived to solicit local priorities. Desa headmen spoke of the need to make the highlanders properly social (*memasyarakatkan*) or, in more extreme versions, to make them into proper humans (*memanusiakan*). The desa headmen who spoke in this way were usually pleading for the Department of Social Affairs to target their desa for a resettlement center to relocate primitive highlanders, officially designated "isolated and estranged people" (*masyarakat terasing*) to the coast, where they could be properly supervised.[23] Several previous attempts at resettlement in the colonial period and since had failed because there was no land for highlanders to farm on the narrow coastal strip, yet desa headmen continued to request resettlement centers because projects of this kind were a source of lucrative contracts and honoraria. On other occasions, desa headmen used a discourse about highlanders' backwardness to disqualify them from development programs involving free farm inputs, credit schemes, or other handouts. They argued that the backward highlanders could not make good use of such inputs, which should instead be given to more advanced coastal dwellers who could provide an example and lead the way.

Most desa headmen were unconcerned about their lack of accurate data about the highland interior, but a few thought that more information would be helpful. The headman of one desa was ecstatic when I gave him a copy of the detailed map I had prepared over a period of months with the help of highlanders who supplied the names of the rivers and hills, based on their recollection of trips they had made to hunt, trade, or visit kin. For me, this map was a remarkable testament to the highlanders' intimate knowledge of a landscape full of meaningful connections. For the headman, it meant something else. "With this map," he said, "I can explain to officials from Palu the difficulties we face in managing these people and bringing development. The officials never go up there. They have no idea what it is like."[24] The map would show the visiting officials why it was impossible for him to civilize the highlanders so long as they remained scattered. He was one of the desa headmen who frequently visited the highlands, and he knew resettlement to the coast wouldn't work. His plan was to persuade Palu officials to build a series of resettlement centers in the highlands where the people could learn to live in real houses and bathe with soap, while continuing to farm on their own land.

Superficially, the idea of building a series of small highland hamlets had merit, but highlanders were skeptical. They needed to live in their fields to guard them from the wild pigs that could devastate an entire corn crop in one night. This meant building a new hut each time they fallowed their fields. But they did not reject the concept of incorporation in a government program.

Although there were reputed to be some especially primitive "bela" deep in the highlands who were stubbornly evading state authority, I did not meet any people fitting that description. Highlanders I encountered, middle hill Muslims and inner hill "bela" alike, were eager for the government to build roads into the highlands and supply schools, health clinics, and the other standard desa services. They were not content with their living conditions. Nor were they seeking "alternative" development paths. They wanted to be included in the national mainstream. They were especially keen on schooling and often mentioned that they were embarrassed by their illiteracy and their inability to speak Indonesian. They knew that their lack of education made them vulnerable to being cheated by merchants, and exposed them to being yelled at and ordered around by desa headmen. It also made it difficult for them to speak up for themselves, and made them feel inferior, a condition they described as shame (*meinka* L) and marked with silence, averted eyes, and hunched shoulders.

Highlanders who explained to me their difficulty in achieving their goals for "development" emphasized that their problem was not simply neglect. They were convinced they were actively excluded by people they described graphically as "crocodiles in the path": corrupt and greedy people who prevented them from receiving their due. Indeed, I noticed that they talked far more often about their exclusion from the gifts they associated with development than they did about the relations through which coastal merchants extracted profits from their labor. Viewing development as a flow of gifts (handouts of cash, tools, seeds, pieces of tin roofing, subsidized rice, roads, schools) had a disciplining effect, as many observers pointed out during the New Order period. A person or group that made trouble would not see gifts flow their way.[25]

Even after the end of the New Order, when repression became less intense, highlanders continued to be absent, or silent, at desa-level planning meetings I observed. Language was one reason for the silence. Even when everyone present spoke Lauje, desa headmen ran these meetings in Indonesian, marking them out as sites of official business in which they didn't expect uneducated highlanders to play a part. Highlanders also stayed silent because they thought speaking up would be futile and probably counterproductive. They would be ignored, or they might even be punished. Even though some highlanders had an incisive analysis and were diligent in finding out just how they were being cheated, they had no way to use this information. So they vented their anger among themselves and shared their analysis with me during long discussions in their mountain homes, but I came across only one instance in which highlanders organized an open collective protest over the way crocodiles had stolen something that belonged to them. The event occurred in 2006, a conjuncture shaped by stronger notions of rights and entitlements, a public discourse about the evils of corruption, and a new confidence among highlanders who had prospered from cacao. I will return to it in chapter 5.

DISTANCING

Among highlanders, the most significant social division was that between the Muslims of the middle hills, and so-called bela of the inner hills, who were animists or recent converts to Christianity. The Muslim highlanders learned about Islam from the coastal merchants with whom they had regular contact because of their long involvement in the production of tobacco. They were not especially devout and their knowledge of Islamic scriptures was limited, but in their own eyes their identity as Muslims aligned them with the people of the coast, all of whom were Muslim, and separated them from the backward "bela" who lived in the inner hills above them.

Just like the Lauje of the coast, Muslim Lauje of the middle hills acknowledged that they shared common ancestors with the "bela" in ancient times. But they too subscribed to the evolutionary narrative that classified the "bela" as primitive. Even when my hosts in the middle hills lived close to "bela" houses, they discouraged me from visiting: "There will be no one home, they have all gone hunting." "They will be too scared and will run away." "The path to the house is too steep and overgrown." "Their dogs bite." They mentioned unpredictability, quick tempers, and a tendency to violence especially if scared, threatened, or insulted. Rina's family had tales of a violent attack on their kin following a failed trade deal in the 1930s, and Rina had to work through her own fears to accompany me on visits to "bela" neighborhoods.[26] Most of the time she would comment afterward about the generosity of our hosts, who had done their best to welcome us, but I noticed that a couple of inner hill clusters we visited made her especially nervous. I didn't know why until she shared with me the stories that circulated on the coast about someone's capacity for violence. This could be direct violence, taking up an axe or bush knife, but more often it involved a capacity to communicate with unseen spirits and direct them to cause accidents or illness. I didn't ask her to revisit these places.

Rina's fears were fed by the tales told by the "bela" themselves: they stressed that they were good people, and happy to receive guests, but they could not vouch for the people farther inland. Yet however far we walked the truly wild folk we were supposed to encounter never materialized.[27] Indeed, when the Canadian development project asked me to take some government officials and NGO people from Palu into the highlands in 1992, the visitors were disappointed that after so many long hot hours hiking up mountain trails, the people we encountered were so ordinary: no paint and feathers, no carvings, costumes, music, or dance, no scary savages or noble ones, just a lot of poor people leading hard lives.

Lauje highlanders living in the middle hills were positioned awkwardly in the spatially ordered social hierarchy of the Lauje area. In their own eyes, they were superior to the "bela" and they were meticulous in keeping their social distance. From the perspective of the coastal folk and the desa headmen, however, all highlanders shared the same deficiencies: they didn't live in concentrated hamlets; they moved their houses each time they left their fields to fallow; they didn't eat the prestige food, rice, as their staple, but "inferior" foods such as corn, cassava, and taro; and their children did not go to school. Middle hill folk judged themselves by these same standards. Although their dress and demeanor enabled them to blend in with coastal people on market days so they avoided the ridicule heaped on the "bela," they saw themselves as poor, they referred to their houses as mere garden huts (*sulaub* L), and they were embarrassed by their lack of education and inability to speak Indonesian. They recognized, of course, that many coastal people also led very tough lives, especially the landless people who lived as squatters in flimsy bamboo huts. Nevertheless, highlanders were not romantic about their autonomy or food self-sufficiency. They could grow their own food, but they were still poor.

Some middle hill folk felt that their social position had deteriorated since the 1970s, when a price collapse of their main cash crop, tobacco, obliged them to move farther inland where conditions were suitable for their new cash crop, shallots. So long as they lived near the coast, some of their children had been able to attend school, hiking up and down daily. As they moved inland their children became illiterate just like the "bela," with all the stigma that label implied. Some ex-tobacco farmers explained that their grandparents had once owned coconut trees on the coast, assets that would have placed them in the respectable middle range of households in the coastal status structure. Instead they "became hill people." Amisa of Sibogo, a woman of about fifty, described how her ancestors were tricked by the coastal elite, in particular the desa headman who ordered her family to cut down their coconut trees to make room for a field of wet rice. He promised to replace the trees, but did not follow through. "After that we stayed in the hills," she said, "so that is why my children didn't go to school." Her story probably referred to the period around 1910 when the Dutch authorities commanded the highlanders to move to the coast and some did indeed plant coconut trees. But their need to access land for food forced them to withdraw back into the hills, and some of them were chased away by coastal dwellers who laid claim to the land. In Amisa's version the story was one of defeat and withdrawal, a spatial and social distancing that made her family into highlanders.

Some middle hill farmers who had kin living on the coast experienced social distance in a bitterly intimate form. In 1996 Amin recounted how he had been snubbed by his relatives. He put it this way: "On the coast there I have lots of family, but if I don't take my own food I don't eat all day. . . . [The teacher] is my second cousin. Why is it that when I meet him it is as if we were not family? Sometimes they are eating in the kitchen, and I just sit [out front] in silence." To avoid embarrassment, he had cut off relations with his better-off kin. Amin was acutely sensitive to social stigma. In the 1990s he carried yams down to sell in the weekly market, a practice he felt marked him as a poor man. Carrying down half a ton of shallots or cacao, in contrast, was something he could be proud of: coastal people and desa officials took notice. By 2006 Amin had become one of the most successful cacao and clove farmers in Sibogo. He planned to build a brick house on the coast, not to live there but to use on market days, and to demonstrate his newfound status. At home in the hills, he built a solid wooden house with a zinc roof and three bedrooms, equipped with pink plastic chairs, a satellite dish, and TV. Just like the coastal elite, his family ate the prestige foods rice and fish at least twice a day, and they drank coffee with sugar.

Extractive Relations

In the period before 1990, coercion and attraction together shaped the extractive relations between coastal merchants and the highlanders who furnished their source of profit. This form of extraction is sometimes described as extraction by "extra-economic" means, a confusing designation if we understand economy broadly as the social organization of production, consumption, and exchange.[28] More accurately, the means were noncapitalist as highlanders controlled their own land and were not compelled to sell crops or labor in order to survive. For the merchant-chiefs to extract profits or taxes from highlanders, they had to coerce them or induce them to enter a relationship. Rina's elderly father captured the dynamic when he recalled how groups of "bela" in the interior had been incorporated into the trade-taxation system run by a charismatic merchant-headman in the 1930s:

> You couldn't make the bela work—they were like wild chickens of the forest. We were afraid to go up there. Some died up there without ever paying tax. The former headman used to coax them, gently. . . . In 1934 he went up into the furthest interior with a ward head respected by the bela. After that, many came down for the first time. They stayed at the headman's house. It was full of people. 50 or 60 came down at a time. He told them to bring rattan, cinnamon and damar. That way he had all of them within his realm. He was the one who tamed them. Before that, some of them had never brought down damar and they had never seen the sea.[29]

From then on, Rina's father recalled, "bela" would hike down to the coast and contract with the headman or another merchant to collect a particular forest product (e.g., damar resin) at an agreed price and take an advance, enough at least for a few packs of salt. When they brought down the goods, the Chinese merchant for whom he worked instructed him to deduct some of the money to pay the head tax, and give them the balance in cash. He explained that the reason the "bela" were willing to bring down forest products and pay their taxes was their desire to be "free to go down to the market." Such a desire can be fostered and channeled, but it cannot be imposed. There was a coercive element: highlanders who refused to pay the tax were harassed if they ventured to the coast. But the means of coercion were incomplete. Highlanders could stay in the hills, and conduct their trade through intermediaries. This meant they couldn't wander among the market stalls to examine the goods and select their own knife blades and clothing—a privilege for which some highlanders were prepared to pay, and others were not.

Scenes I witnessed in the 1990s echoed the ones Rina's father described. Large groups of "bela" still hiked down from the inner hills to the coast to trade and visit the market, and they often slept at the desa headman's house, where they expected that their loyalty would be rewarded with hospitality and protection. A visit to the marketplace had a palpable allure. Whole families, or groups of families, hiked for two days from the inner hills, far more people than were needed if pragmatic buying and selling was their only purpose. They were attracted by the world of goods and the bustle of a crowd of

1.4. Inner hill folk at the coastal market

people gathered in one place, which they contrasted with the dull isolation of their highland lives.

Elderly Muslim Lauje in the middle hills gave different, but equally relational accounts of why their parents had consented to pay taxes. Taxes were what the government demanded, hence paying taxes distinguished them from the "bela" who were too primitive to understand about taxes or obey official commands. They made a similar observation about the unpaid labor service (*kerja bakti*) that was the principal form of rural taxation under the New Order. Desa headmen ordered them to work on construction and maintenance projects, especially during the 1970s when the coastal road was being built. No doubt it was a hardship. The work was strenuous, and they had to bring their own food and stay on the coast for periods of about two weeks. But they argued that it was their work on the road that opened up the Lauje area and ushered in the era of development, an important accomplishment in their eyes. The "bela" did not participate.

FOOD

Lauje highlanders supplied most of the food staples (rice and corn) consumed on the coast from the time people first settled there. A rain shadow that kept the coast and foothills dry for most of the year meant that coastal dwellers could produce at most one crop of corn, and by around 1910, the coconut trees that dominated the coastal strip had squeezed out food production. A collapse in the price of copra in the 1930s caused severe hardship for all the coastal dwellers whose livelihoods had come to depend directly or indirectly on this crop. Rice was imported in the wooden boats that plied the coastal markets from the 1930s, but these imports were not routine and few people could afford to purchase rice from this source. Highland food production was thus essential for sustaining lives. It also sustained the profits of coastal merchants as it reduced the price they had to pay for other commodities (copra, tobacco, shallots) by lowering the cost of reproducing labor. Yet highlanders could not be coerced into supplying coastal folk with food. They had to be attracted.

For as long as anyone in the Lauje area remembered, groups of two to thirty people would hike up from the coast and the dry foothills carrying coconuts, salt fish, knife blades, or sarongs and sometimes cash to buy or barter for corn, a practice called *modagang* L. Highlanders who had produced a bumper crop of corn welcomed these visitors from afar because if one person had a bumper crop often all the people in their neighborhood had plenty as well, so they couldn't sell it or give it away. Nor could they store it for more than six months. In 1992 I spent a very uncomfortable night in a house about eight hours' walk from the coast that was full of rotting, bug-ridden corn. The owners hadn't sold it, because no one came to buy it and they did not think it worth their while to carry it down to the coast to sell at the market. They noted that the small sum it would fetch would hardly cover the cost of the meals they would have to buy at the food stalls before they hiked back up.

I heard different opinions about whether barter was somehow more appropriate than transactions in cash. Some highlanders said food could be bartered but shouldn't be sold. Others said it was just a matter of preference and practicality. Cash was sometimes used, but barter often made more sense to both sides. For highlanders to spend cash they had to hike down to the market: it was convenient to have trade goods brought to the door.

Lowlanders could add value to their trade goods by putting in hard work as porters, and an attractive item like a pretty sarong might entice a highland woman to give up some of the rice she had in store. Usually, however, highlanders kept their rice as a reserve and traded only their surplus corn. They traded food among themselves as well because the diversity of highland soils and microclimates meant that a corn harvest could be plentiful on one hill slope and disastrous on the next. Coastal people had no mechanism to coerce highlanders into selling food if they didn't like the terms of trade, nor could they coerce highlanders into producing more food than they needed for their own consumption. Desire for trade goods encouraged some highlanders to plant big fields, but sometimes a bumper crop just happened because work, seed, soil, sun, wind, and rain came into alignment.

WAGE LABOR

Lauje men from the middle hills worked away from home in ebony extraction between 1930 and 1980, taking out the last stands of this valuable timber.[30] The work required hundreds of men to work together in supervised crews, levering, rolling, and hauling the huge logs to the edge of the rivers where they were too heavy to float, but could be dragged down or sometimes lifted out by helicopter. The merchants who organized and financed ebony extraction built barracks to house the workers on the spot and fed them from a centralized canteen, implementing a form of labor discipline that mimicked factory or plantation conditions. When one stand of ebony was exhausted, a process that could take several years, the workers moved on to the next location.

Some highlanders worked for a decade in these ebony camps, leaving their fields as soon as their crops were in the ground. Although the pay was low it was the only regular wage work available in the area. They could forgo this work since they had their own source of food, but relational considerations entered in: the money they earned enabled them to pay a bride price to their prospective in-laws, a route to marriage that was more prestigious than performing labor service or eloping with the bride. It enabled them to buy clothing so they could visit the market without the shame of wearing rags, like the "bela." In the authoritarian conditions of the early New Order period (1965–80) the level of coercion increased and desa headmen contracted highlanders from the middle hills to work in the ebony camps without pay for a few weeks each year, an illegal extraction they glossed as part of highlanders' obligatory unpaid labor service (kerja bakti).

During the 1980s and '90s, the larger species of rattan vine suitable for use in the furniture industry was the main forest product extracted in industrial quantities. Some inner hill men also participated in this work. It was organized very differently from ebony extraction. Highlanders were contracted by merchants to collect rattan on a piecework basis that put all the costs and risks onto the workers: the cost of buying food to sustain themselves while in the forest, the work of building a shelter to sleep in, the cost of buying batteries for their flashlights, the uncertain outcome of searching for the rattan which grows wild, and the risk of injury as they climbed or felled huge trees to access the spiny vines and hauled heavy loads down to the collection point.

Rattan and ebony merchants used cash advances to draw in and entrap workers. These advances concentrated powers of attraction, coercion, and authority into a single package. The merchants worked through agents whom they sent up into the hills bearing large amounts of cash. The agents attempted to entice workers with an immediate payment, commonly amounting to one or two months' pay. For young men these relatively large sums of money enabled them to buy clothing or make an offer of marriage. Married men gave the advances to their wives so they could buy salt, kerosene, and other necessities during their absence. From the moment the advance was received the worker was "hooked": caught like a fish on a line. Some still obtained cash at the end of their period of wage labor. Others returned home with debts they could only redeem by leaving to work again for the same boss. Highlanders described this condition as being tied at the throat, like a bull in harness, or trussed up in rattan like an animal hunters had strung on a pole to carry home. Some workers spent the advance money within a few days of receiving it, often through gambling binges organized by merchants or their agents, under the protection of desa headmen, local police, and army officers, each of whom took a cut.[31]

Ebony and rattan merchants mitigated the risk of giving cash advances to mobile hill folk by using desa headmen or their deputies as agents, since these men could use the authority of their office to enforce debt collection. Desa officials relied in turn on their representatives in the highlands—the neighborhood heads—to monitor the repayment of advances and harass recalcitrants. Using desa officials as agents also reduced the risk of default by the agents themselves, who handled large sums of cash. A desa official was less likely to abscond. Workers did not have this countervailing power and could be cheated of their pay. They were especially vulnerable in the case of rattan extraction because rattan that has come down from the hills, as one young collector pointed out, will not go back up again. Without a commitment from a rattan "boss" to purchase the load at a given price, a collector would receive very low offers for the rattan he had hauled so laboriously to the collection point. Some workers said their "bosses" still owed them money, having failed to pay them the balance they were due after their rattan was weighed and the advance deducted. It made sense, in this context, for them to take a big advance in case the "boss" defaulted. Sadly, in cases where desa officials doubled as rattan merchants or agents, they often abused their authority coercively to intensify extraction and accumulate more profit.

TOBACCO AND SHALLOTS

Tobacco was the main cash crop produced by thousands of highlanders in the period 1820–1970. It was grown in the foothills on the slopes facing the coast, where the rain shadow and sea breezes provided ideal conditions for drying the tobacco leaves after harvest. The main mechanism of extraction was monopolistic trade enforced by debt. Although tobacco is a "cash crop," former tobacco farmers recalled that they seldom saw any cash. As soon as the new tobacco plants were in the ground the farmers would begin to take goods such as rice and clothing on credit from their tobacco merchant. This continued throughout one growing cycle and was carried over to the next. Men tried to keep their debt down by doing wage work in the ebony camps between planting seasons, leaving their sisters or wives to manage their farms. They cleared fields so the women could grow corn and rice higher in the hills where rainfall is more abundant, but conflicting labor demands and the necessity of staying close to the tobacco to guard it from wandering cattle precluded adequate food production. Drought could cause failure in the food crops, while excessive rain could ruin the tobacco which rotted in the fields or on the drying trays. One way or another, dependence on credit became routine, and a "good" merchant would carry tobacco farmers through a bad season and also help in special circumstances such as illness, death, or marriage. Merchants weren't obliged to sustain them, however, and they cut off farmers who were poor producers.[32]

Tobacco farming was also associated with routine gambling, often organized by the tobacco merchants themselves. The gambling took place in one of the highlanders' homes, or on the coast, in the back of a merchant's store. An older woman who described her husband's gambling binges when they were a young couple in the 1950s recognized a plus side to gambling, in a hard life with few luxuries. Her husband worked hard—harder when he was gambling since he made his tobacco garden bigger than usual, and "when he won," she said, "we would eat as much fish as we wanted." Gambling had much more serious consequences after land became individual property, as farmers who gambled could lose not just their money or their crops but their land, and with it the means to farm again another day, a point to which I will return.

Once trapped in debt, the price tobacco farmers received for their crop was very low indeed. Not surprisingly, some tried to sell secretly to different merchants for a better price, evading the claims of the merchant to whom they were indebted. Merchants and farmers were both trapped, as a merchant who stopped lending to an indebted farmer had no hope of recovering the loan. As Tabang, an ex-tobacco farmer from Sibogo observed, "many people down there on the coast became rich from our tobacco. If we couldn't pay off the debt it was carried to the next year because we had no other income. So the debt was never paid off. As long as we kept planting, the boss still trusted us." The debt was carried over to the children after the parents died. Idin, another ex-tobacco farmer, put his assessment this way: "We planted tobacco for hundreds of years, and we didn't get anything at all—it was just used up on food." He made this comment in 1996, by which time he had prospered from cacao, his implicit point of comparison.

If the highlanders' returns from producing tobacco were so minimal, and the level of extraction by the merchants was so high, why did farmers keep producing this crop? They controlled their own means of production—their land and labor. They could have defaulted on their debts to the merchants and moved away. Some did indeed take this course, especially in the 1970s as the tobacco era came to an end. Ex-tobacco farmers moved out to desas where there was still unclaimed forest not too far from the coast. Some stayed in their home desa but moved higher into the hills to grow food and a new cash crop, shallots. But for more than a century thousands of Lauje highlanders in the middle hills continued to plant tobacco, and they stayed in place. I have already noted the ecological limitations: a farmer who fled to the inner hills, where rain is more abundant, could no longer grow tobacco and would have to find another source of cash. The material characteristics of the place (soil, rain, distance) worked together with the spatialized social distinctions I have explored in this chapter. Tobacco farmers could not live on the coast, since tobacco required continuous attention, but their social orientation was toward the coast and Islam. Although they were familiar with the inner hills, having hiked there to trade, escape to a life among the primitive "bela" held little attraction for them. Status concerns, maintaining a position in the social hierarchy centered on the coast, and trying to avoid being mistaken for "bela" when they hiked down to the market, served in multiple ways to keep tobacco farmers in their place.

Shallot farming set up different relations between highland farmers and merchants. Shallots were prone to fungal and other diseases. High risk made merchants unwilling to make cash advances or to supply shallot sets (bulbs for planting) on credit. As a result only a few highlanders were able to sustain shallot production, namely those who were successful in growing the crop and adept at saving money to use as capital to buy fresh sets when needed. These farmers prospered, but they were not compelled to keep growing this crop if the returns didn't seem worthwhile. They still had plenty of land on which to grow food. The neighbors they hired to help them, especially women who did the tedious work of weeding large fields, also had their own farms and could survive without wages. Nevertheless, since highland women did not do wage work outside the desa, they appreciated having a source of cash nearby. It meant that they and their children could avoid the shame of going down to the market in ragged clothes.

PRODUCTION FAILURES

A final element in the set of productive and extractive relations that linked the highlands to the coast needs to be mentioned. It puts a twist on my observation that for two centuries, highlanders fed the people of the coast. Roughly every five years highlanders experienced a catastrophic collapse in their food production when afflicted by the extreme and prolonged droughts associated with the El Niño weather cycle.[33] Despite their finely honed techniques—planting different varieties of rice, corn, and tubers in separate plots with different sun, soil, and wind exposure—during severe droughts everything they planted shriveled up and died. In centuries past, Lauje aristocrats and coastal merchant-chiefs had sometimes supplied rice seed to highlanders who had lost their entire crop and eaten their reserve seed in the depths of famine. But highlanders could not count on this coastal elite to provide them with a "subsistence guarantee" except, perhaps, as debt-bondsmen or slaves.[34] Nor could they count on neighbors to help them as everyone's production collapsed at the same time.

In the 1990s, highlanders had vivid stories about the extended droughts they had experienced and their struggles to survive. These were terrifying times for them, offering a glimpse of what climate change will mean for people whose survival depends directly on their farms. They relied on famine foods, a wild root they call *ondot* L (*diascorea hirsuta*) in the middle hills, and wild sago in the inner hills, but when demand was high, these sources of food ran out. Drought was accompanied by epidemics of dysentery as water sources became polluted, and dozens of people could die in a short period. The American missionaries based at Ogo'alas described their harrowing experience as witnesses to the extreme El Niño drought of 1977, when inner hill neighborhoods they visited had many dead, and the survivors were too weak to bury them.

Far from living in a state of food security, highlanders were all too aware that their staple food production could fail.[35] Even in non-drought years rainfall was erratic, and attacks by birds or monkeys could devastate crops. Wild pigs could ruin entire fields of corn. An early, hopeful rumor about my presence in the highlands was that I had come to bring some poison or electric fences to keep the pigs from destroying their food. Middle hill Muslims were especially desperate for a solution. Although they were not devout, they were strict on maintaining the taboo against eating pork, as it distinguished them from the pork-eating "bela." The "bela" had a double advantage on the food front: they set traps and hunted the pigs that approached their cornfields, so they had more corn in their diet and also more protein. But they too could suffer from food collapse. Everyone faced the problem that the work of clearing forest and weeding the fields was strenuous, and people who were old or sick, or whose work was disrupted by childbirth, illness, or the death of family members, could not be assured of a harvest.

These were the conditions under which highlanders found the idea of plucking cacao from a tree that would continue to yield from one year to the next with minimal maintenance so appealing. By the time of the El Niño drought of 1997 they had planted cacao and they could borrow money from cacao merchants, their debts secured with their land which by then had become individual property. Borrowing to meet urgent needs put some highlanders on a downward spiral that led eventually to the loss of their land. But they argued that they were still better off with these tree crops than they had been without them. Access to credit helped them to survive a crisis, even if it jeopardized their security in the long term.

A brief comparison across conjunctures shaped by El Niño droughts helps to specify the elements that increase or reduce security. In *Silent Violence*, Michael Watts explores how farmers and pastoralists in northern Nigeria were made more vulnerable to drought as their previously diverse forms of production were undermined by the colonial regime. Mike Davis makes a similar argument about India in *Late Victorian Holocausts*, elaborating further on the severe burden imposed by colonial taxation. In contrast, in his book *Fertility, Food and Fever*, David Henley argues that the arrival of cash crops such as coconut in the northern part of Sulawesi early in the twentieth century gave people access to cash to buy imported rice and helped to reduce drought-related mortality. In 1998, highlanders who had stands of cacao to rely on during a drought expressed its benefit in just these terms. Yet Henley's analysis misses a crucial element: not everyone owned coconut trees. Planting these crops increased the security of some farmers, but undermined the security of people who ended up landless, making it more difficult for them to survive not just in drought years but in normal years as well. A similar process occurred with highlanders' cacao. As I will show in chapter 4, droughts weren't external to the process of land concentration, they were active in producing it, as they compelled some people to sell land and enabled others to buy it at low prices.[36]

Conclusion

The social relations of hierarchy, extraction, and rule forged between Lauje highlanders and coastal folk over more than a century were built upon a combination of powers far more intricate than is suggested by the antinomies state/non-state, or resistance/consent. For centuries, highlanders engaged in trade with coastal merchants because they were attracted by the goods on offer. Indeed, highlanders helped to constitute this merchant class by "feeding" them with their food, labor, and cash crops. The merchants came to own productive property and capital to engage in trade or advance as credit, and they controlled state-backed powers of coercion, a potent combination.

Highlanders were marginalized by a discursive regime that situated them as backward, and in significant ways they came to see themselves in this light. They paid taxes to secure a kind of freedom, while retaining their autonomous food production in the hills. The price of their autonomy was stigma and low social status, as they lived in mere "garden huts," rebuilt every few years when they fallowed their farm plots. Often they had very little cash in hand to spend at the market. The "bela" were especially stigmatized for their ragged appearance and lack of familiarity with the styles of dress and consumption popular on the coast. Very few highlanders spoke Indonesian, and their children did not go to school. They feared famine and the chronic insecurity caused by droughts, diseases, and feuds, inducing them to seek protection by positioning themselves closer to sources of authority. They kept silent about the corruption of "crocodiles" who excluded them from development goods and hoped that their patience would eventually be rewarded.

Together, the material, cultural, economic, and social elements I have described in this chapter formed the conjuncture I encountered in the Lauje area in the early 1990s. They formed Lauje people into three distinct social groups and brought each group into relation with the others through material exchanges and frames of meaning and evaluation. In particular, they positioned highlanders in the middle hills to take the initiative to launch into cacao. I emphasize positioning because my goal in this chapter was not to identify conscious or articulated reasons—because of "a," we'll do "b." Rather, it was to explore the structure of feeling, the experienced set of relations, tensions, and desires within which this course of action emerged. Among the many elements I have identified, three were especially important: the experience of social stigma, livelihood insecurity, and a desire for access to the roads and schools highlanders associated with a modern village life.

2 | Work and Care

This chapter explores the relations of work and care that connected highlanders with each other in the Muslim, middle hill neighborhoods of Walu, Sipil, and Sibogo around 1990. It introduces the dramatis personae (also listed in the appendix), the people who will figure often in my account, and explores the dilemmas that confronted them in the period when everyone still had a place to farm. Although land was abundant, highlanders stressed that their lives were not easy: it was hard work to clear patches of forest with axes and bush knives, weed huge fields on hands and knees, and guard the corn from voracious wild pigs. This work positioned them in intimate relations with seeds and soil, and also with each other, as it wasn't possible to farm or survive alone. Yet the work was also individuating. Highlanders recognized individuals as the full owners of their productive capacities, and the owner of whatever they produced through their efforts.

Lauje highlanders' stress on the link between work and property is not unique, as it figures in many indigenous traditions across Southeast Asia and beyond.[1] Their stress on the economic autonomy of individuals also resembles the "possessive individualism" described by the seventeenth-century English philosopher John Locke.[2] But the individuals in Locke's account are abstract and disembodied. It is hard to picture who fed them when they were young or when their crops failed, or who shared the burden of heavy, intimidating physical tasks. For Lauje highlanders, the tensions between autonomy and dependence, working for oneself and caring for others, formed the texture of everyday life. They also shaped the trajectory that emerged with cacao.

Work Creates Property

In 1991 I hiked up with an interpreter into an area where middle hill farmers were growing garlic. The hike had been steep and it rained, so we arrived after dark, exhausted, muddy, and soaking wet. The next morning we were out on the platform behind the house spreading our wet clothes to dry when one of the daughters of the house began to pull out bundles of garlic and arrange them in the sun. "Who do they belong to?" I asked casually. "That one belongs to my mother, those belong to my older brother, those belong to my sister, these here are mine, and those belong to my father," she replied. "Mother and father work together. Today they are weeding her garlic. When that is finished, they will weed his." This was my introduction to the economic autonomy of household members, each of whom created personal property through his or her work. They also created relations of kinship and care by entering into exchanges with others. In this case, husband and wife were exchanging days of work on a reciprocal basis (*mendunduluan* L). The daughter who laid out the bundles of garlic was just helping out (*mendulu* L), treating her work as a gift, a sign of care that she was free to make (or withhold) because her labor belonged to her, not to her parents or siblings. Although most households were based on nuclear family units of parents and unmarried children, and these households were units of daily food consumption as well as sites of comfort and conviviality, they were not units of production, savings, or investment. Indeed, they reversed the familiar sequence of evolutionary accounts that treat unified families and communities as the starting points of history, with the rights of individuals emerging later. They didn't oppose gifts to rights, but took their capacity to make (or withhold) gifts as a sign of their autonomy.[3] So what were the practices that produced highlanders as autonomous individuals, and linked them to one another?

HUSBANDS AND WIVES

In Sibogo, in 1993, Malia, a successful shallot farmer, paid her husband Tabang to carry her shallots down to market. He checked out the prices with the shallot merchants and hiked back up to report. "He doesn't dare interfere with what belongs to me," Malia observed. "He didn't want to sell them himself because he isn't the owner." She paid him at the going rate for his work as a porter, the same rate he could obtain by working for a neighbor. To pay him less would give him a claim on the product: he would become a joint owner. Like the couple with the garlic, they cooperated on tasks like planting

2.1. Couple planting shallots

2.2. Porter carrying shallots

in which men used a long pole to make a hole in the earth, while women placed the seeds. Tabang weeded his own shallots, and if he asked Malia to do this task while he went off to earn wages outside the desa, he paid her for the work by giving her a share.

Tabang and Malia were a stable couple so these practices weren't a sign of conflict. Rather, Malia argued that separate ownership of their cash crops clarified where each of them stood and meant that when they went down to the market they each had their own money so they could buy whatever they wanted. When their children were small, Tabang took his turn staying at home to care for them and carried infants to the field to be nursed so that Malia could keep working. Some couples also maintained separate ownership of their food crops (rice and corn), but Malia and Tabang worked on these together and considered them jointly owned. Cooked food served in the house was different: regardless of who had grown it or paid for it, a married couple and their unmarried children shared whatever was in the pot. "We work separately," Malia observed, "but we eat together."

Elok, Sibogo's chief of custom, acknowledged that separate crops and separate, often secret savings were a common arrangement. He knew something about this, as part of his job was to resolve marital disputes. The arrangement he thought ideal was one in which husband and wife produced crops jointly, but the wife kept all the cash, saving if possible for tough times between harvests and giving her husband money for his own expenses when he needed it. As feminist scholars point out, the role of women as family treasurers can mean the opposite of women's autonomy, if it makes them responsible for stretching inadequate funds.[4] Women "treasurers" often found it difficult to make ends meet in Sibogo. Malia had to budget carefully as she relied on income from her shallots to buy rice, a crop she had stopped planting as she found it too time-consuming. Yet no one I talked to thought a hardworking woman farmer should be left short of funds. The wife of Ayub, a successful farmer on Walu, was proud of how her husband insisted that she should feel free to treat herself to personal expenditure from their common fund: "Whenever I go down to the market he says to me 'be sure to take money with you, maybe you'll want to buy yourself a new blouse or sarong.'" She took his insistence in two ways, as a confirmation of the property due to her in return for her work, and as a sign of his affection.

Contrary cases proved the rule. Idin, an ambitious farmer in his midforties, was an extreme example. When I first knew him in the early 1990s, Idin was beset with incurable boils. He never wore pants. He spent his days at home in a sarong, "just drinking coffee and smoking," as Malia's sister Ramla observed, "and watching his wife carry timber." Idin's wife Sina crossed the lines of the usual gender division of labor by doing the heavy work of building a house and clearing land, tasks strongly marked as male. She even surprised herself. "I thought I couldn't do those things," she remarked, "but in the end I did them anyway." Despite Sina's outstanding strength and diligence and the prosperity she brought to her husband, neighbors pointed out that she wore ragged clothes. To get cash for her own needs she gathered fallen candlenuts to sell, an activity only poor people engaged in. The neighbors felt Idin was doubly at fault: he did not do his share of the work, and he failed to recognize and reward his wife's work. Ramla was adamant: she would not stand for such treatment. Stressing the exhausting physicality of long, hot tasks like weeding a huge field stooped low, or on her knees in the dirt, she said she would insist on her share "because I would be the one tired out working." She was not alone in her suspicion that Idin had acquired the power to communicate with spirits and was using it to control Sina and extract her labor.

Married men usually did the work of clearing a fresh patch of forest each year to make it ready for their wives to farm. After they cut the forest they left the fallen trees to dry for a month or so, then burned them to kill the weeds and create a fertile ash. The forest they cleared might be primary forest with huge trees that needed to be felled with an axe, a task that took months to complete. More often, it was secondary forest with smaller trees and bushes that could be cut with a bush knife. Rights to use secondary forest were inherited by men and women equally, so the patch of forest a man cleared that year might belong to his side of the family or to his wife's side, or sometimes to both if they had common ancestors (I explain the land tenure system in detail in the next chapter). The land could be used for a second year before being left to fallow, but usually men cleared a new plot anyway so a couple had several plots in production, each at different stages of fertility. They planted each plot with different varieties of corn, rice, and cash crops to help spread the risk of crop failure and also to spread the work load. Farm plots in their second year needed a lot of weeding. There was no taboo on men weeding but it was usually women who ended up doing most of this tedious task. Women sometimes referred to themselves jokingly as *tope lamung* L, people of the lamung, a reference to the special short-handled, flat-bladed weeding knife they wielded from dawn to dusk.

Depending on the size of the trees, and the size of the farm plot, land clearing could be a big or small task, but either way it was firmly gendered male. Widows and unmarried girls who wanted to farm independently had the right to make use of a patch of their inherited family land, and they made their own farming decisions, but they still had to find a way to access men's labor to get the land cleared ready to plant. They could pay someone a wage, if they had the money, or they could ask neighbors to help by attending a collective work-party called a *sug* L. The cost of a sug was the food for a festive midday meal for three to thirty people, depending on the size of the task, and the obligation to reciprocate with a day of work on a future occasion. Another route women could follow to access land was to ask to borrow a corner of a cleared garden from a neighbor, a practice called *momasusu* L. But access to land for momasusu was a gift, not a right, and it wasn't guaranteed.

Leka, a widow and mother of five children, had formed a combined household with her elderly widowed father Dekon. She hoped that he would have the strength to clear a field so that she could stop doing wage work for other people, and establish her own farm. She did not ask her brother Sampo to momasusu because his garden was too small, nor did she call a work-party as her neighbors were also struggling. Meanwhile, to stretch her wages, she joined other widows and women without gardens who purchased food staples (corn, cassava) from neighbors and kin and carried them home by the back load every few days. This practice was called modagang—the same word used to describe the long-distance treks coastal people made into the highland to buy or barter for food, which I described in chapter 1. Modagang within the neighborhood was always for cash.

Although highland marriages could be tense, divorce was not common. There was only one case in Sibogo in the period 1990–2009 when the widow Samina divorced her second husband, the Imam. I stayed at this couple's house for two months in the early 1990s, when Samina was working hard planting cacao as well as food for the family. Although her husband had put no work into the cacao, she was reconciled to the idea that he would insist that the trees were jointly owned. Since both of them had children from their first marriages, she wanted to divide the cacao so each could leave a share to his or her own children. She promised to keep on weeding his cacao so long as the ownership of her share was clarified. He refused. When they divorced around 2000, he decided to register the divorce formally with the Muslim court in Tinombo town, but he refused to follow the court's ruling that the property they had acquired during the period of their marriage should be divided equally. Instead, he sold all their jointly owned gardens without her consent and kept the proceeds to himself. In telling me this painful story,

Samina kept emphasizing the work she had invested in the trees, and the ownership rights that she was quite sure were her due.

PARENTS AND CHILDREN

Highland parents treated their children as autonomous economic actors, with the right to enjoy the fruits of their own work. From the age of about ten, they gave both boys and girls access to a small patch of cleared ground and encouraged them to plant their own shallots or groundnuts. In the past, highlanders recalled, children had their own tobacco plots, and some had food-crop gardens too.[5] Far inland at Gau'ma, Mopu's wife described her childhood experience this way: "We children kept our rice in the same store hut as our parents, but in separate places. If we were going to cook rice to eat together, our parents brought out one bundle of rice to thresh, and each child did too. If a guest came to the house it was the same. We each took out a bundle of rice to eat together with the guest." In her example, the incentive for a child to grow food and lay claim to it was the pride of contributing to the family pot, or to a special meal that built up relations with a guest. The century-old market for highland food crops that I described in the last chapter added a further incentive to work hard and claim individual ownership. Linajan's mother, another elderly woman from the inner hills, recounted an event in the 1940s when she had produced her own crop of rice. Although her family was living far from the coast, a lowlander came by and offered her a decorative metal box for keeping betel nut in return for ten bundles of rice. When she asked her father's advice about whether or not to make the sale, her father said to her, "Don't be sad about it. The rice, it would be eaten, but this thing will still be here. Even grandchildren will be able to use it." Her father advised, but clearly the decision was hers to make. A parent wouldn't sell a crop belonging to a child.

In Sibogo in 1993 no children had their own food plots as they preferred to put their energy into growing shallots and groundnuts, which were more lucrative sources of cash. They sometimes helped their parents on the food plots destined for family consumption, but parents mainly did this work themselves. In Amisa's household, where I asked her literate son Hamdan to keep a record of the daily work activities of each household member over a period of a few months, Amisa spent more than a month weeding and guarding her rice field alone. Her husband spent his time off in the forest collecting rattan and timber to build an extension to their house for the upcoming wedding of their daughter. He had planted groundnuts on a plot of land cleared for him as a gift by his married son Atar (momasusu). He had agreed to give half the value of his groundnut crop to a daughter who weeded it for him. The couples' unmarried daughters and a daughter-in-law each had their own groundnuts, and often worked together in the "day for a day" exchange system (mendunduluan). Amisa was too busy for groundnuts, but she did find time to plant some cassava in the garden of her married daughter Alia, who never seemed to get around to it, and whose children often showed up at their grandmother's house hungry. She also went to help the wife of another married son, Nijo, to bundle up her harvest of fresh corn because she had a small baby and couldn't keep up with the work. Through these practices, work and care flowed between individuals both within and across household boundaries, while there was no confusion about who owned which crops, or how each person's work would be rewarded.

Malia's children were younger than Amisa's and didn't yet farm independently, but she had already started to pay them when they helped her weed her shallot fields. She saw this practice as part of their training. Given an incentive, she argued, they would learn to work hard and grow up to become autonomous adults who could take care of themselves. She also paid one of her older children to care for the younger ones to free up her own time. When she sold her shallot crop she gave each of the children some money and took them down to the market so they could choose a new piece of clothing. She expected them to start clearing their own land when they became teenagers, the boys by working on it themselves and the girls by organizing collective work-parties. For Malia and Tabang, their practice of exchanging days of work growing tobacco on Sipil as teenagers in the 1970s was a prelude to courtship: he cleared land for both of them, she weeded both crops. They also joined the work-parties organized by their siblings and neighbors.

Highlanders placed markers in their fields to recognize separate ownership of the crops planted there. Ayub argued that it was taboo (*pepali* L) to keep a large field intact: it should be divided into strips (*belang* L) for each household member. To break this taboo, he suggested, would offend the spirits of the earth and water, and cause illness. The exception was when a married couple was using the whole field for family food, and no one else had any crops growing there. The large work-parties I saw in Mopu's neighborhood in the inner hills in 1992, in which thirty people were out each day planting whole hillsides with rice, were engaged in both a collective endeavor and a highly individualized one. Each hillside was divided into separate farm plots belonging to households, each plot further subdivided into belang for household members and for others who had claimed a corner for their own use (momasusu). The work-party I attended was called by an unmarried girl who was the owner of the rice crop we planted that day, and who supplied the food for the midday meal consumed by all the people who came to help her.

Idin, once again, provided a counterexample. He didn't reward his children for their work, or recognize their contributions to family food provisioning. Neighbors thought Idin's desire and capacity to control and exploit the labor of his wife and children was unnatural. They believed his powers lay in the spirit realm as he wasn't violent or bad-tempered; he was jovial and generally fun to be around. There were a few men who exercised control over their families through direct violence. When a farmer on Walu sold a huge corn crop for a good price but failed to give his children any money, Ramla was outraged, but not surprised: "He beats his wife and children. None of his teenage daughters have married because he doesn't let them go anywhere. . . . He just keeps them working. One of the girls is very young but he has already taught her to weed. He even makes his children fetch water so he can bathe in the house. If it was me, unless I really couldn't walk to the river, I would never ask my children to fetch water for me to bathe at home." Ramla was horrified by the idea that a healthy adult man would demand this kind of subservient labor from his children. Personal hygiene, minimally, was a person's own responsibility. Lauje men, I noticed, washed their own clothes; their wives or daughters did not do this for them.

Most parents in Sibogo in the 1990s did not expect their children to repay them for the work of providing for them when they were young, but they did hope for loyalty and affection. Idin was irritated when his children wanted to go to earn wages outside the desa: "We raise them when they are young," he complained, "but when they are big, someone else gets the benefit." Malia contrasted the behavior of her oldest son, who slept a lot and kept asking for money, with her second son who volunteered help on his own initiative: "If he comes back from wage work and sees his father's garden needs to be cleared," she commented, "he just takes up his bush knife and does it." Tabang's elderly mother didn't seek a material return from her children, but she did want a sign that they cared about her: "I fed them so they grew up, but now they don't want to feed me. . . . They tell me to get food for myself. If they sent me some money, even just a little, I would be very happy, but they don't send anything, and they don't even mention my name. If not for these children who live near here [Tabang, Samir] I would never taste salt." She was blind by 2006 and couldn't walk. Despite her complaints, she was very well cared for. I missed seeing her in 2009 because she had asked to be taken to visit another of her children some distance away. She was being carried by two of her grandsons in a sarong slung between two poles when I passed her on the trail. I didn't know that she was the person sitting inside.

Neighborly Relations

In the 1990s the highland neighborhoods of Sibogo, Sipil, and Walu had quite a stable membership, and dense ties of kinship, friendship, and neighborliness linked individuals across household boundaries. Individuals related to each other through reciprocal exchanges from which they expected an approximate equivalent, and also through gifts of food, work, and care. Highlanders took pride in being generous, but they didn't like to think that others were taking advantage. Hence deciding when they could legitimately stop the flow of gifts to keep their property for themselves was a delicate matter.

Drawing a boundary between kin and non-kin didn't provide a solution, as most neighbors were also kin. The Lauje kinship system is bilateral, and highlanders gave equal weight to relatives on both their mother's and father's sides.[6] Neighborhoods also tended to be endogamous: almost everyone married someone who had grown up in the same place, so families that didn't share a common ancestor were soon entwined through marriage. I saw this pattern emerge over two decades in Sibogo where the generation I first met as youngsters later intermarried. Idin's daughters, for example, married sons of Tabang and Elok. Jopri, one of Malia's brothers, married Amisa's daughter. Amisa's son Hamdan married Sara, a daughter of the widow Samina, and so on. Second and third cousins could marry, and first cousins could marry too if they sponsored the appropriate rituals. Highlanders expected siblings to be especially close.[7] Even siblings who lived next door could drift apart, however, unless they sustained their bonds through ongoing exchanges.

TRANSFERS OF FOOD

To explore the tricky balance between working for oneself and caring for others, I tracked transfers of food between households and the terms on which the owner of the food, the person who had grown it, could hold on to it. Highlanders noted that they had to share cooked food with a guest who came to the house, especially if the guest saw it. This version of courtesy prompted stories like the one told by Amin, in which his stingy kin on the coast left him sitting hungry in the front of their house while they ate secretly in the kitchen. The material quality of crops was relevant. Tubers would eventually rot in the ground, and owners with excess supply often gave them away for free. Amisa and Malia, who had large patches of taro, yam, and cassava, often received visitors who asked for some, and they told them to go dig up as much as they could carry home. Their most frequent visitors were three widows from Sipil who hiked over to Sibogo for this purpose, often arriving together. They offered to buy the food (modagang), but Malia and Amisa usually refused the money, a gesture called *nosola* L.

Malia said she was happy to give food away but she didn't like to ask for it. She would ask for cassava or yam for free (*momongi* L) from her mother or mother-in-law because the food would go straight into the tummies of their grandchildren. But she would not ask from anyone else, even her sisters who lived very close by. She and her sister Ramla often sent gifts of food over to the sister married to Alip, whose children were always hungry because Alip rarely cleared a garden. Idin was discreetly generous to a widow who lived nearby, struggling to raise her seven children, and he often instructed his wife Sina to take over some bundles of corn. "She doesn't want to ask," he said, "so I have to keep checking to see if they still have food in their house." Sina also appreciated the widow's pride and the brave effort she made to try to manage without help: "She once told me if there was a way a person could work all night, she would do that so she would never run out of food."

In the early 1990s, I saw bundles of uncooked corn moving around Sibogo in three forms: as goods for sale, as gifts for which no return was expected, and on the basis of balanced reciprocity (a loose expectation that the recipient would make a similar gift when his or her own harvest came in). Since corn harvests were staggered, everyone kept an eye out for where some delicious fresh corn might soon be available. The owner usually sent word to neighbors and kin announcing that the corn was in and inviting them to come over to get some. This meant inviting some people and not others. Amin was adamant that he only needed to send invitations to his parents and siblings, but if someone came to the house when the fresh corn was being brought in—that is, forced the issue—he would have to give them some. Malia put the arrival of kin and neighbors, with or without invitations, in a more positive light by linking it to the work they put in helping her to bundle up the corn. "Sometimes ten people come to help," she said, "whoever hasn't harvested their own corn yet." She implied that she might get some corn in return (when other harvests came in), but she also recognized the neediness of some of her helpers, and the ambiguity of the bundles of corn she gave them to carry home, which could be seen as gifts or wages.

Since highlanders did not count the bundles of fresh corn they ate themselves or gave away, quantities were hard to track. The highest estimate I heard was half the total crop either consumed or dispersed as gifts immediately after the harvest. With the remaining corn, owners signaled their intentions by physically dividing the corn into a portion that was for sale and a portion to be stored. They made the part they intended to sell into bundles and waited for someone to come to buy it (modagang). The buyers were often neighbors who found it convenient to buy food from a nearby source. They had no problem with the idea that the person selling corn would expect some return for his or her work. But buying and selling among neighbors wasn't the same as a transaction between strangers. It demanded delicate calibrations over quantity and price.

Several farmers in Sipil complained of feeling pressured to sell more corn than they had planned, at a price that was below the return they felt they deserved. Among them was Amisa's brother Nasir. "I just harvested two thousand cobs," he reported. "Then friends and family came asking for help so we had to give it to them. In this complex we are the only ones with cassava and yam. Others don't have anything at all. That is because they are fed up, since the wild pigs just eat what they plant. For people who come to buy corn I sell one hundred cobs for Rp 500. If they bring money, I take it. If they don't, I still give them some. Yam has a really high price now in the market. People come to the market from far away to buy it. I don't take yam down to the market anymore." His comment about the yams flagged Nasir's sense that the opportunity cost of giving yam away for free was increasing. Because his neighbors didn't grow enough food themselves, they curtailed his freedom to profit from his work. No doubt he did find ways to limit the flow of food to others, but he didn't cut it off.

The standard way to limit the amount of corn available for sale was to place the portion intended for family use on a storage rack outside the house (a *pakele* L) where it would dry and could be kept for up to six months. Cooking it involved removing it from the cob and pounding it into a grain that could be cooked in boiling water like rice, though it was much coarser. The rule was that people did not ask to buy food from the pakele, which bore the implicit sign "family food supply." Highlanders explained the way the pakele signaled meaning in several ways: some said it was taboo to ask to buy corn until after

2.3. Taking the last of the corn down from the pakele

the owners had put the part they wanted to reserve onto the pakele; some said people who had no corn came to help put the corn on the pakele, knowing that from that day onward they couldn't expect to buy any more; others said there was a ritual to complete before the corn could be taken down from the pakele, so a person who just showed up casually looking for corn would be out of luck. A quick calculation showed that in 1996 Amin sold about one-third of his crop and successfully reserved two-thirds for his pakele. In the same year, Idin had no pakele since he sold all his corn. Elok recalled a tactic he had used a few years previously: he didn't have time to make a pakele so after selling bundles of corn to twenty people and still more came, he carried the remaining corn over to his son's house where it would be out of sight.

Elok had grown very large fields of corn expressly for sale since he was a bachelor. He claimed that he kept the price of his corn low because he had made a pact with the spirit owners of the earth and water: they would keep away the wild pigs and other pests, and he would respect the customary injunction against treating food as a source of excessive profit. It was a pragmatic bargain, expressed in a small ritual at which he called the spirits by their secret names, and gave them some food offerings arranged on a woven bamboo tray (*salasa* L). The idea that the spirits would disapprove of excessive profit was a common one in the highlands, but the details—how much profit was excessive—were negotiable.[8] Elok talked explicitly about his sense of moral conduct, arguing that it was better to give food to someone without money than to someone with money, a principle he obviously balanced with the reality that he planted the corn with income in mind. He mostly sold his corn to neighbors, because fewer coastal folk hiked up to buy corn since the price of the food they could buy at the market had come down with improvements to the coastal road. Idin, as usual, was more direct about his profit seeking: "Lucky for me all those people on Sipil are so hooked on gambling because if not my corn here would have rotted. They were so busy gambling they didn't have time to farm, so my corn sold well. I made a good profit. . . . One night I bundled up ten thousand cobs, and the next day they all came to buy it."

WHY WERE HIGHLANDERS BUYING FOOD?

There is a puzzling element in this conjuncture that needs to be explained. Since land was freely available in the highlands in the early 1990s, why did anyone need to buy food? Why didn't they just grow their own? Some food buying was simply a way to even out the gaps between harvests as highlanders planted corn at different times. But there was more to it. The people referred to rather scornfully by Idin as "those people on Sipil" bought food routinely and had tiny farms or no farms at all. Some Sibogo folk faulted them for being lazy, feckless, and foolish, or fixated on short-run returns. Idin took note of their gambling. Malia's mother emphasized their chronic tendency to freeload off kin. "That is how it works on Sipil," she said. "If one person has some corn, the whole hillside goes to modagang there so however big the garden, the food is quickly finished. I once heard one of them complain: 'it is you who make us run out of food because you come to modagang every day.' . . . If you think about it, if they worked and their children helped they could have big farms, but they are so lazy, the whole lot of them. Only the women work hard, going everywhere to modagang."

Malia's mother made these observations as we sat in the doorway of her house, watching some women from Sipil walk by carrying heavy loads of food in baskets on their backs. She was sympathetic to the women's plight and recognized the hard work they put in just to find sources of food and carry it home, compounded by the shame they felt at their neediness and exposure. Ramla concurred that men who failed to clear adequate gardens put their wives in a very awkward position: "If men like that were borrowed goods," she quipped, "it would be better to return them. If you keep them all you get is more babies!" She was stressing that the burden of reproductive work, not just bearing children but making sure they were fed, fell heavily on women. As returns from rattan collection declined in the 1990s, men who left to work for wages brought little money home. Their wives depended on their own wages from weeding and searched for cheap food to make their funds stretch.

Sina did not agree that men from Sipil who came asking for work or looking to buy corn were lazy. Being married to Idin, who did no physical work at all, gave her a uniquely positioned perspective: "They work really hard," she observed; "they work much harder than Idin, so why don't they want to have their own gardens?" She added this: "Idin always tells them, 'you should farm so you don't have to modagang,' but they reply 'Idin should just keep farming so we have a place to modagang.'" She too was puzzled. The problem of the laziness of the poor, as other scholars have observed, is commonly enunciated by people who are relatively rich and like to think that they have earned their wealth through diligent effort.[9] Like Sina, we should hesitate to concede to this assessment. But if not for reasons of laziness, why did people from Sipil routinely buy food?

The specific history of the land and people of Sipil, taken together, yield an explanation. Land was indeed freely available on Sipil, but it was less fertile than the land in Sibogo. It was former tobacco land that had been thoroughly worked out. Ex-tobacco farmers from Sipil had moved in to Sibogo after the collapse of tobacco in the 1970s to find more fertile land for food and shallots (a history I explore in more detail in chapter 3). The people who stayed on Sipil made a different adjustment. The men stepped up their commitment to wage work outside the desa, mainly in rattan extraction which boomed in the 1980s,and the women did wage work in Sibogo. In the early 1990s, it was easy for Sipil women to find work because the large shallot and cornfields planted by Sina, Malia, Amisa, and others needed lots of attention. So long as Sipil folk could buy corn cheaply from their kin on Sibogo (and as we have seen, they sometimes forced the issue), they could make ends meet.

From their perspective, buying food was economical. At the price charged by Amisa's brother Nasir in 1993, Rp 500 for one hundred cobs of corn, they could buy six hundred cobs for one day's wage, Rp 3,000, and they did not need to run the risk of failed harvests or marauding wild pigs.[10] This explains their reply to Idin: "You should keep planting food, so we have a place to modagang."

Sipil folk's way of making a living was undermined during the 1990s by a constellation of elements. Sibogo farmers started planting cacao and stopped growing and selling cheap food. They had less need to employ wage workers, and returns to men's work as rattan collectors in the regional economy also declined. The timing was terrible. By 1998, when Sipil folk had run out of options for regular wage work at decent pay and looked again to the land to see what they could grow there, they found it was already in short supply. Sibogo folk faulted them again, this time for their lack of foresight: when they should have been at home planting cacao, they were away working somewhere else.

Working for Others

Lauje highlanders' emphasis on the economic autonomy of individuals was compromised when someone needed paid work so badly that they could not negotiate. In the early 1990s, workers in Sipil were already on the cusp of this predicament. Their employers on Sibogo handled it with different degrees of delicacy.

Idin had devised a way to handle the continuous need of Sipil folk to buy food and turn it to his advantage: "They are not ashamed to modagang. They come to ask for help. They say look, it is almost dark but we don't have food, so I have to give them some. . . . They ask me if there is any work here, and as payment I give them cassava or bananas." Cassava and bananas were cheap food so the pay Idin gave them for the work they did when they arrived late and desperate wasn't generous. Note that they were not begging. Sina confirmed: "They never ask for food for free. If they don't have money they ask for work. They get started and we pay them in the afternoon. . . . We pay them in corn and give them a meal. Up to eight people come at one time. In the afternoons I don't have time to work myself because I'm busy preparing the bundles of corn for each of them. I add some cassava too. . . . Right now we have no work for them so I send them away." Although the Sipil people she sent away were her kin, she did not feel obliged to give them work on every occasion. Sometimes, she carried debts forward, giving food to a person who promised to come back to work at a later date. And she didn't squeeze their pay down to the minimum, she added a bonus of cassava.

In the history of Southeast Asia, debts incurred due to a shortage of food or the need to pay fines or taxes were an important mechanism of bondage, also described as debt slavery.[11] In the Lauje highlands in the 1990s, I did not hear of debt burdens that were so onerous they amounted to debt slavery, and I could not discover a Lauje word for a debt slave. There were a few people who worked consistently for other households for pay in cash or kind, possibly under conditions of debt, but they tried to present themselves as autonomous farmers, like everyone else. Several employers tried to minimize the implications of having a claim on someone else's labor. Amisa's son Nijo, for example, mentioned that one of the widows from Sipil had asked him for corn some months previously and said she would come to help weed on another occasion. She kept her word, but Nijo stressed that if she had not come, he wouldn't have insisted. He did not want to present himself as someone who would take advantage of the widow's need. Leka explained this kind of relationship from her own perspective. She had asked Malia for some corn a few months before, so when Malia held a work-party she came to help. "I told Malia next time you have a lot of work, send me word." Leka's work on this occasion was a disguised form of debt repayment because Leka never held work-parties herself so Malia would not have to reciprocate the day's work. Like Nijo, Malia did not want to appear to be calling in debts, but she did acknowledge the wage aspect of the transaction: "If I didn't have so much work that needs to be done, I would just give the corn for free."

Highlanders also handled straight-up wage work not preceded by debt politely. "That is how we do it here," Amisa's oldest son Atar explained to me. "We don't say come and work. We ask someone for help, then we give them money." Despite her need, Leka stressed that she could provide or withhold her labor at will: "Malia comes here to ask me for help when she cannot keep up with her weeding. She came a few days ago and I told her I would go there soon." "Soon" flagged a respectable delay, Leka's way of reminding me of her autonomy.

Sina sometimes handled the awkwardness of the wage relation by mixing genres, providing lunch for her workers as if the event was a work-party. She was concerned to maintain a semblance of reciprocal, neighborly exchange even though the situation was unbalanced. She needed workers routinely, while the workers were chronically in need of work and food. She knew that her capacity to plant extensive gardens was only possible because of the continuous supply of willing workers from Sipil. In parts of the highlands where everyone farmed and had enough food, some people still did wage work if they had some time to spare between their own farm tasks, needed cash for a particular purpose, or wanted to help a neighbor as an expression of care. But they weren't compelled. The only way a highlander could access a large number of workers to complete a big task in a short time was by holding a work-party of the conventional, reciprocal kind in which the person who held the work-party returned a day of work at a later date.

ELOK'S SUG

Elok often held work-parties. He had a slightly different view of the kind of reciprocation due to him. Grumbling one day that his nephews had not come to one of his work-parties, he pointed out that helping them with marriage negotiations or settling a dispute could take days of his time. As a senior man and chief of custom, who frequently gave up his time to serve others, he felt he was owed some days of work as an expression of gratitude and respect. He calculated that for an outlay of Rp 10,000 on food, he could have thirty people come to work on his farm. With the going daily wage at the time around Rp 3000, hiring workers would have cost him Rp 90,000. Other farmers made different calculations. Nijo's wife was frustrated by the uncertainty of work-parties. The workers might leave when the work was only half done. Or she might cook for a lot of people but few came. She preferred to hire wage workers from Sipil so she could calculate exactly how much work would get done at what price. Then, there were contingencies such as rain. Sometimes, all these contingencies and calculations were present at once.

It rained during one of Elok's work-parties that Rina and I attended in 1993. This was Elok's explanation for why fewer people came than he expected. Elok was aware that a poor turnout also put his social standing on trial. Discussing the event later, Malia hinted that people were growing tired of Elok's frequent work-parties that began to seem excessive, because "he wanted his garden to be big." Those who came despite the rain arrived late, and worked for only a couple of hours. As we all sat crowded in Elok's small bamboo house, eating the meal his wife and her sister had prepared, Elok dropped strong hints that the workers should stay and wait out the rain, going back out to work for a second stint after lunch. But he did not want to appear too demanding so he made the hint through a story. This is how he put it: "I once went to a work-party where we worked from eight to two; the work was so heavy I would not go there again; I was sick for two nights. Over here on Sibogo we work from eight to eleven, take a break for lunch, then work again from two to four thirty."

The rain didn't stop so I couldn't tell whether Elok's hint would have succeeded in persuading the workers to put in a few more hours clearing a patch of secondary forest, the task Elok had set for them. Reflecting later, Elok expressed regret at the wasted food and opportunity: "I forgot to tell them," he said, "if it rains don't come tomorrow, come the next day." He mentioned that his workers had offered to come back another day to finish off, but he did not want to ask them. What would have pleased him most was for the workers to come back uninvited, making a gift that demonstrated their respect and affection.

BEYOND THE DYAD

The relations of work and care I have described so far were dyadic, linking two people either within or between households. This was true even for a work-party attended by thirty people, like the ones I saw in Mopu's neighborhood in 1992 in which, over a period of a week, a whole hillside was planted with rice, or the ones I observed in Sibogo when a large group of neighbors turned out to help prepare for a wedding. All the people who came to contribute their work did so because of their relation to the host, and their presence or absence further shaped the bond between them. Burials were the exception: regardless of their relations to the deceased or their family, everyone who was close by rushed over to show solidarity and do whatever was necessary to wash the body and get it into the ground quickly. They brought small gifts of food and cash to help with the immediate expenses. Funeral feasts were delayed, sometimes for years, until the family had gathered the necessary funds. They were often held together with weddings as a side event since kin and neighbors, and if possible also the Imam or pastor, were already gathered and the necessary infrastructure (extension to a house to provide shelter for guests, big cooking pots, stacks of borrowed plates and glasses) had been assembled.

Building a bond between two people wasn't easy, but it was clear that two autonomous individuals were responsible for making and sustaining it.[12] Highlanders found it much more difficult to organize collective action on a territorial basis. Neighborhoods were tightly knit through kinship, as I explained, but they were not bounded at their edges, since the houses were spatially dispersed and moved every few years, and many individuals had links to other neighborhoods through descent and marriage. Further, the presence of a cluster of households in proximity and their degree of cohesion could wax and wane, as I illustrated with the example of Mopu's neighborhood which dispersed after his death. The annual cycle of rituals related to rice production was modest and didn't involve entire neighborhoods. There was a small ritual performed in the middle of a rice field by the pasobo who planted the first seeds of the season, after which others could go ahead and plant when they were ready. Some households organized a small ritual after the harvest, alone or with a few neighbors, but it was optional and only held if the harvest had been good. Highlanders had just one ritual event they recognized as a collective project of a neighborhood as a territorial unit. This was a ritual supplication to the spirits said to be the "owners of the earth and water" (*togu petu, togu ogo* L). But it was weakly institutionalized and difficult to pull together, as a set of events that occurred in Sibogo in 1993 will illustrate.

Rina and I were visiting Emsalin, an older man, well liked and respected, when Sina came to his house to tell him about a strange and terrifying incident the night before. She was sleeping with her daughters in one of their garden huts, while Idin and the boys slept in another hut, their usual practice when the corn was ripening and it was necessary to guard it from wild pigs. The women heard a noise at the door like a dog, and they thought it was Idin playing a trick to frighten them. In came two birds. They screamed and chased them out. As the creatures walked toward the stream they realized that they were more like humans, or maybe pigs. Not long after, Idin arrived to see what the screaming was about. "We need to feed the spirits," said Emsalin, upon hearing this story. "Those were not pigs, they were the spirits of the earth. It is because we haven't been doing the ritual [for the spirits who own the water and earth]. The person who should do it is Alip. I'll tell Alip we need to do this so they don't come back."

As people discussed this strange event over the next few days, I heard different opinions on the nature of the pigs. Malia suggested that they were humans who took on animal form, called *pongko* L, and the pongko was in fact Idin. She thought he had spirit knowledge that enabled him to transform himself into an animal and terrify people, a capacity consistent with his unnatural ability to control the labor of his wife and children. Emsalin did not name Idin. He stuck to the argument that the strange event marked a collective affliction and demanded a collective, ritual response. The proper way to do the ritual, Emsalin explained, was with the participation of all the households in the neighborhood, each of whom should bring food to load up the offering tray (the salasa L). The place to conduct the ritual was by the stream that is the dwelling place of the spirits that were acting up. But how to make it happen?

Emsalin's first problem was that Alip, the person he thought was competent to do the ritual, was not willing to step forward because another man also claimed to have the requisite spirit knowledge, and wanted the role. Since both Alip and the other contender had acquired their knowledge in dreams and trances, and neither of them had done the ritual before, there was no means to adjudicate between them. Alip was surprised that Emsalin and others had such faith in his powers, since he was not sure he really had any. There were about a dozen people in Sibogo who were known to have trances in which they became possessed by spirits. These trances sometimes occurred spontaneously without warning. They could also be provoked, and Emsalin used to organize collective trance sessions (*tantaloan* L) for this purpose, because he thought that to have the capacity to trance and not express it could make a person ill. But most of the people who were occasionally possessed by spirits did not claim to have knowledge that was beneficial for public purposes such as healing other people (the role of the *sando* L), or communicating with the earth and water spirits that had sway over the well-being of entire neighborhoods.[13] They were also wary of being accused of using their spirit knowledge to send spirits to harm others. This accounts for Alip's reluctance to insist that he was uniquely qualified for the role.

Emsalin's second problem was that the officially appointed neighborhood head was not an effective leader. He had alienated many people because of his sporadic attempts to enforce a ban on gambling and because of his unfair dealing concerning land, a story I take up in the next chapter. When he called a work-party, few people showed up. He was one of the crocodiles who prevented highlanders from receiving their share of government handouts. He also lacked charisma. No one listened when he spoke. He was often absent on wage work. Although organizing rituals was outside the official job description of a neighborhood head, he had the authority to issue commands, or at least to set a date and request everyone to assemble with their offerings of food. The desa headman was encouraging. He wasn't among the contingent of purist Muslims on the coast who argued that the food on the offering tray would be eaten by birds, not spirits. Yet the neighborhood head did not respond, and Emsalin did not want to assert himself as leader or proceed alone. All he could do was keep talking about the need for the ritual and hope that enough pressure would build to prod the neighborhood head to act.

The collective ritual was held three times in Sibogo between 1993 and 2009, and each time it was a struggle to pull it together. The one I attended in 2006 fell far short of Emsalin's aspirations: only a few households were present, and the food offerings were incomplete. Emsalin's effort to rebuild the small neighborhood mosque stalled for the same reasons: lack of leadership from the neighborhood head, and noncooperation from the residents who claimed that their neighbors were shirking their share of the collective work that had been agreed to. When they gathered on the appointed day to go to the forest to find and carry down timber, few people came. Freeloading in a relationship between two people was problematic, but at least each party knew where it stood. The problem with freeloading in a collective endeavor was that other people could profit from your work just by staying home.

SEEKING ONE'S FORTUNE

Lauje highlanders' ideas about individuals, their autonomy, and the proper way to organize intimate relations were reflected not just in their material exchanges, but in other domains as well. I noticed, for example, that Lauje highlanders paid close attention to the likes and dislikes of small children. Rather than try to mold children, parents thought they should try to understand their distinct personalities as the basis for forming a relationship with them. Variations on the idea that each individual is distinct are common across the Southeast Asian region. Anna Tsing gives an example from Kalimantan, where Meratus Dayak emphasized that it was the practice of living and finding one's "luck" or *rajaki* (D) that differentiated individuals. Rajaki, she writes, is

> the "luck" one can strive to increase through knowledge and ritual and one can look for as game in the forest, honey in the trees, a good deal in the market place, or a winning number in the lottery. The demands of following one's rajaki separate individuals each trying to find their own living. At a basic level, the individual is the subject of rajaki; or, one could equally say, the discourse on rajaki creates individual subjects with separate needs and desires. . . . Talk of rajaki explains why people, even kin, may go their separate ways.[14]

Lauje highlanders believed an individual's life path could be disrupted by malevolent spirits sent by jealous kin or neighbors. Manipulating these spirits required spirit knowledge that anyone could potentially obtain secretly through trances and dreams, so it was hard to know who had this knowledge or how they would use it. Malia was certainly afraid of spirit attack, especially in the days when her shallot farming was successful. She sought to deflect attacks at the source by hiding her wealth and by being generous with gifts of food to keep envy at bay. The point was not that her wealth was illegitimate: everyone knew that Malia's relative wealth in those days was the result of her skill and hard work, which were widely admired. Envy, in this context, was niggling and unspoken—a sentiment that other people might have, but no one would like to acknowledge. Envious people attacked their victim's capacity to work by making the victim sick or lame, an attack that spread out to the victim's family. During Amisa's illness, her married and unmarried children stopped work for several months, abandoning crops in the fields and running through their savings. Amisa's children suspected a woman on Sipil of causing their mother's illness and death, but they did not accuse her as she was kin, and breaking the bond with her would disrupt many other valued ties.[15] Like Malia, Amisa was generous to people around her, but this wasn't sufficient protection.

Since spirit attacks could come from many sources—envious neighbors, random strangers, carelessly kicking a rock, or showing insufficient respect during ritual incantations—highlanders sought to acquire a uniquely personalized, invisible barrier (*penangkis* L). The power concentrated in the penangkis came from their own spirit knowledge, gained through dreams and trances, or from ritual specialists who transferred the necessary knowledge for a fee. Highlanders often asked Rina about my penangkis, which they thought must be very powerful since I seemed to move about freely without falling ill or fearing attack. Adults devised penangkis to protect their small children, but from the age of about ten when children started to take on responsibility for their own lives, they sought the necessary protection on their own initiative. It was only bizarre events like birds that turned into pigs, or collective afflictions like droughts or epidemics, that provoked a demand for a collective response, though it wasn't always forthcoming.

Conclusion

Lauje highlanders in the early 1990s considered individuals—women, men, and children—to be the owners of their capacity for work and the property they created through their sweat. They thought attempts by men to control the labor of their wives and children were unnatural and unfair. But they didn't live as atoms. They built relations both within and across household boundaries through exchanges of work and care that were sometimes reciprocal, and at other times one-sided. Their practices were formed through their long exposure to markets. The possibility that someone from the coast might hike up to buy their rice and corn encouraged individuals to assert their ownership to food crops, even when they hadn't grown them expressly for sale. Another crucial element was the abundance of land, which put the emphasis on work as the source of value. The materiality of crops was also formative. Rice had to be planted in coordination with neighbors and with their help—to plant it alone was futile, as it would be eaten by birds. Corn could not be stored for too long, so giving some away to neighbors and getting some back when they harvested made sense. There was a materiality to big tasks like clearing forest for a new farm plot as well. Technically, it could be done alone, but highlanders said it was less intimidating and more fun to do it in company. Yet they could not take the help of their neighbors for granted. Recall the poor turnout for Elok's sug, and the hint that he was asking for help too often.

The tension between working for oneself and caring for others was part of the texture of everyday life. No one was perfectly generous or completely heartless, and how people positioned themselves along this continuum, or were positioned by others around them, was a matter of subtle adjustment. Rather than describe highlanders as strategizing individuals busily manipulating everyone around them, however, I have emphasized how they became subjects with particular habits and desires. Their everyday practices of exchange were routine and unremarked until there was a breach—a failure of generosity, or a problem with freeloading kin. I paid particular attention to these breaches because they shed light on practices that were normally taken for granted, and because highlanders themselves discussed them, and in so doing, made their values explicit.

Highlanders' stress on the right of an individual to the property he or she created through work was an important element that enabled the arrival of cacao in the highlands and the enclosure of land. Individuals—not nuclear families or households—were the owners of their capacity to work. They were "free" to work on their own projects, to make a gift of work, or to sell their labor to someone else for a wage. But even when they sold their labor, they didn't treat it as a commodity, a thing detached from the social person whose body did the work. As I will show in chapter 4, the idea of labor as a commodity that could be "freely" bought and sold remained an awkward one for highlanders. Even after some of them became landless, they struggled to find ways to sustain a sense of themselves as autonomous persons who decided when, where, and on what terms to add their sweat to the soil. They found it painful to be in a position where they had no choice.

LOOKING AHEAD

In the early 1990s, farmers in Sibogo were full of projects—ideas about what they wanted to plant and how they hoped to live in the future. Their projects were fueled by their observations from places where they had traveled to work or visit kin, intensifying their feeling that they were far behind in matters such as housing and education. Before I left Sibogo in 1993, I went round asking people what sort of changes they thought I'd see on my next visit. Many people talked about a future in which they might be able to build a house on the coast, equipped with electricity and TV, but they didn't think that would happen soon. They would still be living in Sibogo but there would be improvements. "Next time you come back, this place will be all white"—a reference to the flashes of shiny white caused when the sun reflected off the new zinc roofs that were beginning to replace the old thatch. Or, more modestly, "it won't be a struggle any more to buy salt." Or finally, "you won't see us running off to find ondot L," the wild tuber used as a famine food during droughts, but also used by families that were chronically short of food regardless of the season.

Highlanders also reflected on how centuries of hard work in the old manner—growing food, planting tobacco and shallots, earning wages—had enabled them to survive but not to achieve the improvements they desired. Amisa's sons Atar and Nijo, also Alip, Tabang, and Amin, had spent much of their youth in the forested interior of various desas where they worked hauling ebony and rattan, leaving their sisters and wives to maintain their farms in their absence. None of them had accumulated any wealth from tobacco. Only a few people on Walu and Sibogo had been able to accumulate wealth from shallots, and shallots couldn't be grown on Sipil where the land was too poor. Even in Sibogo, planting shallots was a risky business. In the early 1990s, everyone's shallot harvests failed repeatedly due to fungal disease. Malia ran through her capital with several failed attempts to grow this crop before she finally gave up. The erratic return from shallots was another element in the conjuncture that led toward cacao. Although Idin had been able to build a fine house on the coast with profits from his shallot production, it was cacao that got everyone's hopes up at Sibogo. "If we had cacao in the past," Tabang reflected, "we wouldn't still be living like this, after so many years." But planting cacao meant enclosing their common land, a move that had the unexpected effect of re-forming relations among neighbors and kin, changing the organization of work and space, and reconfiguring almost every aspect of daily life and interaction. How highlanders went about enclosing their land is my topic in the next chapter.

3 | Enclosure

In 1990, Lauje highlanders didn't have a word in their language equivalent to the English term "land." They had words for forest in different stages of regrowth, and a word for earth (*petu* L), most often used in the couplet that referred to the spirit owners of the earth and water, togu petu, togu ogo.[1] By 1998 the word *lokasi*, an awkward import from English (location) via Indonesian, was in common use. It referred to land as a unit of space that was interchangeable with similar units, individually owned, and freely bought and sold.[2] The new word signaled the emergence of new practices and relations. These were not shifts that highlanders planned. They didn't hold neighborhood meetings or talk about the need to create lokasi. Land-as-lokasi was a by-product of highlanders' decision to plant tree crops, mainly cacao, which they hoped would improve their incomes and their social standing. The effect was enclosure: the permanent withdrawal of plots of land from the highlanders' commons.

It seems like such a mundane matter. Farmers often switch from one crop to another, and highlanders had made changes before, when they switched from tobacco to shallots. To appreciate why this shift had such far-reaching effects, we have to attend to its materiality. Tree crops like cacao do something by their permanence. When highlanders planted cacao in their fields, the presence of the trees disrupted the cycle in which they cleared a patch of forest, used it for a few seasons, then left it to fallow. The trees also changed the ownership status of the land, transforming it into individual property, since no one else could use the land thereafter.[3] Excluding other users, and other uses, wasn't new: planting a field of corn also required exclusion, at least until after the harvest.[4] The new element was permanence, and the puzzle is why highlanders accepted permanent exclusion from their formerly common land. Why didn't their customs of shared access prevent enclosure, or perhaps furnish means to adjudicate and limit it? As I will show in this chapter, custom didn't stand outside this process as a stable point of reference. It was selectively revised through words and deeds, through the work of putting seedlings into soil, and sometimes through setting fires or watching productive trees go up in smoke.

Land Relations before Cacao

Many studies of property relations among indigenous people refer to the notion of "customary law," envisaged as an institutionalized body of rules and practices of the kind that sometimes receives official recognition in formal legal codes.[5] Studies of common property regimes similarly emphasize the importance of institutions, minimally a clearly bounded territory, a bounded social group that holds rights in this territory, a system for managing the common land supported by an authority with recognized jurisdiction, and a capacity for enforcement.[6] These models don't fit well in the Lauje highlands, because highlanders didn't live in "communities" with clear territorial boundaries. Potential farmland was abundant so they had no need to manage it tightly. Colonial rule was so light in the Lauje area that colonial authorities had made no attempt to research or consolidate Lauje custom, and Indonesian national land law hardly recognizes customary rights, so nothing had ever been written down or made official.

According to government maps, the Lauje highlands are classified as state forest, under the control of the Department of Forestry.[7] Building on the colonial legacy, the Indonesian government designates about 70 percent of the national territory "state forest," but the Department of Forestry had no interest in the Lauje highlands after the most valuable species, ebony, had been exhausted. Forest officials made no attempt to evict the twenty thousand Lauje who lived and farmed in the highlands, probably because they did not know they were there. It wasn't just that highlanders' practices were illegible to the department, in the way James Scott describes.[8] Their very presence was invisible. None of the staff I met at the Department of Forestry branch office in Tinombo town in 1996 had ventured to hike up into the hills. They imagined that the highlands were densely forested and sparsely inhabited. They had no access to satellite images that would have revealed farms and fallow fields all the way up to the center of the peninsula. Conversely, highlanders were unaware that their forests were claimed by the state and took their customary rights for granted. When they started to enclose their own land, they managed the process among themselves, without reference to state land law, without the use of documents, and without the benediction of government officials. On the rare occasions when they took land disputes they could not resolve among themselves to desa headmen, this was not because they recognized that the state had jurisdiction over the land, but rather in the spirit I outlined in chapter 1: invoking outside authority added weight to their own dispute-resolution processes.

Among highlanders, the institution that gave authority to their land regime was their general agreement on "how we do things around here," such that if someone did something out of line, neighbors would rally around the injured party and back them up. This informal system of "law," collectively enforced, was sufficient in the past to enable farmers, rattan and resin collectors, and hunters to get on with their work without tripping over one another, and to resolve the disputes that sometimes arose. The terms highlanders used to classify vegetation also defined rights. They distinguished between *do'at* L (primary forest that has never been cleared and doesn't have an individual owner); *ulat* L (secondary forest, owned by the pioneer who first cleared it, or his descendants); *abo* L (a recently fallowed garden on which scrub has started to grow back, but there are still useful plants such as banana, papaya, cassava, yams, chilies, and tomatoes that belong to the person who planted them); and *jo'ong* L, a farm plot in current use, usually planted with crops belonging to different people, as I described in chapter 2.

At the center of Lauje highlanders' approach to tenure was the principle I have already explained: the person who does the work becomes the owner of the property that results, a feature shared by many indigenous tenure systems. Put differently, when forest is abundant, it is the labor of making forests into farmland that creates rights. Hence the pioneer who did the heavy work of cutting down the huge trees of the do'at became the owner of the ulat he created. Since only men did this work, only men were recognized as pioneers. Women contributed by growing food to enable their husbands to do this work, but they didn't assert co-ownership. Pioneers sometimes transferred ownership of their ulat to someone else, usually because they had moved away and didn't plan to return. They didn't frame this as a sale (*mobalo* L), because they didn't (yet) have a concept of "land" that placed it in a series with other commodities (like knife blades) that could be bought and sold. They described the transfer, rather, as compensation for their exhaustion (*ongkole* L) and the cost of the food and tobacco they had consumed while working (*ongkose* L). Being compensated in this way extinguished their rights to the ulat. Some men pioneered do'at with the intention of transferring it, effectively using their skills as woodsmen as a way of earning cash.[9] Usually, however, pioneers retained ownership of their ulat and lent it out to kin, neighbors, or newcomers who wanted to use it for a few seasons. They didn't charge rent.

The benefit pioneers received from lending their ulat was that periodic use prevented the trees from growing too big and made the ulat easier to clear next time they wanted to farm it themselves. After a pioneer's death, his ulat passed to his descendants, but they didn't divide it up and claim ownership of individual plots because they were not the people who had done the work of creating the ulat. It wasn't the result of their sweat. So they too saw themselves as "borrowing" ulat from the pioneer, even after his death. They added more ulat to their collectively inherited pool by clearing more do'at around the edges. This then was one kind of commons: a pool of inherited ulat used by a group of kin in a loose rotation.

A second type of commons, more ambiguous than the first, was the pool of primary forest, the do'at. Jurisdiction over the do'at in each river valley (*ompogan* L) was loosely exercised by ritual specialists (pasori L) who had the power to communicate with the spirits of earth and water to seek their blessing for forest clearing, hunting, or rattan collection. Showing respect for the spirit owners of the place was necessary to keep dangers at bay. Highlanders who wanted to start clearing do'at in a new watershed, or who wanted to hunt or collect rattan there, asked permission from the pasori and elders of the nearest neighborhood cluster. Asking for permission was both polite and pragmatic: fear of spirits, and fear of other highlanders bearing blowpipes complete with poison darts, were good reasons to observe proper etiquette.

No person could own the do'at because the definition of do'at was that the primary forest was still intact: no one had done any work there. But it wasn't a "free for all": access had to be negotiated with the people and the spirits nearby. According to the definition used in property rights theory, the fact that there was an agreed procedure for access to the do'at—people and spirits to ask for permission, and sanctions for breach—made it a commons rather than an open-access resource. Yet Lauje highlanders' bilateral kinship system, dispersed settlement pattern, and shifting residence meant that the boundaries of the do'at-as-commons, and of the social group who had the right to access it, were loosely defined.[10]

Lauje highlanders' shifting cultivation system was fairly intensive. A typical cycle involved two to three years of cropping with rice, corn, and tubers followed by a four-to-eight year fallow in which only bushes or light forest returned. This short-fallow system was recorded by colonial officials in northern Sulawesi in the 1820s, and it was still being practiced in the same areas a century later, indicating that it suited local conditions.[11] The main reason for the short fallow was erratic rainfall. Highlanders explained that the huge trees in the do'at often didn't dry out well enough to burn properly. When a burn failed the plot had to be left for a few years until the tree trunks had rotted and some ulat had grown back. Only the second round of clearing produced a good burn and a large clean plot suitable for growing rice. So they cleared do'at only on occasion, and mostly reused their ulat, allowing enough regrowth so that the burn yielded a fertile ash but not letting the trees become too big.

Highlanders' land use system, shaped by the combination of human use and the materiality of the milieu (soil, rainfall, vegetation), produced a landscape in which patches of do'at remained untouched while the best spots, especially hillsides that were not too steep or rocky and had a convenient water source, were cultivated quite intensively. A further implication of the short-fallow system was that farmers didn't usually plant fruit or other useful trees in their farm plots because they reused and reburned the ulat too frequently for trees to mature. So landmarks such as old mango trees were rare in the highlands, and there were no agro-forest gardens of the kind found in Kalimantan near old village sites.[12] Indeed, Lauje highlanders did not have old village sites because they built their houses in their fields, and moved them every few years when they left the field to fallow.

Since highlanders believed it was taboo to mention the names of ancestors—any ancestors, not just their own—their genealogical knowledge was thin. They had no written records. Hence in the long-settled areas like Sipil they lost track of which ancestor exactly had cleared the do'at in which spot. Besides, this knowledge was not important. Bilateral kinship and the high rate of kin and neighborhood endogamy I described in the previous chapter meant that everyone farming on a given hillside was related. They stressed relatedness more than distinct ancestral lines, and they did not give social or ritual precedence to descendants of the original pioneers.[13] The short answer to my question "whose ulat is this?" was always "we are all kin here, there are no outsiders" or "this is all the ulat of the ancestors." In effect, access to ulat was broadly shared among neighbors, but highlanders didn't describe their shared access as a commons "system," nor did they give their land-sharing practices a specific name. There was no designated elder with jurisdiction over the ulat envisaged as a whole: as a defined and bounded unit of collectively owned and managed space. Instead, the person who wanted to use a patch of ulat asked permission from the person who used it last, especially if there were still residual crops such as bananas growing there. Like the system of jurisdiction over the do'at, the system for borrowing ulat was lightly institutionalized. "We all just borrowed from each other" (*mensangsabolang* L, from *menyabol* L, to borrow), was how Amisa explained it. "We just went on and on like that."

THE DIFFERENCE THAT TREES MADE

Highland pioneers who cleared do'at effectively enclosed it, that is, they took control of a patch of do'at held in common and asserted individual ownership of the ulat they created through their work. But over time the ulat reassumed a collective character, as it became the undivided, inherited ulat of all their descendants who used it for their annual crops. When highlanders planted the new tree crops on patches of the inherited ulat, they excluded their kin from future use.[14] They understood tree-planting as a permanent claim of individual ownership and argued that it had always been so: that was why people who borrowed ulat weren't permitted to plant tree crops, only annuals. The clarity of this rule, which was often stated in the early 1990s, seemed to me anachronistic on two fronts: in the past highlanders routinely "borrowed" ulat, so "borrowers" weren't a distinct social group; and they seldom planted trees because the trees would burn the next time the ulat was cleared for planting. In this context, a statement about "how we do things around here" didn't reflect agreed and stable custom. It was an expression of a custom-in-formation, tentatively legitimized by reference to the past.

More than talk, it was the new tree crops themselves that did the transformative work. Like the "work" of the hedges in the enclosures in Britain in the sixteenth century described by Nicholas Blomley, trees both performed and enunciated a permanent change.[15] Highlanders didn't discuss plans to reassert collective claims to the ulat after the cacao had passed its prime, nor did they consider reserving some ulat for food and cash crops, land that could still be borrowed freely. To do this would have required a more explicit conceptualization of the ulat as a commons, a defense of its social and practical value, and the institution of a tighter management regime than had been necessary thus far. Relevant cultural resources to support the value of ulat-as-commons could be found in highlanders' practices, but so could cultural resources to support individual ownership. It was individual ownership that came to dominate in the early 1990s, when everyone wanted to plant cacao. It wasn't the loss of the commons that provoked debate, it was the question of who exactly was entitled to plant trees where.

Since there was no enforcement of national land law in the highlands, and no paper record of landownership or transfer either before or after highlanders planted cacao, it was only the collective authority of highlanders themselves that could make the new enclosures stick. This meant that highlanders had to consent or at least concede to their permanent exclusion from a patch of ulat where someone was planting trees. It wasn't a smooth process, and there were many disputes. Arguments were sometimes made verbally and sometimes enacted forcefully by planting cacao seedlings alongside corn in a garden and waiting to see if anyone objected. Disputes framed in terms of custom were not conclusive. The notion that every highlander needed access to a place to farm was such an obvious fact of life in the past that it wasn't made explicit, and anyway, ulat was abundant, so anyone who wanted to farm could borrow some. Did this mean that planting cacao on the ulat broke with the "custom" in which kin were entitled to access? Or was it merely a new instantiation of the established principle that the property you create through your work becomes your own?[16] Or was it just an awkward but necessary consequence of highlanders' desire to improve their material conditions, a desire that required them to plant productive tree crops on the ulat, instead of "just going round and round" with annual crops, as they had in the past?

Highlanders' answers to these questions were sometimes debated, but more often enacted through the emergence of new practices, and the erosion of old ones. To explore the process of enclosure, I examine three highland conjunctures in which different sets of relations were in play: (1) Sibogo and Sipil, where enclosure meant that neighbors and kin excluded one another, (2) enclosure across the social boundary separating middle hill farmers from the so-called bela who lived just above them, and (3) enclosure shaped by government-backed "development" projects.

Excluding Kin

"He is a fierce man," observed Amisa, talking about her uncle Dekon on Sipil who was trying to monopolize their inherited ulat and had started to sell it. By fierce (*dodog* L) Amisa did not mean physically violent. She meant that he was loud and angry and it was difficult to reason with him. He insisted on his right to do as he pleased without consulting anyone. The occasion was a Friday afternoon in 1993 when Amisa's adult children had gathered in the room at the front of her bamboo house after the men came back from the noon prayer, and the conversation turned to the matter of enclosure. Amisa's oldest son Atar made the argument that families should meet together to discuss how to divide the ulat, since they had shared rights inherited from their ancestors. Amisa was focused on a particular patch of ulat on Sipil she claimed had been pioneered by her own father. He had marked it with a mango tree that was still growing there. She planned to start planting cacao there the following year, but now Dekon had started to work it himself. She was afraid he wasn't serious about farming the plot and would soon sell it to someone else. To prevent this, she planned a preemptive strike: "Even though Dekon has started working there," she insisted, "I'm going to tell my children to go over to plant cacao because that ulat belongs to me."

Enunciating principles such as the notion that families should consult over the division of their inherited ulat, and they should put it to productive use and not sell it; highlighting visible signs on the landscape that served as evidence of work previously invested (the mango tree); and actively embedding fresh work in the soil by planting cacao were three ways people made claims to ulat on Sibogo and Sipil in the early stage of enclosure. But consultation was rare, and the evidence an individual could use to justify taking possession of a patch of ulat was disputed. Who really planted that mango? Who cleared the do'at in which spot? And how much land was it legitimate for one person to claim before being seen as greedy—as someone who cared only about themselves and prevented others from having the chance to work and prosper? Amisa's plan to work the disputed ulat was a gamble, both economically and socially. It might yield effective ownership of the plot but sour relations with her kin. Or, she might do the work and wake up to find her seedlings burned to the ground, or suffer illness from malevolent spirits sent by someone she had offended.

As a way of enclosing land, doing work had both moral and practical force. Work changed the landscape, and if the change was permanent—like the work of a pioneer in the do'at—it created ownership rights. Since highlanders understood tree planting as a permanent change, whoever did the work of planting trees first became the owner. That was why Dekon had started to work the disputed ulat. His practice so far had been to plant just a few trees to establish his ownership, then sell up. Amisa hadn't tried to stop him until now, but this particular patch of ulat was dear to her because of its history—her father's mango tree—so she was determined to hold on to it. If Dekon objected, she would reimburse him for the work he had put in so far.

Amisa understood why Dekon was claiming and selling ulat, and she wasn't cold-hearted. He was her kinsman, and she was bound to him by ties of affection and common experience as they had lived as neighbors planting tobacco on Sipil. He was an old man now, whose wife had died. He had formed a joint household with his widowed daughter Leka. He and Leka didn't have the time or money to invest in cacao as they were living from hand to mouth on Leka's wages from weeding gardens in Sibogo. Selling land provided a welcome but temporary solution to their desperate situation. Amisa thought it was woefully short-sighted: "If they sell it all they will end up living suspended in the air," she observed. "They will have to hang from a tree."

Amisa's big worry was that Dekon might already have sold the disputed ulat to Idin in secret. When Amisa's children went to work the land, Idin would tell them to stop because the land belonged to him, as he had purchased it from Dekon or seized it as payment for Dekon's debts. Idin would say that if the ulat didn't belong to Dekon, that was a problem for Dekon to sort out with his kin. Incidents like this had already occurred on Sipil. A few months previously Idin had taken possession of land with fifty kapok trees planted on it, which he claimed as repayment for a debt incurred by Leka's husband before he died. Idin claimed that Leka's husband had pledged the kapok trees as guarantee but there was no proof either way. Leka's brother Sampo, another fiercely outspoken man, was furious about this. He thought Idin heartless and devious because Leka was depending on the yield from the kapok as a source of income. He couldn't help his sister much as his own situation was far from secure. Because he didn't regard the sale as legitimate, he had a mind to cut down the disputed kapok trees and plant cacao instead. Idin suggested that the Sipil folk were telling me tall stories: they were all chronic gamblers, and that was their real reason for selling land.

Highlanders who cut down or burned trees on disputed land were attempting to annul a claim to ownership by physically annulling the value of the labor invested. In effect, they stole labor, and even if they didn't succeed in reclaiming the disputed land, highlanders treated their actions as a serious offense. Victims demanded compensation. Amin recounted an incident a few months earlier that had made him very nervous: "There was cacao and clove over there, it was already yielding, and they cut it down and planted cacao and clove all over again. They said it belongs to lots of people, not just to one. But the person who cut it down, it wasn't theirs either." Amin concluded that he didn't want to plant his trees on inherited ulat where disputes with kin could arise years after the trees were planted, wasting his investment. Instead he wanted to pioneer in the do'at where his ownership would be clear. But he hadn't found a suitable location so in 1993 he was the only one among his neighbors who still hadn't planted any trees. By 1996 he had found another solution. He paid his father for some ulat his father had pioneered on Sipil, a transaction witnessed by his siblings so they wouldn't be able to claim it as part of their own inheritance.

In taking this approach, Amin drew on the established principle that paying money for something both changed and clarified its status by cutting the bond between the person who did the work and the property they created. Recall how Malia paid her husband Tabang for his work as a porter so he could not claim to be a joint owner of her shallot crop. By paying his father for the ulat, Amin broke the link between the ulat and his father's work, and he also freed the land from future claims by his siblings who would otherwise have a shared right to it. Although he paid a good price for the land, he didn't describe the transaction as purchase of a commodity. He framed it in the old terms, as compensation for his father's sweat. It was his payment that did the transformational work. After he had paid his father, Amin became the socially recognized owner (*togu*, L) of a new object, a lokasi, and could do with it as he wished. He held on to this particular plot, but my records of land transactions in different neighborhoods showed that plots that had been "freed" by being sold once changed hands several times thereafter, while other plots continued to be owned by the person who first planted cacao on them. Land purchasers I interviewed often mentioned that they preferred to buy land that had already been sold at least once, so they could be sure it was an unencumbered lokasi, fully detached from its origins in someone's work.[17]

Just as work—or in Amin's case, cash—excised land from the commons, it also created individual ownership rights for household members. In 1993 I watched a daughter of the widow Samina sweating under a load of cacao seedlings she was transferring to her garden plot, where she had already dug holes to plant them. Her stepfather the Imam, also looking on, said the girl had refused his offer of help because "she didn't want me to claim a share." On the same principle, parents usually gave children some of the trees they had helped to plant. Amisa's daughter-in-law noted that the division in her family had been done strictly according to the work each child put in. She was rather frail and her parents had given her fewer trees than her siblings because she hadn't worked as hard. Idin didn't give his children any of the trees they helped to plant, arguing that if he did they might sell them. He pointed to the example of Amisa's nephew from Sipil, who had helped his father Nasir plant cacao trees then promptly sold them, saying that because he helped to do the work he was the joint owner.

Some married couples planted trees separately. Other couples planted them together and viewed them as jointly owned, sharing the cash they earned fifty-fifty, or leaving it with the wife as treasurer, as they had done previously with shallots.[18] Idin told me about men on Sipil who had planted trees jointly with their wives, but secretly sold the trees to cover gambling debts. He knew a lot about this since he was usually the one who bought the trees. "I wouldn't dare do that," he chuckled. "I'm afraid my wife would hit me."

Amisa planted her own trees and before she died she gave some of them to each of her children and her husband. For Amisa's family cacao came along at just the moment when she had a house full of teenagers, and she encouraged all of them, boys and girls alike, to plant their own trees. Over the next few years when each of them married, they had a steady source of income from their trees that helped them to avoid the livelihood crises that often plagued young couples in the period when they were preoccupied with pregnancies and childcare. The striking contrast was with families in Sipil—Amisa's kin—in which the teenage boys were mostly away doing wage work outside the desa and lost out in the enclosure process. Elok's sons were also absent, much to his frustration. He and other members of the older generation who lacked the stamina to plant much cacao themselves, and didn't have money to pay workers or buy seedlings, looked on with dismay as the inherited ulat filled up with trees. Although highlanders didn't describe enclosing land as a competitive process, the "whoever works it first" rule put a premium on the capacity to act fast.

Paying someone to do the work had the same property-creating effect as working the land directly. Idin used savings from his days as a successful shallot farmer to pay workers to plant cacao on inherited ulat and on other land he bought from neighbors or seized when they defaulted on their debts. As I noted earlier, he did no physical work at all. His neighbors said he "worked only with money." With tree planting as with other tasks, a person who was paid had no claims on the property their work created. So it was the conditions under which sweat was applied to soil—not just the sweat itself—that defined who ended up owning the land. I was struck by the way highlanders extended the meaning of the heavy work of cutting huge trees in the do'at with an axe, the work through which a pioneer created ulat as individual property, to planting cacao seedlings or hiring workers. These are clearly not equivalent in the human effort expended, but highlanders recognized each of them as doing the "work" of generating socially legitimate property rights.

DISPUTED KNOWLEDGE

The question of who exactly was entitled to plant tree crops on which patch of ulat was the most heated front of struggle among kin. Amisa's problem on Sipil, as I noted, was that the ulat she and her kin had been using for generations was "borrowed" from the ancestors: "It used to be like that. Whoever wanted to work that patch, they just worked it. If I wanted it, then it was me next." Recall that Sipil was formerly used for tobacco, and had been cleared of do'at at least a century before. Knowledge of which ancestors had pioneered which patch of do'at and how they were related to the present generation had long been lost. "All the old people are dead," Amisa's brother Nasir lamented. "If only we had known how important it would be, we would have asked them more questions but we never asked." Amisa's claim to know for sure that her father had pioneered the spot where he planted the mango tree was plausible, as remnant patches of do'at that had been passed over at first were cleared later, when land pressure increased with added population. It was possible to reconstruct the history of places where the do'at was cleared within living memory, but anyone who claimed to know the history of whole hillsides where ulat had been used for multiple generations had some persuading to do.

In struggles over the ulat that routed through claims to knowledge, older men tended to have some advantage. Ayub of Walu was a man with multiple powers, a bit like Mopu. In the rice-planting days, he had been the pasobo who conducted the ritual for planting the first rice seeds of the season. He was able to gather his young kin—children, nephews, and nieces—to live near him, and he asserted jurisdiction over the ulat of his dead siblings. He also had money saved from his days as a successful shallot farmer. He was able to translate these powers into a claim on a large area of ulat on Walu, which he planted with cacao. His niece, the widow Samina, recalled that Ayub used to show her a patch of ulat where she could plant her corn and rice, but she never knew if the patch he designated was one he had pioneered, that he was allowing her to borrow, or one that had been pioneered by her own father on which she and her siblings should have first claim. She couldn't ask her father because he died when she was young.

Ayub was also willing to use force to back his claims. He prevented Samina and her children from planting tree crops on Walu when the cacao era began. One of her daughters decided to press on and plant clove trees on ulat she thought was Samina's by inheritance, but years later when the trees started to yield, Ayub paid some workers to harvest them as if they were his own. He also persuaded some neighbors to plant cacao on "his" ulat, with the promise that he would give them half of the land and the trees when they began to yield. His gain was access to their labor for free and a consolidation of his claim to the ulat. But when the time came for division, he claimed all the land and trees as his own. Without a written contract, his bullying was enough to intimidate his neighbors into giving up their share.

Knowledge, and more specifically a claim to genealogical and landscape knowledge, was both a source of power and its effect. Powerful people could make their claims to knowledge stick, while other people found their knowledge ignored and their claims denied. Older men like Ayub claimed to know who had pioneered the do'at because they had gone along to help out in their youth, before the younger generation was born. Women had a hard time being heard on the topic of do'at pioneering, although older women I talked to often had detailed knowledge. Tabang's elderly mother, born around 1930, knew a lot about the older generations' kinship ties, and about the history of the landscape as well, but she wasn't able to use this knowledge to give her own claims traction.

> My father pioneered the do'at. I know it was do'at because the fallen trees where my parents sat me down to rest were huge. If it was too hot, I sat down in the shade of the fallen trees. My father was almost killed by a falling tree. Luckily he ran in time. He left his bush knife behind, and we never found it. With my mother I planted corn and tobacco. If we'd had cacao or cloves at that time, my family would have lots because my father really cleared a lot of do'at. . . . If you don't have any signs, you can't claim. . . . If I could have guessed it would become like this I would have planted something there, like an areca nut tree.

The old lady's knowledge was embedded in experiences, sensations, and events—the size of the trees, the shade they provided, the lost bush knife, and a close escape. They were part of her claim to be the rightful inheritor of her father's ulat, but she was not forceful in pressing it. Indeed, she was sure that a lot of the ulat on Sipil that Dekon was selling to Idin had been pioneered by her father. Dekon and her father were half brothers. When I asked her why she didn't press her case, she had several reasons: Idin's trees were already growing in the fields, and she did not have the money to pay him for them; Dekon was clearly in the wrong but he was her uncle and she didn't want to make trouble for him; she was "not clever at talking"; and she had no proof. In the 1990s, the kinds of proof that were persuasive enough to support the claims of someone otherwise lacking in social power were fruit or nut trees (which were seldom planted) and grave sites (which weren't always marked). Tabang's mother didn't have the right kind of evidence. Nor was she willing to alienate kin to get her own way.

Remarkably, none of the disputes over enclosure among kin on Sibogo and Sipil were taken to the neighborhood head or the desa headman for settlement. However disgruntled highlanders felt about being excluded from a patch of ulat because one of their kin had planted trees on it, they settled the matter among themselves. Ties of friendship carried the same weight. Natun sold some ulat that belonged to Tabang but Tabang didn't challenge him about it "because Natun is a friend," he said. "I don't want to quarrel with friends." Tabang valued the quality of his relationships with others, the social bonds on which his sense of well-being depended. Amin also valued good relations with his kin, hence his desire to avoid conflict with them over inherited ulat by pioneering do'at himself, or by paying for his father's ulat to settle its status. Amisa was frustrated by Dekon's land selling, which she thought was short-sighted, but she knew his life was hard and she didn't judge him in moral terms. For these highlanders, care for others and retaining the esteem of neighbors and kin continued to be important both personally and practically.

Many highlanders thought that Ayub and Idin were greedy and too aggressive in seeking to enrich themselves at other peoples' expense. However most acts of enclosure—the quiet, mundane planting of trees in the ulat—didn't become the subject of moral censure or debate. For the most part, highlanders consented to these enclosures, and to their own exclusion, not by debating it but by recognizing and helping to enforce the new ownership rights that emerged. Where I saw the individual ownership and increasing commoditization of land as a rupture or turning point—an intimate iteration of the "great transformation" Karl Polanyi described—highlanders emphasized continuity and what they took to be common sense: work creates property, and people who worked harder, or faster, or more skillfully ended up with more. Moral arguments became more explicit in the struggles that emerged between middle hill folk and the "bela" who lived just above them.

Crossing the Social Boundary Line

In chapter 1 I explained that there was a sharp social boundary separating Muslim Lauje of the middle hills from Lauje of the inner hills, the so-called bela, who were animist or Christian and reputedly very primitive. There were several clusters of "bela" living just above the middle hill neighborhoods of Sibogo, Sipil, and Walu. In general, Muslims and "bela" maintained their social distance, and there were few marriages across the divide, but economic exchanges were common. Some women from the middle hills worked for the "bela," weeding their large cornfields and helping to bundle up corn for sale. "Bela" food was especially important for middle hill folk living on the worked-out tobacco lands of Sipil and Walu who eked out their wages and supplemented their inadequate food production by hiking up to buy food from this source. They also borrowed ulat from "bela" to grow their own food.

Since middle hill farmers and "bela" did not share claims in a commonly inherited ulat, borrowing ulat across the social divide was based on a different principle from borrowing ulat among kin. It was governed by a loose, unstated understanding that since ulat was abundant, there was no reason to withhold access from someone who approached the owner politely and asked for permission to borrow it for a few seasons. Middle hill farmers' desire to plant cacao on the borrowed ulat created a new situation, since it meant a permanent transfer of ownership. They also sought access to the remaining do'at, as they filled their ulat with cacao. In making and responding to these claims, highlanders from both groups made moral arguments, and evaluated each others' conduct in terms of what was humane and fair, or greedy and unreasonable.

The two main "bela" clusters above Sibogo and Sipil had prominent leaders, each of whom responded differently to the middle hill farmers' requests. From the perspective of the middle hills, one of the "bela" leaders, Tempo, was a generous, almost saintly man with a strong sense of shared humanity that made him overlook social and religious differences and recognize their needs. They judged the leader of the second cluster, Linajan, to be a man driven by greed and a desire to monopolize land and power. Both men were pasori and were renowned for their spirit knowledge. Middle hill folk stressed that Tempo used his spirit knowledge to protect people. Natun recalled how he had visited Tempo en route to collect rattan in the forest, and Tempo told him not to be afraid, "it is all OK," he said, "I'll be listening from here and I'll be with you as you go." Tempo was gentle—he didn't assert power forcefully. In contrast, middle hill folk suspected Linajan of using his spirit knowledge to cause illness and death. He also threatened physical violence and was reported to bully his adult children and appropriate their labor. Not only did the two men have different ways of relating to others, the Sibogo farmers thought Tempo had legitimate jurisdiction over the ulat he was managing while Linajan did not. The contrast between the two leaders' practices, and middle hill farmers' evaluations of them, gave me the opportunity to explore how enclosure was practiced and legitimated across this social boundary line.

CHALLENGING LEGITIMACY

Claims to knowledge of the detailed history of place figured prominently in disputes over the ulat. Everyone agreed that the ulat being used by the middle hill farmers at Sibogo was pioneered by "bela" from the inner hills, mostly Tempo's kin. For decades, tobacco farmers from Sipil and Walu had borrowed this ulat from the "bela" to plant rice and corn, since their tobacco land was too dry for food crops. Some of the tobacco farmers pioneered remnant patches of do'at as well, so they planted their food on both their own and borrowed land, creating a messy mosaic that only someone with detailed landscape and genealogical knowledge could decipher. In the 1970s when the price of tobacco collapsed, some of the former tobacco farmers from Sipil and Walu moved up to live permanently in Sibogo and started to use the ulat more intensively for food and for the new cash crop, shallots. Then in 1977 and again in 1983 and 1987 there were catastrophic El Niño droughts, which forced the highlanders to scatter.

In response to these droughts, Tempo's kin withdrew from Sibogo to their sago groves near the center of the peninsula. Tempo later moved back to Sibogo but many of his kin stayed in the interior after the droughts ended, anxious to keep control over their vital famine food. The middle hill farmers who had moved up to Sibogo fled in different directions. Some fled inland to ask for help from the "bela." Some fled along the coast to Sigenti, a desa with extensive coastal sago groves that were not affected by the drought, and which the owners let them work on a half-share basis. Many of the drought refugees stayed in Sigenti after the droughts ended, but some of them including Amisa, Tabang, Malia, and their families returned to Sibogo. Hence they were the people who were living and farming in Sibogo in 1990, when the cacao era began. It was only at that point that the precise history of the ulat became important as the middle hill folk needed permission from the "bela" do'at pioneers or their descendents to plant cacao on borrowed land.

Linajan did not claim that his ancestors had been do'at pioneers in Sibogo or in the upper part of Sipil, the two areas where middle hill farmers wanted to plant cacao. Nasir from Sipil claimed that he knew which "bela" had pioneered the do'at above him as they were still there in his youth, but most of them had since moved away. He emphasized that Linajan was a newcomer who had moved in when one of his children married a descendant of the "bela" pioneers. When I asked Linajan why he wanted to live above Sibogo his reasons were pragmatic: he liked living close to the coast. If he left his house before dawn and walked fast, he could hike down to buy salt or fish at the market and be back home again by midday. Despite his newcomer status, he asserted jurisdiction over all the ulat above Sipil, stating grandly but vaguely that it belonged to his "ancestors seven generations ago," a claim he did not attempt to support with a detailed genealogy.

Linajan encouraged his kin to plant cacao on the ulat over which he claimed jurisdiction, but he prevented Sipil and Sibogo farmers from doing the same. These farmers accused Linajan not just of grabbing land that didn't belong to him, but of attempting to monopolize it: keeping it from people who needed it as a basis for their livelihoods. In making this claim, they drew on a "custom" from the old repertoire—that landholders lent ulat freely to someone who needed a place to plant crops—and used it to make the moral argument that access to ulat *should* be extended. The conjuncture, however, was different. In the old days, as I explained, lending ulat was often convenient for the lender, as it prevented the forest from growing too tall and hard to cut and burn. With the arrival of cacao, it was permanent transfer of ownership that was now at stake.

Tempo and his father had both pioneered some patches of do'at in Sibogo in the decades before the 1970s, when the former tobacco farmers from Walu and Sipil started moving up from below. Most of the do'at, Tempo acknowledged, had been pioneered by his kin who had retreated inland during the prolonged El Niño droughts and were still living far up in the interior. Unlike Linajan he didn't make a grand claim to have jurisdiction over all the ulat. Rather, he drew on his detailed knowledge to mediate transfers of the ulat belonging to his absent kin, among them an energetic pioneer named

Manutar. While the farmers at Sibogo applauded Tempo for his generosity in recognizing their need for land, Tempo's version of the story was a bit different. He explained to me that he had only lent ulat to Sibogo people for short-term use. Sibogo farmers who wanted to plant cacao should pay for the land, since they would acquire permanent ownership. He was feeling pressured by the actions of the Sibogo farmers he called "the people from below," who were planting cacao without permission.

Knowledge about the exact nature of the rights Tempo had granted to Sibogo farmers was hotly contested during my second visit to Sibogo in 1993 because Tempo had just been killed by his son-in-law Banio who shot him with a poisoned blowpipe, allegedly by accident while out hunting. Banio threatened to take back Tempo's land, and even Tempo's wife and children were not secure. Banio had a volatile temper and he had already shown he could be violent. He was also quite savvy, as he managed to escape punishment for Tempo's death by sweet-talking the police, speaking to them in their own language, Bugis, which he had learned on his travels. All this made Sibogo folk afraid of him. To defend their claims to the ulat they were busy planting with cacao, they needed to demonstrate that either Tempo or Manutar hadn't just lent them ulat, but granted them ownership.

As usual there were no documents to confirm the land transfer agreements that Tempo was said to have made, all of which were verbal. A few of the agreements were made in the presence of witnesses, but highlanders didn't use witnesses routinely—it wasn't necessary in the past, when they loaned ulat freely. Only do'at pioneers made permanent transfers, and they had the undisputed right to do as they pleased. Elok, whose house was close to Tempo's, claimed that Tempo had been explicit in making him a gift. "He told me to work his ulat so I would not move away because he regarded me as his kin and he wanted me to stay near him." Tempo's children had witnessed the gift, so Elok was confident that they all knew the transfer was permanent. Amin noted that Manutar, whom he recognized as the pioneer of the ulat he was working, had come to visit and given his benediction with these words: "If you want to plant here, even cacao, you can go ahead because this is my ulat." Emsalin quoted Tempo thus: "He said just work it, if it belongs to me, it also belongs to you." Because Emsalin was still anxious, Tempo clarified further: "Actually the person who cleared the do'at here had no children but he was my uncle; it is OK, there won't be any problem."

Tabang claimed actual kinship with Tempo through a great-grandmother who had married into a "bela" family and moved to the inner hills. He often described Tempo's encompassing sense of kinship and shared humanity. More specifically, he told of how both Tempo and Manutar had come by and seen the tree crops he had planted—one thousand cacao trees and more than a hundred clove trees. They told him explicitly they had no objection. This was a bit different from asking permission first and it effectively forced the issue, creating the pressure Tempo described to me: his sense that "the people from below" were taking advantage. Tabang argued that it was actually quite unclear who was the pioneer in which spot. In the absence of this knowledge even the saintly Tempo was on thin ground.

Knowledge, especially thin knowledge, jostled uneasily alongside the emerging argument that monopoly was illegitimate and sharing access to ulat was the morally appropriate thing to do. Sipil and Sibogo folk stressed that Linajan tried to monopolize more ulat than he needed, and more than he could possibly use. Tabang acknowledged the "custom" that pioneering created ownership rights, but he suggested that the need of others could trump those rights, and he proposed a time limit: "Even if I was the one who pioneered the do'at," he said, "if someone else started to work there I wouldn't complain because I figure they also want to work. If you want to keep your ulat, you should hurry up and work it yourself." Tabang's brother Samir, who lived close to Linajan's cluster, was convinced that Linajan's project was indeed to monopolize:

> They have so much ulat, they don't finish working in one spot and they've already moved to another. They cut and it doesn't burn, so they go back to burn in the dry season, and then they plant it. The reason is so that we from below don't take that spot. . . . We can't access the ulat up there now because they made a boundary. We still want to work but we don't have any ulat. They have the ulat but they don't want to share it. They have so much ulat even if three families worked it they couldn't finish. The fact is, they are controlling half the mountain.

By 1996 Linajan would no longer lend out ulat for growing corn. He would only let people use "his" ulat if they planted cacao on it and agreed to share the land and trees fifty-fifty after three years. But Sipil and Sibogo folk were reluctant to agree to this arrangement since they regarded Linajan's claim to the ulat as illegitimate. If they worked for a half share, Linajan would be getting the benefit of their labor for free.

Knowledge of the spirit world played a role in these land struggles. The only person who was really sure of his right to land at Sibogo was Elok, and that was in relation to the remnant patches of do'at he had pioneered himself. He had learned the secret incantations needed to appease the dangerous spirits that lived in a clump of huge trees that were still standing because other people had been too afraid to cut them down. The proof of his mastery was that he cut the trees down, and he didn't fall sick. Spirit knowledge was a big part of Linajan's power and his capacity to bully people to get his way. According to Tabang, Linajan had sent spirits to disputed ulat that Tabang was working and suddenly, overnight, the thriving rice plants in Tabang's field emptied out. The grain inside the husks disappeared. Soon after this incident, Tabang's sister who was working a section of the ulat died and Tabang stopped working, fearing more attacks. To protect himself he gained some spirit knowledge of his own, and the result was that Linajan's next attack bounced back on Linajan and made his own son fall sick. In 1995 Tabang's son tried again to work the disputed ulat, and he also died. After this bitter experience, Tabang sold the disputed ulat to someone from the coast, using the sale to get some return for his work while preempting Linajan's claim. Spirit power was consequential. It stopped Tabang from working and he felt this failed initiative put him years behind his neighbors in establishing cacao.

Some of the disputes with Linajan were adjudicated by the Sibogo neighborhood head and eventually sent to the desa headman for settlement. Elok and the Imam participated in these settlement processes, which usually resulted in a ruling about who was in the wrong, the culprit's acknowledgment of their wrongdoing, and payment of a fine. But Sibogo folk didn't believe the adjudication was fair. They thought the neighborhood head was a weak man who was so terrified of Linajan's spirit powers that he always ruled in Linajan's favor. Money was also a factor. Disputes with Linajan resulted in Tabang and several other highlanders paying him fines. Amin won his case against Linajan, a success he attributed to his strong arguments, and his willingness to speak out. He thought Tabang had been too timid and didn't put up a strong fight. Not having enough money to pay a fine deterred many highlanders from pressing claims, even when they were sure they were in the right. It also made them reluctant to insist that their case be heard at the desa level, where the costs in bribes and fines was higher than at the neighborhood level.

Linajan had plenty of money. He had abundant land, hence lots of food and no need to spend money buying rice; he regularly employed wage workers to expand his farms; he was a moneylender; and he was still having success with his shallots. Like Idin he used his wealth to build a house on the coast and he bought himself a bicycle. Although no one ever suggested this to me, I think it is possible that some of the invective against Linajan was related to this status transgression—that he, a primitive "bela," should have become more prosperous than the middle hill folk, who thought themselves more civilized.

WHO HAS JURISDICTION OF THE PRIMARY FOREST?

By 1996 farmers at Sibogo and Sipil began to feel that there was a shortage of land, and when I visited again in 1998 Amisa's sons were twiddling their thumbs. Their problem, as they stated it, was that they had no more lokasi—no place on which to expand their farming enterprises. Their ulat was full of cacao, and few people were willing to lend ulat even for short-term crops. No one in Sibogo had planted rice since Amisa's last harvest in 1994. The status of the remaining ulat had been more or less settled among kin, sometimes by planting a few trees on it as markers, sometimes by means of payment, as in Amin's case. Farmers who had run out of ulat did as they had done in the past: they turned to the do'at as a frontier on which they could expand their farms. They quickly cut down the remaining pockets of do'at close to Sibogo and Sipil, causing some spectacular landslides on the steeper slopes, but this source was soon exhausted. The next target was the do'at in the inner hills, but it was far from clear who had jurisdiction over the do'at and who would be successful in enclosing it.

The farmers at Sibogo and Sipil argued that no one—least of all Linajan or Tempo's aggressive son-in-law Banio—had the right to monopolize the do'at. Anyone could clear it and when they did, they established the complete ownership rights of a pioneer. The job of the pasori of the past, they argued, was to commune with the spirits to keep rattan collectors, hunters, and do'at pioneers safe: they didn't have the right to monopolize resources or keep other people out. Jurisdiction wasn't ownership. The distinction was clarified by old man Dekon on Sipil, whom Rina and I came across one day on the trail, quite enraged. He complained that he had found a fallen tree blocking the path to a patch of do'at above Sipil where he planned to collect rattan. Someone—he assumed it was someone in Linajan's cluster—had placed the tree as a barrier to signal their claim over the rattan in that patch of do'at, even though the person hadn't collected it yet. He rejected this attempt to monopolize the resource: "It doesn't matter how many bush knives they have up there," he said, full of bravado. "I'm going to collect that rattan because I also want to eat salt. With the money from the rattan, I want to buy salt." Salt is a modest commodity, one even the poorest people bought when they could. Reference to salt dramatized Dekon's argument that Linajan was depriving him of access to basic necessities.

Blocked by Linajan on one side and Banio on the other, the farmers of Sibogo and Sipil turned to a different source of authority. They argued that only "the government" (*pemerintah*) had the right to control the forest. Unless "the people up above" (the polite way of referring to the "bela") had paid taxes on it, or had "become the forest department," they had no right to keep others out. More specifically, they informed me, their desa headman had given them permission to pioneer in the do'at as soon as their ulat was full of cacao. This headman, like most of the other headmen in the Lauje desas, was keenly interested in expanding the production of cacao which had brought prosperity to the coastal zone as highlanders had money to spend on food and clothing at the market, and cacao merchants were doing very well. He also knew that his superiors in the district administration expected him to help curb forest destruction by "backward" highlanders, hence his ruling that they should fill their ulat with cacao before they started to pioneer in the do'at to expand their land base.

Encouraged by the headman's support, a group of Sibogo farmers took the initiative to form themselves into what they called a "farmers group," a term usually used in the context of government and donor-sponsored development projects. They made plans for an expedition to stake out a claim to a new lokasi—a large patch of do'at about six hours' hike inland. But the plan was stalled because Banio had preempted them by taking up a group of twenty people from Tempo's cluster to demarcate a large area—the best location—for themselves. They hadn't cleared the do'at, but they had felled some trees in the middle and around the edges, clear signs of their intention. For the Sibogo group to go up after them would provoke a confrontation. Minimally, it would provoke a dispute that would have to be adjudicated by the desa headman and might result in expensive fines. At worst there could be violence. Although the desa headman had encouraged them, he was not consistent and they suspected he could be bribed, so they dared not go ahead. Besides, they had seen from their reconnaissance trips that the lokasi they were interested in was already full of brightly colored paint: many people, not just Banio's group, had put their signs or initials on the trees and rocks, staking out their claims.

Staking claims to the do'at by spraying paint was a new practice. In the past, someone who wanted to claim a patch of do'at they planned to work in future had to put in some hard work there, clearing some of the forest to signal the seriousness of their intention. Banio's group had done this, but the other signs were just paint. Paint could wash away. It wasn't clear the claims would hold. Nevertheless, the Sibogo group read the paint as a sign intended to exclude them, one that had traction because it wasn't just any paint: the names painted on trees and rocks included the subdistrict head, the police chief, and army officers, people who had both authority and the capacity for violence to back them up. The frontier had turned wild. For farmers at Sibogo who saw themselves as "small people" these powerful players were too dangerous to cross, so they had to give up on their plan.

In the following decade, a few Sibogo farmers found ways to access a steep patch of remnant do'at above Sibogo after Andi, another son-in-law of Tempo, assumed jurisdiction. Around 2000 the desa headman created a new official neighborhood combining Tempo and Linajan's clusters that had drawn together around a new church. He appointed Andi to the post of neighborhood head. Andi was the prayer leader in the church, he was literate, and he spoke Indonesian as a result of his mission education. With these roles and qualities as his sources of authority, he allocated lokasi in the do'at to several middle hill farmers who had both money and social standing: Idin, Emsalin, and Amisa's son Hamdan, among others. He permitted them each to clear four to ten hectares, setting these ambitious and successful farmers up with ample land resources to make their cacao-farming ventures prosper. Explaining to me how he had been able to acquire this new land, Emsalin stressed that he didn't buy the do'at from Andi, "because the do'at belongs to the government." He had just paid Andi for the work of marking out the plots. The "work" was again rather light—not much more than spraying some paint, though Emsalin didn't mention this. He hedged on the question of Andi's authority to allocate land in this way.

Andi himself didn't claim jurisdiction in the old terms: he wasn't a pasori like Tempo or Linajan, whose jurisdiction was linked to their spirit knowledge. Instead, he emphasized his role as neighborhood head, arguing that this role gave him the right and responsibility to allocate land in his neighborhood. It wasn't a right supported by national land law, but he stressed that his main concern was to prevent conflict, especially conflict between Muslims from the middle hills, who had a legitimate desire to expand their farms, and inner hill Christians like Linajan and Banio, who were attempting to assert a monopoly. Andi's concern about conflict prevention picked up on events in other parts of the province of Central Sulawesi around 2000 where conflicts pitting Christians against Muslims had resulted in many deaths and thousands of people had been forcibly displaced.[19] I didn't visit the Lauje area during this period, so I don't know for sure how far this conflict resonated in the highlands, but in the 1990s tensions between middle and inner hill Lauje in Sibogo were not expressed in terms of religion. Middle hill Muslims evaluated inner hill folk on more particular, intimate grounds, contrasting the virtuous Tempo with the greedy and aggressive Linajan.

Andi's concern to keep the peace didn't extend to finding land for farmers of Sipil and Sibogo who had lost out in the enclosure process. In our discussions, he recognized that some middle hill farmers were desperately short of land and quite impoverished, but he didn't think their problem was his to solve. Unlike Emsalin and Idin, these people did not have sway with the desa headman, and they were not in a position to make complaints against Andi or cause him trouble. Lacking money and clout, and unable to make moral arguments that had traction, they were firmly shut out of the do'at frontier.

Official Development Schemes

In the two conjunctures I have examined so far, the initiative to plant tree crops came from highlanders themselves, and the struggles that took place during the process of enclosure involved people who had ties to their neighbors and to the places where they were living. Official development schemes introduced new actors into the highlands, and a different set of powers.

CANADIAN CACAO

In 1991 the managers of the Canadian development project I mentioned in the introduction concluded that promoting tree crops would be a good way to introduce highlanders to modern agriculture. It would discourage them from their dependence on "shifting cultivation," thought to be a cause of forest destruction and erosion, and it would give them a new source of income. My survey in 1991 showed that highlanders throughout the middle hills had already begun their own experiments with planting clove and cacao, so the project did not introduce these crops, nor did it supply many of the seedlings—less than 20 percent of the cacao planted in Sibogo, by my count.[20] Highlanders bought most of their seedlings from other farmers, merchants, and traveling salesmen, using their own hard-earned cash. Nevertheless, the Canadian cacao project did shape land relations in two ways, both of them unexpected.

The first effect came from the unequal distribution of free cacao seedlings. The plan was to work with the Department of Estate Crops to distribute the seedlings to farmer groups, favoring "the poor," but inadequate monitoring meant that a disproportionate number of the seedlings fell into the hands of already prosperous farmers. In Sibogo, Idin and the Imam used their influence with desa officials and their leadership of the project-sponsored "farmers group" to allocate themselves about half the seedlings, with the remainder shared among other energetic farmers like Amisa's son Hamdan. The Imam argued against sharing any seedlings with the people on Sipil or with the "bela" in Linajan or Tempo's clusters on the grounds that the more advanced farmers of Sibogo needed to set an example before backward folk would follow.

It wasn't until 1996 that some free seedlings reach Sipil, and most of them were not planted. I was distressed to discover that I was implicated in this outcome, albeit unknowingly. After I left Sibogo in 1993, Ayub's son, who had become a teacher on the coast and had designs on the hillside land, spread a rumor that there were strings attached to the project seedlings and someone—probably me—would come back one day to collect a share. Why else, he asked, did the white woman keep going to visit them? Highlanders led by Emsalin discussed this rumor and concluded that the teacher was wrong: they were confident that I was only interested in finding out about their lives as farmers as I always said. If there was a nefarious scheme behind my presence, they would have seen a sign of it by now. But while the rumor circulated many of the seedlings destined for Sipil died in their poly-bags. The teacher, meanwhile, persuaded a couple on Walu to plant "his" seedlings on their land, with the land and trees to be shared equally. Project seedlings enabled him to acquire other peoples' land and labor for free. The inadvertent result of the project's free inputs, in sum, was to deepen the advantage that a few powerful individuals already had in the struggle over land. By ignoring inequality, the project helped to intensify it. The government officials who were responsible for running the project weren't concerned about these details. They were happy that the hills were being covered with cacao trees, and eagerly anticipated the kudos they would earn when they took credit for the tons of cacao beans that would soon be carried down to the market.

The second effect of the project was to help farmers in Sibogo to consolidate their hold on the ulat they were using, but the way this happened was quite different from the way the project managers expected. The project's plan to distribute free cacao seedlings had run into a problem with officials in the Estate Crops department who were unwilling to proceed without confirmation that highlanders were indeed the owners of their land. The officials usually dealt with farmers who had land titles or who had been granted an area of state-owned land through an official resettlement scheme. They argued that they could not work with highlanders because they were illegal squatters on state forest land. The Canadian project managers took a different approach, quite novel at the time, and argued that highlanders had customary rights to the land they were using. They did not need land titles to prove it, and the land didn't need to be given to them as a grant from the state since it already belonged to them. The project hired a legal specialist and field assistants to interview highlanders about their customary tenure system and duly recorded the core concepts: that land was owned by the pioneer who first cleared the do'at, and ownership of the ulat passed to his descendants. The legal team then set about interviewing highlanders individually, asking who was the pioneer of the ulat they were using, and how they were related to him.

The legal specialist expected that the information highlanders provided would confirm that they were the legitimate landowners according to their customary system. But there was a problem. Many highlanders, including those in Sibogo and Sipil, could not demonstrate their ownership based on the template that emphasized the rights of the pioneer and his descendants. In Sipil they were using the "ulat of the ancestors," but they could not trace which ancestor exactly. In Sibogo, the middle hill farmers were on land that had been pioneered by "bela" who had moved away. The problem the legal specialist encountered was not unique. Attempts by colonial authorities in Asia and Africa to codify "customary law" repeatedly ran into the problem that the "law" was dynamic, as it took its meaning in the context of particular relations. In Sibogo and Sipil in the early 1990s, "custom" had been shaped by the length of time that had elapsed since the do'at was first cleared, the effects of drought, the new significance of land in the context of cacao, and many other elements. Nevertheless, the work done by the legal team, drawing maps and compiling lists of de facto possession, made highlanders feel more secure in their claims, which appeared to have received state validation.

Mapping was completed in Sibogo by 1993 and in Sipil by 1996. Highlanders observed that land struggles among kin had settled down once the team they called the "people from Palu" had written everything down in a book. It wasn't just the content of the information they had recorded that was significant, it was also its form. The inscription devices used by the project's fieldworkers—a map showing land parcels, each with a number that corresponded to a name on a list—lent itself to a sense of land as lokasi: a thing-like, interchangeable unit of space, readily detached from the people whose work had produced it.[21] Unwittingly, I contributed to this process of inscription and detachment. I carried copies of the maps and lists prepared by the land team with me each time I went back to Sibogo and used them to review what had happened to each plot since my last visit. Amisa's sons helped me with this task. Together we pored over the map, and they watched me record changes on the list by crossing out the name of the person who had sold a plot of land and replacing it with the name of the new owner.

THE "PEOPLE'S GARDEN PROJECT" AT PELALANG

The Canadian project at Sibogo was designed to work with the highland farmers in situ, but in the early 1990s most desa headmen argued that highlanders were too backward to become cacao farmers. Their preferred development model was to encourage coastal people to move into the highlands to grow the new crops and show the backward highlanders how to farm efficiently. Pelalang, an inner hill neighborhood, was selected by one of the desa headmen as the site of what he called a "people's garden project," which he marked with a wooden sign. It was the first time I had seen a desa headman mark out a block of territory in the highlands. I immediately asked him whether it was do'at or ulat, and if ulat, who were the people who had a claim on it. But the headman wasn't concerned about these details, as he thought his declaration that this was a development "project" was sufficient to free the land from any prior claims. It was, he stressed, state land over which he had jurisdiction. Besides, he added, highlanders had no right to hold on to the land since they weren't using it productively.

The argument that the work of making land productive creates ownership rights is well worn: it was a principle enunciated by the philosopher John Locke in the seventeenth century, and used by colonial officials to justify appropriating land from profligate natives who failed to put it to good use.[22] Lauje highlanders made the same argument, but they recognized pioneering in the do'at as work that created individual property, and they recognized growing corn and rice as productive use, while the desa headman called these practices "forest destruction" and "producing nothing," or "just moving around."

As it turned out, coastal people who tried to access the headman's "project" land discovered that his authority had not effectively cleared away previous claims. They still had to pay money to "free" the land from the pioneers and their descendants, a move facilitated by a highlander named Katulu who served as broker. Katulu's role marked an important difference between enclosure processes in Sibogo and Pelalang. In Sibogo, Tempo only brokered land to (selected) neighbors living just below him in the middle hills, and Linajan refused to broker any land at all. In Pelalang, Katulu brokered land to coastal people who had no previous connection with the highlands and whose only purpose in acquiring land was to profit from cacao.

The sources of Katulu's authority were complex. His father had been one of the more famous ward heads in the 1930s who helped headmen keep order in the interior. He was Muslim but had married several wives, both Muslim and Christian. Hence his son Katulu's kinship connections spanned the religious, social, and spatial divide separating the middle from the inner hills. He lived on the border between the two groups and served both of them in the role of chief of custom, mediating disputes and solving problems. His spirit knowledge was legendary. Highlanders feared to cross him. Like Linajan, Idin, and some other powerful men, he had an unnatural desire and capacity to control the labor of his wife and children, and his married siblings as well. He was close to several desa officials and served coastal merchants as a labor recruiter for rattan extraction. This was another role he had inherited from his father who had brokered highland labor for ebony extraction. When the interest of coastal entrepreneurs shifted from accessing highland labor and farm products to acquiring land, Katulu was ready to help them.

Most of the land Katulu transferred to coastal Lauje seeking land in Pelalang in the early 1990s was ulat belonging to his kin and neighbors including Gilanan, whose family had a running feud with Katulu. In Gilanan's view, Katulu was grabbing and selling something that did not belong to him. There was no point in trying to settle the matter through the desa headman since he clearly backed Katulu. The coastal people who acquired land at Pelalang paid Katulu for his services as land broker and paid little or nothing for the land itself. Once the land had been detached from its original owners it became a commodity that circulated freely. It was traded mainly among coastal people, some of whom always had speculation in mind and some of whom wanted to farm but lacked the capital to invest or simply lost interest because the road the headman had promised as part of the "garden project" didn't arrive.

Most of the coastal people who arrived in Pelalang had no previous experience in farming, and they had never set foot in the hills until the prospect of tree-crop profits lured them in. They included fishermen and petty traders, and ranged from the higher to the lower end of the coastal elite I described in chapter 1. Anyone who could muster some capital, including Rina and her siblings, tried their hand. For some, a small plot of hillside cacao was their hope for the future. For others, it was one among several sites in which they invested capital as a way to help pay for the costs of children studying at universities in Palu. When the long-promised road finally reached Pelalang in 2005, and the coastal landowners could visit regularly, the value of their land increased exponentially and all of it was planted with clove and cacao.

Gilanan and his kin, meanwhile, withdrew from Pelalang to some ulat above Walu that still belonged to them. Their desa had been divided in 2002 and they had a new headman who had recently returned to his natal desa after a period of work and study in Java. He was eager to improve the lives of the highlanders under his care. He tried to help Gilanan's cluster by getting a school built for them above Walu, and he applied for government funds to build them some free houses. But his plan didn't work. When the new road reached Gilanan's cluster, they lost control of their ulat as more coastal people arrived seeking land. Like other highlanders Gilanan's cluster was caught in a bind. They didn't expect to use the new roads themselves, as they thought they would still walk along the old footpaths that follow the riverbeds, a shorter and more shady route. But they did want roads as a means to access schooling for their children. They knew that until the road was built and schoolteachers could travel up and down by motorbike, the highland school would not function and their children would not learn. But by 2006, the men of Gilanan's cluster were far inland, clearing do'at to replace the ulat they had lost, and the women and children soon followed them. There was some do'at closer to the road and the school, but it had long ago been staked out by the police chief and other powerful outsiders who had advance information about where the road would eventually go. "Desa planning," said the new desa headman in frustration, "what is that? I can make a plan to allocate land, but no one recognizes my authority." He too was up against ruthless people from the coast, who were prepared to back their claims with violence, and against the subdistrict head and other senior officials whom he suspected of using their leverage to obtain land for themselves.

The displacement of Gilanan and his kin from Pelalang in the early 1990s and later from their ulat above Walu was not exceptional. In all of the inner hill neighborhoods I visited where coastal people and successful middle hill farmers were pushing up from below, inner hill folk sold up or were sold out by their kin and retreated farther inland where they put pressure on the inner hill clusters above them, domino style. Alarmed by this pattern, in 2006 Mopu's cluster in Gau'ma were discussing the need to prevent coastal people from buying their ulat, explicitly referencing the land needs of their children and future generations, but it was not clear that they had the solidarity necessary to take a collective stance on the matter. Some individuals had already started to sell ulat, and a new road planned for their area would increase the pressure on them. If we compare across conjunctures, it was Linajan in Sibogo who was the exception because he refused to sell ulat or to permit people from the middle hills to leapfrog over his cluster into the do'at above them, and he was authoritarian enough among his kin to make his rules stick. As a result his cluster was one of the few groups of inner hill folk that stayed in place and prospered through clove and cacao. By 2009, several of his kin had built fine houses, and a number of the young men bought motorbikes they plied as taxis on the motorbike trails that were extending steadily inland.

Conclusion

This chapter has tracked the emergence of lokasi, a thing-like unit of space apparently detached from the history of the landscape and the work of putting axes to trees, and seeds into soil. Its detachment was only partial, however, because of the peculiar materiality of land. Unlike a mat, you can't roll it up and take it away. It stays in place. Hence an individual or group can only be said to own it when the claim is backed by social relations, and more specifically by a system of law and force that recognizes and supports one party's right to exclude others on a permanent basis. Remarkably, enforcement in the highlands remained largely informal, outside the purview of national land law and largely beyond official supervision, even during a period in which land use, land values, and the actors interested in claiming ownership changed drastically. Over time, the new property relations stabilized and most disputes simmered down. One patch of ulat at a time, highlanders conceded to their exclusion from formerly common land, and participated in the dismantling of a commons "system" that had sustained them for generations, even though they didn't give this "system" a name. Through their words and deeds, they selectively revised the content of Lauje custom, the meaning of work, and their sense of what was reasonable and fair.

The powers shaping the enclosure of land included threats and coercion, but also desire: a desire to prosper, and to see kin and neighbors prosper as well. Spurred on by this desire, Lauje highlanders did not invoke custom to prevent enclosure or to manage and limit it. E. P. Thompson reports a similar process in England during the eighteenth century. Although many villagers opposed enclosure of common lands, some supported it because they hoped to claim some land for themselves. In so doing, they thought they could share in the wealth made possible by more productive land uses.[23] Hope turned to despair when they later lost the few hectares they gained as prices turned against them, a process with echoes in the Lauje highlands as I will show.

The main complaint of Lauje highlanders in 1998 was not that some people had enclosed land; it was that their supply of land had come to an end. Yet their experience of coming to land's end was uneven. Some people had plenty of land, while others had none, a divergence that had its roots in the initial enclosure process but involved other elements as well. Farmers in many contexts own land individually and have a socially recognized right to sell it, but they hold on to it tightly. Why Lauje highlanders found it so difficult to hold on to their land is the question I turn to next.

4 Capitalist Relations

In the decade 1998–2009, inequality within highland neighborhoods intensified and took on a new form. Some farmers accumulated wealth and increased their access to land and capital, while others lost their land as they struggled with debts for farm inputs or food, which now had to be purchased. By 2009, some highlanders had no access to land at all, a condition unthinkable in 1990. The relations I examine most closely in this chapter are those that made it difficult for highlanders to hold on to their land and reproduce their farms and households from year to year in modest but stable "middle peasant" style. This is the problem agrarian scholar Henry Bernstein calls the "simple reproduction squeeze," to distinguish it from the difficulty faced by farmers seeking to expand.[1] Highlanders who were just trying to hold on to what they had were caught in a series of tight spots and crises that left them unable to make ends meet, and compelled them to take on debt, or sell land. Although they described these crises as idiosyncratic—an illness, a wedding, bad luck at cards, an attack of pests—the outcomes were both cumulative and systemic, as relations among highlanders took on capitalist form.

Capitalist relations governed by competition and profit can only emerge when land and labor are commodities, freely transacted. But the emergence of land and labor as commodities isn't enough to instill the element of compulsion that distinguishes capitalist relations and makes them competitive. Only when a person is obliged to sell crops as a condition of survival is he or she obliged to sell them at a competitive price—the price set by more efficient producers. Only when people are compelled to sell their labor is the price they can obtain for a day of work governed by competition with other workers, who are equally desperate. Only when land cannot be accessed except through rent or purchase is its price fixed by the sum the most competitive farmers can afford to pay. Hence the emergence of capitalist relations depends upon another process: erosion of noncommoditized relations through which people may previously have been able to access food, labor, land, and help to weather crises.[2] "Erosion" is the term I choose because it nicely captures the way capitalist relations emerged among Lauje highlanders: not dramatically, but piecemeal and by stealth, rather like the action of water on a stream bed that creates new pathways and makes old ones unusable or irrelevant, without anyone willing it to be so.[3]

To recap from chapter 2, the relations of work and care that characterized highland neighborhoods in the era before cacao didn't amount to a cozy utopia. There were tensions and fractures, and some peoples' lives were harder than others. Highland neighborhoods weren't self-contained. Highlanders sold crops and worked for wages to acquire the goods they needed (clothing, salt, knife blades, and so on). But their access to ample land and help from kin who made gifts of work or food to ease them through difficult times protected them from the capitalist imperative of competition. Whether or not they produced "efficiently," they could continue to farm from year to year, and generation to generation, supported by the social relations that linked them to each other and to the land.

After the commons was dismantled through the processes I described in chapter 3, land became a commodity that was easy to sell, but impossible to access for people who did not have capital of their own, or sources of investment credit. "Free" labor, Marx's ironic label for people who have no choice but to work for wages, was slow to form as highlanders resisted routine wage work, which affronted their sense of how an adult person should live. Nevertheless, by 2009 some highlanders—I estimate at least half the residents of Walu, Sipil, and Sibogo—depended on scarce, occasional wage work for their survival. Access to capital, the third factor of production, was increasingly channeled along competitive lines. Coastal merchants and highland moneylenders refused credit to losing ventures or charged such high interest that a loan could only be repaid by selling land. Yet the emergence of capitalist relations is not an inevitable progression or evolutionary unfolding. Before I tease apart the elements that gave this conjuncture a capitalist form, I first provide an overview of the changes that struck me when I returned to the Lauje area in 2006 after a gap of eight years.

Changes

On the coastal strip, social and economic relations seemed to be much the same as they were in 1990. The skinny, unproductive century-old coconut trees still took up most of the space, and the class divide between the landowners in their brick houses and landless people in their flimsy huts was as stark as ever. The electrical grid had reached the coast, though service was erratic and many people could not afford the rates. The big change for me personally was the cell phone network that enabled me to keep in touch with family in Canada, something that previously required a two-day trip to the provincial capital, Palu.

Rina agreed to work with me for two months, handing off her market stall to a niece who could manage the small volume of trade she expected in the quiet period between cacao harvests. This was a time of year when highlanders had no money to spend on clothing, her specialty, and coastal folk who made a living indirectly from highlanders' production were short of cash as well. The latter included suppliers of house building materials and consumer goods, and Rina's friends who sold kitchenware and food at the weekly rotating market. Another group were young men who had bought motorbike taxis on credit to ply the rough roads and trails that now reached up into the foothills. When money from cacao was scarce, they had difficulty paying their monthly installments and their motorbikes could be repossessed. Money was especially tight in 2006 because of the high price of rice.

As Rina and I hiked up into the hills, changes in the landscape were striking. There were lots of cacao and clove trees, but we didn't see a single rice field, and we saw very little corn. The houses we passed by or stopped in to visit were of two distinct types. There were large, comfortable wood plank houses with tin roofs, bedrooms, pink plastic chairs, wall clocks, DVD players, diesel-powered generators, and satellite dishes for TV. There were also bamboo and bark huts, as tiny and precarious as before though more difficult to build, as their owners explained, because the forest materials they needed to construct them had become scarce and could only be found far inland. The materials themselves were still free, but the highlanders' time was constrained. They needed to save from their tiny wages to accumulate a stock of food before they could go off to the forest to gather what they needed. Although in the past we had stayed in these houses—that was all there was in the 1990s—their owners were now more embarrassed to receive visitors and directed Rina and me toward the more solid houses of some of their neighbors, which were better able to accommodate guests.

The bigger houses had well-stocked kitchens, and our hosts fed us in the coastal style with rice at every meal, and sometimes fresh fish if someone had hiked down to the market, or a fish seller made the trek uphill. As we walked around visiting people during the day, however, we were often hungry. In the 1990s every house we stopped at to chat would rustle up a plate of fresh corn, cassava, or yam for the guests. In 2006 many of the kitchens of the tiny houses had no stocks of food and there was no pakele outside the kitchen door, loaded with dried corn waiting to be ground. In houses where there was a stock of rice, the owners had taken it on credit from their cacao merchant, and they kept it hidden, eking it out very carefully. There were no bundles of fresh corn moving from house to house as gifts or for cash. This was one of several shifts that I flagged as significant ruptures, signs that old social relations had eroded and new ones were being set in their place. Highlanders' observations were more pragmatic: since neither they nor their neighbors were growing any more corn, the matter of its distribution was moot.

Some people still made treks to modagang in the inner hills where they could sometimes buy corn for a price that was a bit cheaper than corn sold at the coastal market, but these treks often failed as the "bela" were also busy with cacao. Many people talked about the high cost of rice and recalled days when food was plentiful. Yet no one agreed with my suggestion that a return to food production, or perhaps a balance between food and cacao production, might make them more secure. This was the plan they themselves had enunciated in the 1990s, but it had turned out to be unworkable.[4] The corn and cassava they tried to plant on their small remaining patches of land yielded very little, as they could not leave the land to fallow, their usual means of restoring soil fertility and keeping weeds at bay. The weeds grew back vigorously when they tried to burn them, while their attempts to hoe them produced erosion as the thin topsoil washed away, leaving their fields stony and barren. No one had tried to make terraces as they couldn't see a solution to the linked problems of thin topsoil, low fertility, and weeds.

Ironically, highlanders found that the best method to get rid of stubborn weeds was to shade them out by planting cacao. The cacao also provided protection from erosion by holding the soil with its roots, and spreading a leafy canopy to reduce the impact of wind and rain. Meanwhile, the wild pigs had become increasingly voracious as their food sources had dried up, and even

4.1. Old-style house in a cacao grove

4.2. Still leading hard lives

4.3. New plank house, Rina on the step

the strongest fences could not keep them out of a patch of corn. So highlanders who could not grow enough food to feed their families had reached the point of compulsion: they no longer had a choice. They had to try to maximize the cash revenue from their tiny plots and hope it would be enough to buy food. Since cacao was the most productive crop available to them, they planted more of it. From then on, it was the ratio between the price of cacao and the price of rice that determined whether or not they could hold on to their land.[5]

The only highlanders still growing large fields of corn were those who could afford to purchase new land from the "bela" to expand their farms. Their goal was cacao and cloves, but they had the bonus of a few years' supply of corn until the tree crops took over all the space. On Sibogo, Tabang and Malia were the only couple with a large patch of yams which they allowed neighbors and kin to harvest at will. This was a generous gesture, especially appreciated because gifts of food had become so rare. One of the land-short people on Sipil, desperate for cash, was harvesting this free food and taking it down to sell at the market. Dekon's son Sampo was relying on Tabang and Malia's yams to feed his household for three days so they could focus on clearing a new garden. "Those yams belong to lots of people. They come asking for them," Tabang said. He wasn't asserting a concept of common property, but rather taking pride in his capacity to help others and the affection that flowed toward himself and Malia in return.

Rina and I found not only diets, houses, and landscapes rearranged, but also the ways people organized their time and moved through space. The flimsy huts were all inhabited, with women and children at home, even though many of the men were away on wage work in other desas, as they had been in the past. But the big houses were often empty, or left in the care of a teenager while the rest of the family was far inland, several hours walk away, working on new farms where they were expanding their cacao and clove production. Meeting up with these people required making an appointment, sometimes for a week hence when they planned to go back to their big house for a few days to rest. Even when the family was home, these big houses were oddly quiet. I remembered Amisa's house in the early 1990s, a beehive of activity with kin and neighbors dropping in for one thing or another, and compared it with her son Hamdan's much grander abode. Hamdan's only visitors were children sent by their parents to buy cigarettes, sugar, coffee, or snacks from the stall his wife Sara kept in the front room. The children didn't even come into the house. They perched on a ladder by a side door and Sara served from there. Two more of Amisa's sons, Nijo and Atar, lived less than a hundred meters away from Hamdan, yet neither they nor their wives were regular visitors. Each of them kept their privacy.

One of Amisa's daughters, Alia, was struggling to feed her family as she had very few productive trees. She was living in a tiny thatch house, built on borrowed land, that wasn't big enough for her teenage children to sleep in at night. During my 2006 visit, I hardly saw her though she too was living close to Hamdan and Sara. Sara mentioned that Alia did come to visit sometimes, usually to ask to borrow money, obliging Hamdan to navigate the difficult terrain between helping kin and conserving his investment capital. "It is OK to help her once or twice," Sara commented, "but not all the time." Hamdan had become a major landowner and his father thought he was overdoing it. Sara became thin each year during the main cacao harvest, when the couple worked daily from dawn to dusk, trudging between the dozen or so cacao groves they had planted or bought in different parts of Sibogo and Sipil. After ten years of marriage they had only two children of whom the first had died and the second, a girl, was small for her age. "You don't need to add any more gardens," the old man advised, "you are worn out, you should rest." But

Hamdan and Sara were on a roll, and they continued to accumulate, through their own work and, increasingly, by treating money as capital to invest.

Malia's brother Siam and his wife had built a big house on Sipil, but when Rina and I visited them they were living in isolation in their garden hut high above Sipil where they had acquired new land. Their purpose in living there wasn't just proximity to their farm. They had deliberately tried to withdraw from contact with kin on the wife's side, who were numerous and poor, and made continuous demands. As the couple explained their situation and their plans, they stressed contrasts: while they worked hard to improve their lives, their kin just asked for food and said unkind things about them when they rejected requests for help. They complained about thieves—possibly their own kin—who were stealing yams and taro from their gardens, and corn from their pakele. These losses were interfering with their plans, as they were counting on this food to eke out purchased rice. They needed to keep careful control of their expenses to spend time developing their new farm.

Hilo and his wife Dama, sister of Sara, also had a big house on Sipil although Dama said her family was "alone on Sipil." As a description of the spatial layout this was inaccurate. Their house was surrounded by neighbors. Her point was that these were neighbors occupying a different social position, people whose conditions of life and prospects for the future had come to diverge sharply from their own. Their daughter was the only youngster from Sibogo or Sipil currently in high school in Tinombo town, a source of pride to her parents and also a worry as they had to ensure a continuous flow of funds to support her. Their son had failed to complete primary school, but Dama stressed that he did not mix with the kids on Sipil, who were too lazy to work but already adept at gambling. He preferred to stay with one of his aunts or uncles at Sibogo, where the habits were different. Through micro-practices such as these, social divisions linked to differential wealth were becoming entrenched.

Several successful women farmers told us of their plans to move their families down to the coast: the schools there were much better, as was the social milieu. Besides, there was less work for them to do in the hills now that they didn't have huge corn and rice fields to weed. As soon as they had enough cacao and clove in production, they thought their husbands could manage the upkeep alone. They would just visit the highlands occasionally when extra hands were needed and focus their attention on raising their children and supervising their schoolwork. This gendered division of labor, and the separation of the work of raising children from work in the fields, was quite new in the hills where previously children learned by working alongside their parents, and then by planting crops of their own. In the poorer families we visited, parents didn't talk about their plans for the children's future, but they did worry about what would happen to them since they would inherit little or no land. In Sibogo parents sent their children to the small school that had been built around 2000, but the quality was poor. It had only one teacher for the six grades, and he lived on the coast, showing up only two or three days a week at best. He used the Lauje language most of the time, so the children did not learn much Indonesian. Very few children completed six years of primary school and passed the final exams. Besides Hilo's daughter, only two children had gained admission to junior secondary school on the coast. They were boys who attempted to support themselves by doing odd jobs, but they both dropped out after one year.

The large, somewhat festive and largely reciprocal work-parties to clear and plant corn and rice fields had disappeared. Again, highlanders explained the shift in pragmatic terms. They had no more need to gather large groups of workers, nor to coordinate among neighbors. It was the attempt to "share the birds" that previously drew them together to plant whole hillsides with rice in a short period of time. The new tree crops required very little work. Clove trees only fruited in alternate years. Well-fertilized cacao produced pods weekly, with a concentration in one major harvest season per year. Couples with few trees did all the work themselves, and those with a lot of trees hired occasional labor for tasks they couldn't complete. The most sociable moments in cacao production were sessions when families gathered in the shady cacao groves in the late afternoon to split the cacao pods, extract the seeds, and load them into sacks to carry back to spread out on the drying trays next to the house. Neighbors sometimes came along to help split the pods, enjoying the casual chat and the relatively light work.

Highlanders didn't express concern about giving up self-provisioning in favor of cash crops, even though this might appear to be a more alienating form of labor. Indeed, I discovered in 2006 that highlanders who had been planting cacao for more than a decade were not even sure it was food. Hamdan asked me about this one day when he came into his house after spreading a huge pile of cacao on a platform to dry. He said he had tried nibbling the cacao beans but they tasted so terrible he couldn't imagine what use they could be to anyone. I reached up to a shelf where Sara kept the commercial foil-wrapped snacks she sold to neighborhood children and found one that listed cacao as an ingredient. Both empirically and existentially, the link between his mound of cacao beans and the brown-colored confectionary was hard to explain.

Although social relations created through reciprocal exchanges had eroded, highlanders still did not live as atoms. They called formal work-parties for house building when many hands were needed to raise the house frame and secure the roof. They counted on neighbors to help at funerals and weddings, which had become more elaborate. Preparations for a wedding could take weeks, as highlanders mobilized to build additions to a house, organize firewood and supplies, deliver invitations, set up the stage, secure the awnings to cover the area where guests would sit, and host guests who came from afar. Close kin were most deeply involved. During our visit to Sibogo, all of Amisa's children were preparing for the wedding of Alia's daughter, showing solidarity with their sister despite their limited social interaction.

The routine occasions for men in the middle hills to gather were Friday prayers at the small neighborhood mosques, arenas of formal equality in which social distinctions were muted. For women and children, there were nightly sessions for watching TV or video at the houses of rich neighbors. Some owners charged a fee for this privilege, on the grounds that they needed to cover the cost of fuel for the generator. Others let neighbors watch TV for free, making their profit by selling them snacks, or by collecting a fee for the use of electricity to charge their phones. Teenagers used the TV sessions as an opportunity for courting. Men, especially poorer men, tended to stay away, ashamed perhaps at the social distance that had opened up between them and their neighbors.[6] When I occasionally joined the crowd watching TV in the evenings, I was struck by the content, especially the advertisements for laundry detergents that showed smiling, healthy children in superclean homes, wearing super-white clothes—clothes that definitely hadn't been washed in a muddy mountain stream. Reality wasn't the point of watching TV, however, and highlanders' favorite programs featured flying ninjas and plenty of magic. They didn't watch the news. Even if they did, they would not have understood much, as their Indonesian-language skills were still limited.

Economic inequality among highlanders was directly linked to the buying and selling of land, though the extent of land selling was difficult to quantify in the absence of official land records. In Sibogo, where I kept records of land transactions from the time of initial enclosure around 1992, fifty of the ninety-eight farm plots had changed hands through purchase by 1998, a sign of the difficulty some farmers had in holding on to their land during

4.4. Family in a cacao grove splitting pods

4.5. Spreading cacao to dry near the Sibogo school

the initial years of tree planting. Between 1999 and 2006, there were very few transfers of landownership in Sibogo, but the apparent stability was deceptive because the successful farmers were acquiring land in other parts of the hills. Idin, Hamdan, Hilo, Amin, and Emsalin, for example, had each acquired ten to twenty farm plots on Sipil and in the inner hills some distance away. Whenever anyone needed to sell land, they were ready to buy it.

One justification the larger landowners gave for continuing to accumulate land was the need to provide for their children, who wouldn't be able to pioneer in the do'at, as previous generations had done. The enclosure of land was enclosing households as well, making them more tightly bound as economic units. Highlanders could see that young couples' livelihood prospects would depend crucially on the property their parents were able to give them. I noticed that Amin was attempting to control his children's labor, much as Idin had done a decade before. At that time, neighbors thought Idin's conduct was strange, but Amin and other landowners later followed his lead. They discouraged their children from going away for wage work and urged them to stay home to help build up the household's stock of land and trees. Parents gave children a share of this property on marriage and tried to reserve enough for younger siblings. The poorer households, in contrast, were still loose at the edges, much as they had been before. Men and teenage boys were absent, trying to find sources of income wherever they could, mostly outside their own desas. Parents without land had no means to draw in their childrens' labor, or to hold them close.

Highlanders with little or no land were living from hand to mouth. Timit from Sipil was a distressing example of someone who was working as hard as he could, but was unable to earn a living wage. When we visited him he had just come home from a month of work in another desa hauling timber out of the forest. The pay he earned was the equivalent of just two kilograms of rice per day. With the savings he managed to bring home after paying for his own living and transportation costs, he did not buy rice. Instead, he spent his week "at home" hiking up into the inner hills looking for cheaper food like cassava and yam as a way to stretch his tiny funds before he left again for wage work. He had no way to acquire capital or access credit to buy land or inputs, and even if someone had given him land for free, he could not have worked it as he needed daily wages to sustain his family. He was just twenty-five, and exhausted. His father had died young, and his mother did not enclose much land when the cacao era began, leaving him and his siblings with none.

Some of Timit's age-mates had acquired land through marriage into land-holding families. The social divide wasn't sharp enough to prevent contact between youngsters, a situation that could change if landholders followed through on their plan to move to the coast or send their children to school there. As in the past, young people chose their own marriage partners and they weren't necessarily strategic. In 2009 I asked Atar how his niece, Alia's daughter, who married in 2006, was getting along, and more specifically whether her husband had inherited any land. He responded that neither of them had anything at all and their prospects were dim. His niece was pretty like her mother, and he thought both women could have received better offers. But he accounted for the outcome by noting that each person is destined by fate (or god) to have one uniquely suitable marriage partner (their *jodoh*), so there was nothing more to say about it.

In 1998 I had seen some indications that enabled me to predict who would prosper. Hamdan and Idin were clearly on the rise. Other people surprised me. Amin had few trees in 1998 and was still carrying down backloads of yam to sell at the market. By 2006 he had become one of the richest men in Sibogo. Tabang was living in a better house, but he was borrowing it from a brother who lived elsewhere. He was embarrassed because the house was still an empty shell with clothing hanging from the rafters and no furniture. The sisters Ramla and Malia, married to Amin and Tabang, still visited each other freely, but Tabang was ashamed to visit his old friend Amin because he felt the difference between them had become too great. Following his land dispute with Linajan and the deadly spirit attack, which I described in chapter 3, Tabang had sold the disputed plot to a person from the coast. Amin later bought the plot. Tabang recognized the sale as legitimate: he needed to sell, and at the time he was grateful that someone was willing to buy. But still, it hurt. He said he closed his eyes whenever he walked past those beautiful trees and pictured the wealth they could have brought him. What was it, then, that put Amin on a path to accumulation, and left Tabang and his wife Malia—a woman renowned for her hard work and skill—barely holding on?

Mechanisms

Considered as mechanisms, in a stripped-down form, the key elements that enabled some highlanders to set up productive tree-crop farms were the ones identified a century ago by Lenin in his study *The Development of Capitalism in Russia*: technical efficiency in production, determined by access to capital or credit to acquire the necessary inputs; economies of scale; usury/money lending; and extraction of surplus value from wage workers.[7] These mechanisms did not operate alone, but combined with the character of crops; habits and desires; local and global prices; droughts, diseases, and other elements to form the conjuncture at which capitalist relations took hold.

SOURCES OF INITIAL CAPITAL

Technical efficiency and scale were closely linked to highlanders' access to capital in the initial phase, when cacao seedlings were going into the ground. For reasons I will soon explain, merchants based on the coast who bought highlanders' cacao did not supply them with investment credit in the early years, so highlanders had to rely mainly on their own work and savings to generate capital to invest. Ayub and Idin used their savings from shallot production to buy land and hire workers. Access to this initial capital positioned them to accumulate quickly. Amin's surprising rise to fortune was enabled by money he had obtained from the sale of some coconut trees he had planted in another desa where his family had moved in the 1970s, after the collapse of tobacco. When his wife Ramla wanted to return to Sibogo to be close to her family, he sold the trees and wisely put the money in the bank. Years later when this rather cautious man finally became convinced that investment in cacao and clove would pay off, he used his savings to buy trees that were already in production, quickly recouped his initial investment, and began to accumulate. These examples aside, few highlanders had access to savings in the early 1990s. Most of them scraped together the capital they needed from wages or from occasional trade, often combined with work as porters. Amin and Tabang once hiked for three days across the peninsula on the narrow trails, carrying forty kilograms of trade goods in each direction to take advantage of price differences between the two coasts to gather the funds to restart their shallot production.[8]

Amisa's teenage sons, who were supplied with food from their mother's extensive rice and cornfields, could spare the time to stay at home and invest in their farms. In contrast their cousins on Sipil were often away hauling rattan and timber for very low wages. The only decent wages available to Lauje highlanders came from work on the biannual clove harvest in desas along the coast that had a lot of clove in production. *If* clove prices were high, and *if* highlanders were able to secure harvesting jobs, they could make good money in a short period. In 2006 several near-landless highlanders told me they hoped to use their wages from the next clove harvest as capital to buy land and invest.

Timit's neighbor Nisran on Sipil was the exception that demonstrates just how difficult it was to generate investment capital from wages. Nisran received no land at all from his own or his wife's family, and like Timit he worked hauling timber out from the forest on piece rate. It was backbreaking work. But Nisran could haul twice as much as his peers. He stressed that he didn't waste time, as others did, smoking or drinking coffee. He felt he had superhuman and possibly supernatural strength. "I'm still in the forest," he said, "but in my mind, I'm already at the timber depot. So I set out and hey, I've arrived." He invested his earnings in buying land on Sipil, and he also hired workers. He calculated that he could earn three times as much hauling timber as the daily agricultural wage, so it was more cost effective for him to haul timber and pay someone else to work on his farms. Indeed, he was adept at calculation. He would give the timber foreman a chit detailing exactly how much he should be paid for the logs he had hauled, based on the number of cubic meters. He had stopped school at primary-level two, barely knowing his letters, but he taught himself to read and write through text messaging on his cell phone. Neighbors agreed that Nisran's capacities were unusual and added that he earned far more than average from clove harvesting because he used both hands and didn't hold on to the ladder. In a context where several clove harvesters died each year in falls, his path to accumulation seemed to be enabled by spirit powers. His story contrasted strongly with that of Timit, who was caught in a low-wage trap with no way out. Timit didn't have Nisran's supernatural strength. All his energy was taken up by the struggle to feed his family.

SPENDING, SAVING, AND HOARDING

Reducing the cost of consumption and reducing the flow of gifts to neighbors and kin (which meant weakening social ties) enabled some highlanders to save money to invest. Nisran did not smoke or drink coffee, two of the small luxuries of highland life. When I stayed at his house in 2006, I noticed that a cousin who slept over had brought some cooked food of her own and discreetly served herself in the evening, a break from the custom in which the house owner as host shared cooked food with whoever was present. Hamdan's brothers observed that Hamdan did not smoke and he kept on planting corn long after he could afford to buy rice. They also mentioned that he had been less than generous in helping with the costs of his siblings' weddings, and he had continued to work while their mother was sick—a serious breach of proper relations of care, in their eyes. A contrasting case was Emsalin who had become a successful tree-crop farmer but struggled financially because he was generous in helping his adult children and had also taken in two orphaned nieces. During our visit one of his married daughters came by his house to pick up a sack of rice he had bought for her so she could spend a month working on her new cacao farm without worrying about food. He also supported his grandchildren, especially the eight children of his oldest and most feckless child, the gambler Osan. Emsalin's wife prepared food for up to twenty people every evening at their house.

A gambling habit worked against building up investment capital and a viable farm. A few notorious gamblers including Osan lost all their land to gambling. Many highlanders lost some. Amin attributed his rise to riches in the period 1998–2006 to his decision to stop gambling, triggered by a particular event. He and Ramla had struggled financially when they moved back to Sibogo in 1992 on short notice following the death of two of their young children. Eventually they scraped together the money to buy two goats to sacrifice in the name of these children, and Amin went down to the market on the coast to buy the goats. On the way he stopped to gamble in the back room of a merchant's store, and he lost all the money. Ramla was so furious with him that she threw a pile of money in his face. He hadn't gambled since then and their fortune had improved greatly. Tabang once gambled away a large sum of money that belonged to someone else. When Malia found out she slapped him in public. Since then he had gambled less but he recognized that if he had been able to stop entirely, like Amin, he would have been able to build up his farming enterprise.

Weddings could bankrupt a family or enhance their social prestige. Either way they interfered with accumulation, so a balance had to be struck. As in previous decades, young people in poor families simply eloped and some young men worked for their in-laws in bride service, but highlanders who had prospered wanted to demonstrate their new social status.[9] The gold standard was to hold a lavish wedding feast on the coast, attended by desa officials and other members of the coastal elite. Highlanders held these events in rented space in someone's yard, where they had access to electricity to power lights and amplifiers for a rock band, the prized form of wedding entertainment. But not everyone took this path. In 1993 Amisa risked her family's prestige by agreeing to a low bride price and a simple highland wedding for one of her daughters. The groom and his family could have paid a higher price and Amisa also had savings, but she argued that a big wedding would waste money that the young couple could invest in their farms or use to build a decent house. A few people sold land to pay for weddings. There was a famous example in Pelalang where an older man who had pioneered a lot of do'at sold all of it to pay a high bride price for a young wife, leaving his children with no land. The land clearly belonged to him, but at the new conjuncture when land had become scarce and expensive, highlanders judged his conduct to be both foolish and selfish.

Weddings weren't the only events demanding new skills to balance spending, investment, and proper relations of care. Idin was notoriously skilled at managing money. As Elok once pointed out, "Idin doesn't work himself, but his money is always on the move." Idin's habits changed, however, after he suffered a stroke. He began to carry his money in a sack that was always by his side, even when he went to defecate, much to the amusement of his neighbors. A few other older men did the same, all of them ridiculed for conduct that no longer fit with the times. Neighbors commented that it made no sense to hoard money when there were opportunities for profitable investment. But they also had harsh judgments for people who were overly focused on accumulation. Tabang and Malia told me a story about a neighbor who insisted on going out to work one morning even though one of his grandchildren was ill. By evening, the child had died. They read the neighbor's behavior as confirmation that he valued money more than kin. Indeed, they said, he was obsessed. He reportedly told his children "a day without work is money lost." Malia observed that he "prefers to see his corn rot rather than give it away to others, even to his own married children." In telling me this story, Tabang and Malia were also drawing a connection between their practices of care, signaled by the yams they gave away for free, and their rather limited economic advance.

FARM SIZE AND PRICES

The size and quality of the land farmers enclosed early on or were able to purchase was a critical factor in their upward or downward trajectories. Idin and other highlanders with access to many plots of land were able to put some plots under cacao while still producing food on the remainder. In this way they could sustain their families until their cacao began to yield, steadily convert more land to cacao, and buy up more land year by year. Farmers with only a small area of land were extremely vulnerable during the period when they had no more land for food but their tree crops hadn't yet begun to yield. They quickly succumbed to the "simple reproduction squeeze." Land quality was equally significant. While Sibogo farmers often suggested that their kin on Sipil were too lazy to plant trees, Sipil farmers pointed out that Sipil was less fertile than Sibogo. It was former tobacco land and thoroughly worked out. It wasn't suited to cacao. The cacao they planted didn't grow well and had few fruit.

Sibogo farmers also claimed that their kin on Sipil were unable to manage money and wanted to consume in ways they couldn't really afford: taking too many sacks of rice on credit instead of eking it out with cheaper foods, or selling land soon after planting trees in order to enjoy immediate consumption instead of waiting patiently for the trees to yield. These criticisms were justified in some cases but often they were not. They misrecognized the squeeze that poorer households faced as they struggled to sustain their families with little land and low wages, and their need to sell productive property to survive a crisis period. When pushed to the limit the priority had to be short-term survival, even at the cost of long-term security and the potential to advance.

Relative prices were crucial in farmers' capacity to hold on to their land. Most important was the relation between the price fetched by the new crops and the price of food that the farmers now had to purchase. Neither of these prices was determined locally. In the early 1990s when they started to plant cacao, highlanders weren't thinking too hard about the price of rice relative to cacao as they considered rice a luxury food, and they planned to keep producing corn and cassava. In 1997–98, the price of rice increased significantly but the price of cacao increased even more: it quadrupled, not due to any shift in global demand but because of the crash of the Indonesian rupiah vis-à-vis the dollar during the Asian financial crisis.[10] The financial crisis had nothing to do with the Lauje highlands but it had a particular effect there: the high price of cacao produced a windfall of cash for farmers who already had cacao in production, giving them the means to buy land and expand their operations. It also encouraged highlanders to convert their remaining land to cacao, and they were not alone in making this decision. The hike in price intensified the "boom" in cacao throughout the island of Sulawesi, as farmers planted large areas to this crop in a short period. The price squeeze for people who were barely holding on came in 2005 when the price of rice began to rise, peaking in 2008 during the world food crisis.[11] By this time, land-short highlanders were not growing any food at all. They had no choice but to borrow money to buy food, placing them on a downward spiral.

THE MATERIALITY OF CROPS

The capacity to hold on to land was also shaped by the material features of cacao and clove, the two main tree crops grown in the hills. In the 1990s when highlanders started to plant tree crops, they favored cacao because it is farmer friendly in its initial stages. Entry costs are low, just some seeds or seedlings and a patch of ground. The trees start to yield after two to three years and produce some pods every week during the early years, helping farmers to earn money from their trees quickly and get through the difficult conversion phase. Cacao planted in fertile soil doesn't require chemical inputs to give a good yield at first. All this changes, however, as the trees age. They need increasingly intensive inputs of pesticides and fertilizers to keep on yielding from years five to fifteen. This feature makes it difficult for cacao farmers to simply hold on: without a substantial investment in expensive chemicals, or funds to purchase new land where they can again take advantage of nature's subsidy or "forest rent," their production declines sharply.[12]

With cacao, farm size and technical efficiency are integrally linked: successful cacao farmers had enough income from their trees not just to keep the family going, but to keep their trees producing as well. Farmers who could not afford inputs saw their productivity drop down to zero by year ten. Highlanders were desperate for advice about how to treat their diseased cacao but no government extension workers with relevant expertise came to help them.[13] Their main sources of information were salesmen promoting agricultural chemicals at the rotating markets, and their own observations. Cacao merchants I interviewed also faulted their clients' mentality: they couldn't persuade them to treat credit as an investment fund to increase productivity. Merchants watched with dismay as their clients' production declined, and their own profits dwindled. Highlanders insisted that fertilizers and pesticides were too expensive, an assessment based on the debt they were already carrying for food and their lack of confidence that the investment would produce results. They pointed out that farmers who did buy chemicals but didn't know how to use them, or used too little, saw no improvement. Yet they recognized that neighbors with sufficiently big and productive farms were able to keep the trees yielding and use their profits to acquire new land.

Clove trees had a different trajectory. In the 1990s they were not popular because they took at least five years to begin to yield, and even after eight years they only produced a good harvest in alternate years. For land- and food-short highlanders, they took up too much space for too long, without any return. Farmers also found the price fetched by cloves too low to cover

4.6. Cacao merchant; the sign below the Islamic inscription says "Reminder: when you harvest you must repay your loan as agreed."

production costs, especially harvest labor, so they left their trees untended and some farmers cut them down. The price of clove rose significantly after President Suharto left office in 1998 and his family's monopoly exercised through the clove marketing board was lifted. By 2006 highlanders began to recognize other advantages of cloves. The trees were less prone to disease than cacao, and they required an input of labor only once a year at harvest. But only farmers with plenty of land planted clove trees. Land-short farmers could not afford the long wait or the erratic yields. Rather like shallots and another highland annual, chili peppers, clove trees could pay off with a jackpot: money to build a new plank house with a tin roof and to buy a TV and a CD player all at once instead of through saving. But they were not a reliable source of income for people who needed to buy their food.

The contrasting experience of Dayak rubber smallholders in the 1970s is instructive. These farmers had sufficient land to plant rubber without jeopardizing their food supply. Some of them accumulated up to thirty hectares of rubber and employed wage workers. But abundant land meant that their accumulation didn't come at the expense of their neighbors and kin.[14] Rub-

4.7. House and consumer goods, paid in full with one spectacular clove harvest

ber also has material qualities that make it especially farmer friendly. It isn't prone to disease, so farmers don't need to shower it with expensive agricultural chemicals to keep it productive. They can stop tapping the rubber trees for years and the trees live on, like a bank account ready to supply cash when needed. Hence rubber smallholders don't have to farm efficiently just to hold on to what they have. They can produce inefficiently, or even haphazardly, without losing their assets. Lauje highlanders—rich and poor alike—were far more constrained.

CONTINGENCIES

Contingencies were prominent in the experience of highlanders, although as many studies of rural life confirm, their effects were not random. Adverse prices, drought, illness, death, childbirth, and the expenses of family weddings affected all highlanders, but while these challenges could be weathered by rich people, for people whose resources were already stretched, they could tip the balance and lead to a downward spiral. Contingencies also arose in linked bundles as I found out when I visited Sibogo in 1998. I hadn't planned to visit the Lauje area that year but I decided to spend two weeks there after completing some other work because I had read an alarming report in an international newspaper: Tinombo was mentioned as the location of death by starvation due to the prolonged El Niño drought of 1997. When I arrived coastal officials firmly refuted the story about starvation, a suggestion they found embarrassing. Highlanders in Sibogo observed that they hadn't even had to turn to the old famine food, ondot, because they had been able to borrow money from cacao merchants—a benefit they contrasted sharply with the terrifying experience of hunger during previous droughts when they had no land or trees to pledge against food for survival. But as I dug deeper I found that the drought had a polarizing effect.

The obvious consequence of the drought was that everyone's food crops shriveled up and died. Much of the cacao survived but did not produce any fruit. The result was not only a crisis in production and income on Sibogo, but also a crisis of employment on Sipil, especially for women who relied on wages from their work on Sibogo to support their families. Land transfers were another effect. My record of land transfers on Sibogo showed that many of the plots of land that changed hands shifted during or shortly after the drought year as highlanders with cash in hand bought land from desperate neighbors. The El Niño drought in 1992–93 had furnished similar opportunities. Then there were the illnesses that followed from the drought, with its triple jeopardy of poor nutrition, polluted water, and lack of funds or energy to seek medical help on the coast.

A distressing visit to Tabang and Malia led me to write in my notebook: "There is no food at all at Tabang's house; the children are filthy and sick." This was not something I had previously observed in their house, as Malia was a competent mother, farmer, and manager of funds. There was deep sadness in Idin's house too where two children had died within hours of each other, probably from gastroenteritis. Sina hadn't farmed at all in the year since the children died and she left a whole field of groundnuts to rot unharvested. Fortunately, she said, they had income from cacao to tide them over. One of Alip's children had also died and he was so distressed he had hardly left his house in months. Unlike Idin he had no savings and conditions in his household were even more dire than usual.

It is worth recalling that highlanders didn't necessarily see events such as drought, illness, or death as contingent. When many people were afflicted at the same time, they thought the harm was caused by spirits of the land and water that ought to be placated by collective ritual action, in the way I explained in chapter 2. They sometimes attributed individual good fortune to a pact made with these spirits, and bad fortune to a failure to properly acknowledge them when collecting rattan, clearing land, or planting and harvesting crops. Mostly however they thought individual misfortune, especially illness and death, was caused by malevolent spirits sent by kin and neighbors with the deliberate intention of preventing the victim from prospering.

Some highlanders thought spirit power was involved in gambling too, as people who won made deals with spirits who took their side.[15] Because gambling was banned by desa headmen, highlanders tried to hide their gambling from me, even though they knew I knew it was taking place. Half-joking, half-serious, Idin once suggested that Rina and I should talk loudly or maybe start singing as we walked along the trails, and especially as we approached a house we planned to visit, in case the people inside wanted to hide their packs of cards. Highlanders' coyness meant that I learned about the consequences of gambling for land loss, but I did not learn much about how gambling was organized or how highlanders understood gambling risk.

DEBT AS A MECHANISM OF LAND LOSS AND EXTRACTION

Individual ownership of land made not just gambling but debt more generally a new and potent mechanism of land loss. In the old days the main way highlanders could obtain credit from a merchant was by taking an advance against a forest product (rattan, resin), or against their tobacco crop. So long as highlanders held their land in common, they couldn't pledge or sell it, and a creditor could not seize it as repayment for a debt. Individual landownership changed this situation. Although mortgages and loans—like landownership—were not documented, highlanders who held land as individual property could be pressured to sell it to cover their debts.[16] Pressure was informal. I heard of only one case of nonrepayment that was adjudicated by a desa headman, who became involved only because the debtor had no land to sell and the moneylender, Linajan, was threatening violence.

In the 1990s Linajan and Idin, the two main moneylenders in Sibogo, extended credit to their neighbors as a part of a deliberate strategy to acquire their land, and a decade later there were several more large landowners who lent money and took payment in land. Cacao merchants based on the coast also furnished credit to highlanders, but they had no interest in taking over their clients' land. To do so would involve them in managing scattered plots of cacao in remote locations, a time consuming and risky task. Instead, they made their profit from the margin between the price they paid highlanders for their crops, and the price at which they sold the cacao to dealers based in Palu, augmented by the interest they charged highlanders on their debts.[17] They didn't need to set foot in the highlands. They could just send their agents to wait at the foot of the hill for the sacks of dried cacao indebted highlanders carried down to deliver to them on market days, and load into their trucks.

In the 1990s, volume was the key to the cacao merchants' profits, and their main purpose in advancing credit was to build up a loyal clientele. Competition among merchants kept the interest they extracted from indebted cacao farmers modest. They paid the farmers roughly 15 percent below the market price each time they brought down their cacao, a rate that stayed constant regardless of the size or duration of the debt. The risk the cacao merchants ran was that indebted farmers would sell their crop to competing merchants, breaking the terms of the loan agreement. When they caught farmers doing this they cut them off, forcing them to take loans from other sources that were more expensive.

Around 2005 highland moneylenders and coastal merchants increased the rate of extraction and tightened the credit system by introducing a new mechanism: mortgage of the crop. Under this arrangement, the debtor agreed to repay the loan with a fixed quantity of cacao or clove, priced 30 percent to 50 percent below the market rate. This arrangement freed merchants from the need to monitor the crops coming down from the hills, as farmers could sell part of the crop at market price so long as they fulfilled the mortgage commitment. Roni, the merchant who serviced Walu, defended this arrangement as better for highlanders as well. Instead of receiving 15 percent less for all their cacao, they paid interest only on the mortgaged portion. Access to credit was still a plus. Farmers who could borrow were better off than those who could not borrow and had no option but to sell land. Nevertheless, heavily indebted farmers received little or no cash at harvest time, making them more vulnerable to all the crises that came along. Credit and debt were bundled up with farm size, price, and contingency in enabling some highlanders to prosper, while others were squeezed out.

In addition to the profit cacao merchants extracted for themselves, their extension of credit to highlanders intensified the process of polarization among highlanders in two ways. The first of these was quite unintended. In the old days, tobacco merchants extracted *all* the surplus from tobacco farmers, so none of them were able to accumulate capital to invest, or to lend out with interest. They were left uniformly impoverished, with barely enough food and money to sustain themselves from one year to the next. In contrast, cacao merchants competed with each other for clientele, and their rate of extraction was less complete. Successful cacao farmers paying 15 percent interest could still accumulate, hence they had funds to buy land from their struggling neighbors and kin.[18] But the cacao merchants' unintended stimulus to accumulation worked only because of another element: the highlanders' land had become individual property, and it could be purchased. The two elements together—individual ownership of land and a new capacity among highlanders to retain some of the surplus they generated—created a polarizing effect.

The merchants' deliberate stimulus to polarization began around 2005, when they began to channel investment credit to successful highland farmers who wanted to expand their farms. Cacao merchants I interviewed argued that they could no longer extend credit to the weaker farmers who never paid their debts and did not produce much cacao. Their own capital was borrowed, and they had to pay interest to the bank. To stay in business and compete with their peers, they couldn't afford to allow their capital to stagnate. By enabling the more successful, loyal, and reliable farmers to buy out the weaker ones, they could reduce their risk and increase their profits, while still leaving the land and the organization of production in highlanders' hands. Rilenti, the main merchant who serviced Sibogo and Sipil, extended investment credit to Hamdan, his brother Atar, his brother-in-law Hilo, and also Amin. Hilo was especially ambitious, and when I talked to him in 2006 and again in 2009, he was quite extended. His returns from his own tree crops were modest as he had started late, and he had borrowed large sums to acquire new land. Nevertheless, he had Rilenti's confidence and he was expanding his farming venture aggressively.

Awkward Relations

As highlanders separated into two groups—one group accumulating property, the other losing it—they did not simply co-exist side by side. They were linked through a class relation, since accumulation for some depended on the value they extracted from their neighbors. They extracted value in three ways: they bought their neighbors' land to expand their farming enterprises; they lent them money at interest; and they employed them as wage workers. These class relations were awkward for highlanders to navigate because they cut across ties of kinship, neighborly interaction, and decades of common experience. They were also novel. In 1990, it was not possible to buy land; highlanders seldom had surplus funds to lend to each other at interest; and no one was obliged to do wage work for another person. The awkwardness shaped the form of the new class relations although it did not prevent them from emerging; it limited extraction, but not enough to prevent the polarizing pressures of competition, which were relentless.

DEBT, MORTGAGE, AND LAND SALE

Highlanders often asked their prosperous neighbors to lend them money. These requests put men like Hamdan and Amin in an awkward position. If they refused, their neighbors could accuse them of being unhelpful. If they agreed, they could be accused of charging too much interest and profiting from their neighbors' distress. The complaints I heard were mainly about refusal to lend. Faced with an urgent need, highlanders looked on someone willing to lend them cash as helpful, regardless of the interest charged. A loan enabled them to avoid selling land and gave them the chance to produce again another day. They took the same perspective when it came to land purchase. They were aware that highlanders who accumulated land did so at the expense of the people who sold up: the buyer got the land, and they often paid a low price for it because the seller was under duress. But the person selling wasn't necessarily thinking about the price. In the transactions I tracked, the sellers described the buyers as helpful because they had provided a way out of a tight spot. Another buyer, aware of their desperation, might have offered them even less.

The contrasting experiences of Amisa's sons Hamdan and Atar, both of whom bought land and were involved in money lending, show just how tricky it was to negotiate loans among kin. In 2006 their sister Alia was desperate to have some cash in her hands during her daughter's wedding which was being held on the coast at Hamdan's newly built brick house. She came to Atar a few days before the wedding and told him that if she had no ready cash she wouldn't attend. She would just stay at home in Sibogo and let the wedding go on without her. Atar agreed to take over Alia's last remaining cacao trees on a two-year mortgage, which meant that he would harvest them and keep all the proceeds during that period. "She wanted to sell them but I told her don't sell, after two years I'll give them back to you. If she wasn't my sister I would just have bought them outright. Maybe the mortgage should have been for three years, but I didn't calculate that, I just helped because she is my sister and her life is very hard." Putting the matter this way, Atar claimed to be helping Alia. He gave her the cash she needed, he enabled her to hold on to her trees, and he took less profit from the loan than another, less caring person would have done.

Alia also borrowed repeatedly from Hamdan although it was clear she didn't have the means to repay him, so the loans were really gifts. Over the years, Hamdan had bought most of her cacao trees, which she sold one plot at a time when she was desperate for money, and came to him asking for help. Like Atar, he didn't see himself as profiting from her distress because if he didn't buy her trees someone else would have bought them for a lower price. He too felt that he would have to keep on helping Alia as she was his sister and he couldn't cut her off. Alia's husband's gambling was the source of the problem. More than once an unmarried brother, Amal, had given Alia productive land and trees to try to help her establish a stable farm enterprise but instead she continued to lurch from crisis to crisis.

Alia's situation was extreme, but Hamdan often felt himself under pressure to lend money to kin and neighbors whose requests were not backed by a reasonable prospect of repayment. In 2005 he followed the lead of other merchants and moneylenders who had tightened their credit terms by shifting to the crop mortgage system. He pegged the rate of return at one kilo of cacao per Rp 5,000 in loaned funds, at a time when the market price for cacao was about Rp 8,000. This amounted to an interest rate of 60 percent. In the end, the neighbors and kin who borrowed from him at this rate only returned about half the cacao they had committed. He still broke even because the market price of cacao rose sharply in 2007–9, so the cacao he did receive covered the difference. Possibly, the people who had borrowed money from him took the price increase into account when deciding that Hamdan had already made enough money from his loans. I didn't find out their side of the story. For Hamdan the whole experience was a bitter one. He did not pressure his kin to repay the debt. "I'm just treating it as if it was paid," he said, "or I would have bad relations with them." He hated the awkwardness and the unkind gossip that the loans introduced in his relations with people around him. His response to this experience was to stop lending money to anyone, and concentrate on farming his own land, which kept him quite busy enough.

The risk Hamdan ran when he stopped lending money was that kin and neighbors would accuse him of interrupting the flow of care that ought to characterize highland social relations. He had the money, yet he refused to help. He was isolating himself and as I noted earlier, his house was oddly quiet. He received few visitors. His brother Atar used the crop mortgage system to make advances of rice instead of cash, and he had more success. In 2009 he had loaned out two tons of rice to neighbors, and soon recovered 90 percent of the promised cacao, netting a profit of more than 100 percent. Atar seemed to weather the stress of lending to social intimates better than Hamdan, perhaps because he wasn't as rich, or because he was more affable and less of a puritan—he liked to smoke and gamble. Hamdan was strongly opposed to gambling and wanted the neighborhood head to ban it. One of his neighbors observed, unkindly, that Hamdan had lent a lot of money to people on Sipil during a period the previous year when a gambling binge was going on. Shortly afterward, he built his brick house on the coast, complete with a façade of pink ceramic tiles. Doubtless Hamdan's money lending made him some money but he did not insist on repayment or seize land, unlike Idin and Linajan, the main moneylenders in Sibogo in the 1990s. Idin used to organize gambling at his house and serve as "banker," a position from which he was guaranteed to make money. Nisran and Hilo used an even more cynical strategy: they went to gambling sites using the alibi of selling snacks or cigarettes, but were ready with large sums of cash so they could buy land on the spot from someone who was losing at cards.

LABOR

Exploiting someone else's labor was another way in which one highlander could profit from the distress of another, but this was more tricky to navigate than making loans or buying land, as it pushed against highlanders' sense of personal autonomy, expressed through their capacity to work on their own terms. Even though people who had little land depended on wages, retaining or feigning some degree of control over their capacity to work remained an important source of pride. Freeing up the commodity "labor" was more tricky than freeing up land, because a person who works can't be detached from the labor he or she sells. This is the feature that led Karl Polanyi to classify labor as a "fictitious" commodity, and Marx to reflect on what it means to alienate labor from the person who bears it.[19]

Although highlanders sometimes hired wage workers in the days before cacao, as I explained in chapter 2, wage work was occasional, seasonal, sometimes reciprocal, and usually framed as "helping" to mitigate the awkwardness experienced by both parties. Recall how the widow Leka, who often worked weeding shallot fields for Malia and depended on wages to support her five children, nevertheless stressed that she wasn't at Malia's beck and call. She would "help" Malia when she had time. Malia paid her, but the idiom of helping flagged Leka's sense that she gave Malia a bit more than she received in return. After all, Malia received a garden free of weeds in which her shallots could grow. If Leka hadn't agreed to do the work, the shallots would not be there.

Talking to Adam in 2006 I noticed a telling shift in the way he expressed the wage relation. He was one of the poorest men on Sibogo with lots of children and little land. In response to my question about whether it was difficult to find work in the neighborhood, he said it wasn't easy but there were several people, mainly kin of his wife, who would "help" by giving him work if he asked. In framing the relation this way, he positioned himself as the one who was requesting help, not the one whose help enabled the farm owner to prosper. He had become dependent on the land, capital, and care of others as the means to put his own body to work. Lack of demand for his labor made his situation more desperate than Leka's had been in the 1990s, but like her, he put on a brave face and stressed that he didn't work for wages all the time. He and his wife took pride in the fact that they had a garden. To demonstrate, they insisted on giving Rina and me some yams to take home, small ones that were the only food they had growing alongside some young clove seedlings on a very steep patch of land next to their shaky, unfinished house.

Refusal to work for low pay was another way in which highlanders attempted to assert some autonomy. Idin was notorious for paying low wages to his workers from Sipil, most of whom owed him money, but he went too far on one occasion in 2006 when he tried to underpay the porters who carried down his cacao. Highlanders always paid their porters at a standard rate per kilo, so when Idin offered his porters only half the going rate and tried to confuse the issue by calling the event a work-party, he was quite out of line. Few men showed up. Although he failed on this occasion, Idin's clumsy attempt to extract more than the usual rate of profit indicated another important shift: he could take the risk of offending his neighbors because if they did not want to do the work, others would replace them. The shift was clarified for me when I reviewed a transcript from a discussion about porters I had recorded in Idin's house in 1993. During this discussion, Sina recounted how she had produced a bumper crop of shallots and needed thirty people to carry them down to the market. In addition to the standard rate per kilo, she had provided them with cigarettes and a good meal, complete with fresh fish. It wasn't the first time she had done this. She recalled how, on a previous occasion, her porters had made two trips and she cooked deer meat for them. Idin chimed into Sina's story with this comment: "Well it's true, if they didn't help, who would carry all those shallots to the market? So even if it was expensive, buying some deer meat was the right thing to do."

Idin's comment referenced the dearth of "free" labor in the early 1990s, when highlanders still had access to land and grew at least some of their food. They sometimes worked for wages, but they weren't compelled to do this as a condition of survival, nor were they obliged to attend work-parties. If they were not treated with due courtesy and care, they could stay away. Idin's and Sina's prosperity depended not just on their workers' labor, but on their willingness to do the work. By 2006 Idin's neighbors were more desperate and he placed less value on their goodwill. Even if he crossed the line between legitimate accumulation and the greedy attempt to bully people to do his bidding, he knew he would be able to find workers when he needed them. If necessary, Idin could even have hired workers from the coast. Although none of the prosperous farmers in Sibogo had started to hire workers from outside the neighborhood, the existence of an increasingly large pool of needy people both in the highlands and on the coast made it less necessary for employers to treat workers as whole social persons. They could begin to think of labor as a standardized commodity in which one unit was interchangeable with another. They only needed to calculate how much labor they needed, and where to buy it for the best price.

After Idin died in 2008 Sina handled labor relations differently. She was hard-pressed to manage all the farm plots they had accumulated. Tabang noted that Sina had left some of her cacao fields unharvested. When I asked her why she didn't hire people to do the work, she replied that she was trying to save money because she needed cash to pay for her son's wedding. This was the response of a hoarder, someone who holds on to their money rather than treating it as capital to invest. Tabang wondered if Sina would be capable of maintaining her capital or would let it drain away. But her reluctance to hire wage workers was not simply idiosyncratic. Despite their wealth Hamdan and Sara still trudged between their fields harvesting their own cacao except at the busiest time when they really couldn't manage. The only workers Amin hired were members of his immediate family. With the exception of carrying sacks of cacao down to the market, an occasion for triumphal display, Hilo and Dama did most of their farmwork themselves. It was not just the cost of paying workers that held them back, it was the social awkwardness of the relationship.

Full-time wage work for a single employer was the most awkward relationship, as highlanders associated it with personal subservience. Emsalin expressed his horror at this condition through the example of his son Osan who had lost all his land gambling, including several new plots his father had given him in the hope that he would change his ways. Osan had married young and produced eight children he could barely feed. "Now Osan lives under orders," Emsalin commented sadly. "People tell him do this, do that." There was a man in Pelalang nicknamed "taxi" because he was always available for hire as a porter. Like Osan, he had no farm. He was ridiculed by his neighbors and treated with disdain.

Filip on Sipil, another man with almost no land and many undernourished children, was so desperate he proposed to give up his residual autonomy and bind himself to Dama and Hilo, who lived nearby. He had often asked them to "lend" him food, but then he went further, asking them to order him a sack of rice in return for which he would work for them on any task, for an indefinite period of time. He was effectively seeking to put himself under indenture. To signal this intention, he also asked if he could sleep at their house. But Hilo and Dama did not want this relationship. They found it personally uncomfortable and also impractical: they didn't need a full-time worker, and they had no interest in taking responsibility for maintaining Filip or his family. A few years earlier, they had tried to help Filip by inviting him to plant cacao on some of their land, offering him half the land and trees after three years in return for his work. Their hope was that he would establish himself as an independent farmer, but he did not follow the plan. From Filip's perspective, the plan wasn't realistic: he was compelled to sell his labor daily in order for his family to eat. Free land was not enough to enable him to put himself to work. He also needed capital or credit to buy food to sustain himself and his family until the new farm began to yield, minimally for a few months while he planted some corn and waited for the first harvest.

Although the compulsion to work daily for wages had become the de facto condition of many highlanders by 2006, age and family status made its assault on the autonomy of adult men like Timit, Filip, Adam, and Osan, fathers of many children, especially painful and a source of personal shame. Full-time wage work was socially more acceptable among bachelors, especially teenagers who could describe their activity in terms of seeking capital to invest. Sometimes they were distant kin of the landowner, a status that modified the wage relation slightly and protected idioms of "helping," although it was still awkward. In 2006 Hamdan had recruited a teenage boy named Olut to work for him almost full-time. Olut often slept at Hamdan's house, a practice that could suggest kin-like intimacy or the lowly status of a farm-servant, always at the master's beck and call. Hamdan stressed that he liked Olut because he was hardworking and obedient. When I mentioned to Olut's mother that I had heard a neighbor call Hamdan "Olut's dad" because the two were always together, she was embarrassed. She stressed that her son only worked for Hamdan when he wasn't working on his own farm or helping out on hers. Her point was not that she had a claim on her son's labor; it was rather to assert that the boy was free to decide when and where to work. She was a widow whose husband had once been a prosperous farmer, peer of Idin and Emsalin. She had raised seven children on her own and struggled to hold on to the land she had left. I asked her if Hamdan planned to help set Olut up with land of his own. I imagined he might like the role of kindly uncle or adoptive father since he had no son. But she confirmed that the relationship was strictly wage based. Hamdan had made no such promise. By 2009 Olut no longer worked for Hamdan. He was away working in another desa, trying to save money to marry.

The only enduring wage relation I came across in which a few people worked almost full-time for a single employer was on Walu, and the conjuncture was distinct. The employer wasn't a neighbor; it was Roni, one of the few coastal merchants who bought land in the highlands and became directly involved in managing farms. The workers on his extensive landholdings—half the hillside by one account—were three young couples, three siblings from one family married to three siblings from another. They had little or no land because their fathers had gambled away their land when they were children. Some of the trees they tended for Roni were the very trees their own fathers had planted. Roni paid them on a contract basis for finite tasks like spraying pesticides, or clearing a new field and planting clove. For the work of cacao harvesting, which was continuous because his well-fertilized trees produced cacao pods year round, he paid them per kilo of harvested beans, dried and packed ready in sacks. These methods of payment reduced the need for supervision although he visited his farms and workers almost daily after the long-promised road along the Walu ridge opened in 2005, and fifteen minutes on his motorbike replaced an hour's steep hot climb.

From Roni's perspective the relationship between him and his workers was a perfect match. They needed steady work, which was difficult to find in the hills because the demand for labor was sporadic. He needed honest, reliable, full-time workers at his beck and call. So long as they were available, or other workers like them, he envisaged expanding his farming enterprise indefinitely. After all there were plenty of landless people on Walu and neighboring hills. But from the workers' perspective their relation with Roni was far from ideal. They felt it wasn't good to work for someone else all the time. "Roni always complains the cacao isn't clean enough," one of the women commented, expressing her discomfort at being subject to another person's command. All three couples wanted to work for themselves on their own farms and spoke of their hopes—far-fetched but fervent—to acquire new land. One of the men had heard of some land that would soon be for sale far above Walu, in the coveted area that had been covered in brightly colored paint. He was just waiting for the clove harvest to get the money together. Another stressed that he already had a farm on an adjacent slope. The truth was that this land was extremely steep, dry, and infertile, and his ownership of it was contested. But it enabled him to imagine, or perhaps just to present himself to me, as an autonomous farmer with a plan for how to make his future better than his present.

Although hiring workers was necessary for highlanders who wanted to expand their holdings, they preferred to bypass hired labor whenever possible.[20] Hamdan, Idin, and others quickly adopted chemical herbicides when they became available around 1996, significantly reducing their need to employ the women of Sipil who used to do their weeding. In 2009 Atar bought the first diesel-powered bush cutter, a machine strong enough to clear a year's growth around the clove trees, eliminating another kind of work, this one gendered male. The work of porters was also eliminated when a motorbike trail reached Sibogo in 2008. Work as a porter had been Adam's main source of income, and he showed me the misshapen humps on his shoulders caused by the bamboo carrying pole. No person should be a beast of burden, and someone from Sibogo had died from a hemorrhage after forcing himself to carry excessive loads, hiking up and down four times in one day. Nevertheless, for Adam the loss of this work increased his hardship. Highlanders agreed with my observation that the new technologies deprived landless people of income, but everyone who had the funds adopted them, arguing that they were cheaper and more efficient.

Conclusion

In the early 1990s, highlanders were optimistic that planting the new tree crops, especially cacao, would enable them to improve their material conditions and their social status. What was unthinkable—not imagined and hence not discussed—was the prospect that twenty years hence, a few highlanders would control much of the land while neighbors would be compelled to depend on wages, and they would build their tiny bamboo huts on borrowed land. It shouldn't have been so hard to imagine. There was an example of just this phenomenon on the coastal strip that highlanders could see laid out below them as they hiked downhill. Many coastal folk who planted coconut trees around 1900 had sold them over the years, until all the trees and the land had become concentrated in just a few hands. Most of the people living under the coconut trees were landless workers, who lived on wages that were sporadic and low. Yet highlanders imagined that everyone who planted cacao and worked hard would prosper. They did not foresee the processes that would divide them, nor the mechanisms that would make it so hard for them to hold on with modest livelihoods in the stable "middle-peasant" style. Nor did they anticipate how competition and profit could reconfigure their relations with one another, insidiously, piecemeal, and unannounced.

To explore how capitalist relations took hold in the highlands, I focused on the mechanisms identified by Lenin—technical efficiency, scale, credit, labor—as they were shaped by features of the landscape, drought and disease, prices, practices, and the character of crops. I paid attention to the formation of classes, and to neighborly relations that cut across these classes, modifying them slightly. I highlighted the erosion of choice and the emergence of compulsion as the distinguishing feature of capitalist relations. It is easy to understand why landless people were compelled to sell labor. It isn't quite so obvious why land-short farmers couldn't plant more food, or why rich farmers couldn't be more generous. There were acts of generosity (Tabang's yams, Emsalin's sacks of rice); and there were acts of refusal (Idin's reluctant workers, Hamdan's withdrawal from moneylending). But if taken too far, these acts undermined highlanders' capacity to sustain themselves. Compulsion means, precisely, the erosion of choice. Owners of land and capital had to balance relations of care with the need to run their enterprises at a profit. If they failed to do this, their cacao farms would stop producing, and their source of capital would dry up. Soon they too would become vulnerable to crises, and their more successful neighbors would buy their land. Similarly, competition wasn't a matter of choice, it was progressively built into the relations through which highlanders accessed land, capital, and opportunities to work. Their previous market engagements—though centuries old—did not take this compulsory, competitive form.

Teasing apart the elements that formed this conjuncture enabled me to clarify why capitalist relations emerged at this time and not before, why here and not among the rice-and-rubber farmers of Kalimantan, and which elements were an awkward fit. A conjuncture isn't a seamless whole. Its elements jangle and collide. They foreclose some pathways and open others. Exploring the tensions caused by rising inequality and the politics that arise from this conjuncture is my focus in the next chapter.

5 Politics, Revisited

The end of land as a common resource to which all Lauje highlanders had access, and the need for land-short highlanders to find work or starve, severely curtailed their autonomy. Land's end undermined their capacity to make their own fortunes through their own efforts, frontier-style. The shift was swift and sharp. Fifteen years, half a generation, saw the emergence of a steep and stubborn form of inequality that set neighbors on different trajectories, a situation made worse by the lack of jobs that paid a living wage. It would seem like a conjuncture that was ready to explode, and so it might. I don't claim to know the future. To analyze a conjuncture is to make a cut through history at one point in time. Nevertheless, a conjuncture isn't radically contingent: all the elements that constitute it have histories and there are spatial configurations that make certain pathways easier or more difficult. In this chapter, I take advantage of the specificity of this conjuncture to think through its implications for politics. What happens when the telos of transition narratives doesn't hold, development "alternatives" lack traction, and hope gives way to bewilderment?

According to some political theorists, highlanders like Kasar and Adam, hungry and exhausted, perched in their shaky houses on tiny plots of steeply sloping land, have three "options": loyalty, voice, and exit. They can tolerate their conditions, protest, or find a way out.[1] Although this formulation is overly voluntaristic, it provides a useful framework for examining how highlanders responded to the cramped space in which they found themselves, and the political possibilities that arise from that location.

Tolerating Inequality

Despite the livelihood crisis that beset many highlanders, and mounting inequality, no overt protest drawing attention to these problems had emerged by 2009. Theorists of agrarian politics offer two possible explanations for this condition of nonrevolt. One explanation is that highlanders were protected by the provisions of a moral economy, hence their conditions—though dire—were not desperate enough to provoke an open revolt. In his analysis of peasant rebellion in Southeast Asia, James Scott argued that landless people (laborers, tenants) tolerate a high level of inequality and do not engage in open rebellion so long as landowners continue to act as patrons and provide a "subsistence guarantee." Rebellion occurs only if landowners ratchet up the level of extraction to the point where subsistence is jeopardized, violating the principles of the moral economy.[2] Related arguments stress the importance of solidarity among kin and neighbors, or whole communities, especially those envisaged as "indigenous." Solidarity may be loose and informal, or institutionalized in the form of rights to common land, limits on land concentration, or obligations to share food or work.[3]

Transported to the Lauje highlands, the assumed link between morality and solidarity seems misplaced. Highlanders were not devoid of moral concerns, and in some contexts they evaluated each others' conduct in moral terms. But their focus was less on protecting the weak than on ensuring that every individual received a fair reward for their work. The process of enclosure I described in chapter 3, and the polarization among highlanders that soon followed, reveal the limited protection supplied by Lauje highlanders' practices of kinship and care. As I showed in chapter 4, the new landowners in Sibogo and Sipil occasionally "gave work" to needy kin and neighbors, but they did not feel obliged to hire them routinely. They argued that if their neighbors could not find work in the highlands, they could go to collect forest products to sell on the coast, as highlanders had always done. Highland neighborhoods had never been closed systems, and the new landowners had no desire to constitute themselves as patrons or to assume responsibility for their neighbors' subsistence needs. Nor, crucially, did landless people expect them to take on this role, which didn't have a precedent.

To recap, in the era of shifting cultivation when land was still abundant, highlanders expected each person to seek his or her own fortune through their own efforts. They cooperated in food production, and entered into relations of exchange, but these relations were not of the hierarchical, patron-client variety. They were horizontal and reciprocal. They were also shaped by the materiality of the milieu. A rice crop would be devoured by monkeys or birds if the owner didn't coordinate with others and seek their help to plant and harvest in a timely way. Highlanders' reciprocal work exchanges reflected their shared predicament. They all put themselves to work and accessed land in the same way. One person's prosperity was not gained, indeed could not be gained, at another's expense. Exceptions like Idin's success in profiting from the work of his wife and children proved the rule. The emphasis was on taking responsibility for oneself and extending care to others, not on meeting obligations or enjoying entitlements. Similarly, the old practice of giving away bundles of fresh corn was embedded in the seasonality of production and its materiality as well. The pleasure of eating corn while it was fresh, and the fact that it would rot if stored for more than six months, made it sensible to give away the surplus or sell it to people who came asking. These features were specific to corn. They did not translate into the transfer of sacks of purchased rice, paid for with hard-earned cash. Nor did the old practice of exchanging days of work on a reciprocal basis fit the demands of the new situation in which households had quite different labor needs.

The gradual, unmarked way in which old practices eroded and new ones took their place was a crucial feature of these transformations. Highlanders didn't reject old ways of doing things; old ways were re-signified, or slipped quietly into disuse.[4] Where I saw ruptures and turning points, highlanders emphasized the banal and commonsense adjustments they made without fanfare or debate. Even in the old days, no one gave all their corn away, and some highlanders were more generous than others. As practices changed highlanders didn't contrast a moral economy of the past with a newly immoral one. Their evaluations of moral conduct didn't pertain to epochs. They concerned the behavior of individuals they knew intimately as neighbors and kin, with all their personal quirks and shared and divergent experiences.

Highlanders had little interest in my attempts to draw them into more general discussions about how the new era was different from the old one. In relation to land concentration, they agreed with my analysis that there was a pattern: the rich were accumulating land and the poor were losing it. But they didn't proffer this kind of analysis themselves. Instead, they pointed to the small things—particular events, personalities, droughts, illnesses, debts, prices, and opportunities that had led one person to prosper and another to sell their land. These were accurate observations, and highlanders found them quite sufficient to explain what had happened in their neighborhoods. They agreed with me that in the past, everyone who wanted to farm could access land, but they didn't refer to the old system as a fixed point of equality and virtue from which to construct a critique of the unequal present. They admired people who had succeeded in acquiring lots of land, built fine houses, and escaped the poverty that had colored their lives for so many centuries. Land-short highlanders had specific complaints about the meanness of rich relatives who were not willing to help out with loans or give them work, but they had no problem with the practices of tree planting, land concentration, or money lending that had made these people rich. Few people expressed nostalgia for the era in which they cleared large fields each year to plant corn, rice, tobacco, and shallots. They still described this as backbreaking work for uncertain returns.

If highlanders didn't stress nostalgia for past solidarities or practices of food production, what did they stress? For them the critical turning point—the one that marked an epochal shift—was the closing of the land frontier. Yet their recognition that land really had come to an end was reluctant and partial. Although land-short highlanders who lacked the capital and clout to compete in the scramble for remaining forest patches really were shut out, they continued to express the hope that they could somehow find a way to access land on which to work and prosper.

FRONTIER THINKING

Living on a land frontier formed the structure of feeling of highlanders in decades past: the idea that there was always a fresh patch of do'at to pioneer, if not here then over the next ridge, or the one after that. Their respect for individual initiative was grounded in the hard work it took to clear forest and establish a new farm. It formed their sense that individuals were responsible for their own fate, and failure to prosper was the result of personal deficiencies such as laziness and poor planning. As the land frontier closed and capitalist competition dictated who would be able to farm, the emphasis on individual responsibility no longer reflected actual opportunities. Broad agreement on the virtue of enterprise was increasingly out of touch with the situation on the ground. A crucial element in the conjuncture had shifted, yet the emphasis highlanders placed on individual responsibility remained in place. I don't treat this apparent continuity as a matter of cultural lag. It is a puzzle, as much in need of explanation as the changes I have described.

It isn't surprising that landowners sustained the view that if their land-short neighbors really wanted to work they could surely find new land or increase production on the land they had. This view matched their own experience—they started with nothing, and gained wealth through their own hard work. But why would land-short people sustain the belief that they could prosper through their own efforts? Adam, Timit, and others gave me incisive accounts of the difficulties they faced in establishing farms, highlighting their lack of capital to buy land and their need for daily wages. Nevertheless, they insisted that their future lay in cacao and announced their hope and intention of pursuing the same course that had enabled some of their neighbors to prosper.

The materiality of the milieu, specifically the uneven quality of the highland terrain, was one element that enabled land-short farmers to sustain a view of themselves as farmers whose future would be better than their present. They could still find some tiny residual nooks and crannies, very steep plots, or areas of worn-out grassland that had been passed over as unsuitable in the enclosure phase. Although these plots did not offer a realistic prospect of producing enough cacao or food to support a family, desperate highlanders pinned their hopes on them. Temporality was also significant. They were young enough to remember the events that had led their parents to lose their land and recognized the part they had played themselves: if only I had been here planting trees instead of away hauling rattan, if only I hadn't sold those trees, if only I was as hardworking as Hamdan or as skilled at managing money as Idin. . . . These practices, memories, and ways of understanding changes in the highlands as a string of idiosyncratic, small events, were consequential. They were not a sign of "false consciousness"; they were the real, embodied, mainly implicit structures of feeling that enabled land-short highlanders to maintain the view that any individual with determination and hard work could succeed. Their words and deeds reflected a sense of "not yet" rather than "not ever," as they situated themselves on a timeline moving forward in which their turn would eventually come.

Frontier thinking wasn't for everyone. Some highlanders, Kasar among them, were in despair. On Sipil, Filip described his sense of bewilderment. His old way of living had become impossible, he explained, but a new one had not taken its place. He used to grow corn in the hills and collect rattan on contract for fishermen on the coast who used it to construct their fishing gear: "That was how I was raising my children," he said. "We had our own corn, so we didn't need to buy rice." Now he was reduced to begging for rice on credit from Hilo and Dama and seeking to persuade them to become patrons of a new kind—people who would take responsibility for sustaining him and his family. But they had rebuffed his offer of placing his labor permanently at their disposal, and he didn't have anything else to propose.

An older woman on Sipil linked loss of a previous livelihood to the failure of cacao to deliver as promised, despite her diligent efforts. Her analysis included a tinge of nostalgia, not for a lost way of life but for lost productivity: "We used to grow so much food here, people came to modagang. For four cassava plants, we could get one or two sarongs. . . . Now our cacao is diseased and has no fruit. We would like to be the same as others and we want to work, but we have no more land. My husband works hard, we have both worked hard always, why is our life still so hard?" Her account emphasized that hard work and skill should have produced results, as it had in the past. It didn't stress the elements I highlighted in my analysis: the poor quality of their tiny plot of land, the high price of credit, and competition from more efficient farmers who had squeezed them out.

At bleaker moments, impoverished highlanders turned critiques against themselves. Mostly, they just left the matter of who or what was responsible for their condition unresolved. Whether these land-short households sustained a sense of hope, or expressed their situation in terms of bewilderment and despair, in 2009 they did not show signs of becoming what Marx called a class for themselves: a group capable of acting collectively to advance a class interest.[5] Just to endure under these conditions was a major accomplishment and it took up a huge amount of energy.[6] No one observing from the outside could fault these often-hungry highlanders for not doing more.

WEAPONS OF THE WEAK?

A second possible explanation for highlanders' apparent tolerance of inequality, also drawn from the work of James Scott, is the proposition that highlanders had a nascent class consciousness, but they did not protest openly. Instead, they acted covertly, using what Scott called "weapons of the weak" such as theft, arson, gossip, and slander.[7] Theft of cacao was indeed widespread in the highlands. Landowners were concerned about it and some of them had organized night patrols to try to prevent it. Larger landowners like Hamdan, Amin, Idin, and Hilo with holdings dispersed throughout the hills were especially vulnerable.

Although theft might be seen as an implicit critique of unequal access to land, an assertion of the moral rightfulness of taking a share in order to stay alive, and an indication that the attempt to justify inequality in terms of merit was unconvincing to the poor, my discussions with highlanders did not support this interpretation. They recognized that people without cacao were more likely to steal out of need, but they did not offer a justification of theft framed in class terms—as a struggle between owners of capital and workers, envisaged as groups whose interests were distinct. Once again, we can draw insight from the conduct of the notorious Idin. In 1998, some sacks of Idin's cacao disappeared from where he had stored them under his house, and neighbors suspected that Idin's daughter Nisa had taken them. They were quietly sympathetic. For them, Idin's transgression wasn't that he was a rich man who deserved to be brought down, or even that he employed workers and profited from their labor. The problem was that he had failed to pay Nisa for her work, or give her a share of the money he made from cacao. Hence she had the right to take some sacks of cacao as payment of what was due.

Nisa took action, and she also married and moved out from her parents' home. She was able to start her own farm enterprise based on land and trees her parents gave her. This indeed had been Idin's goal: to accumulate so that he could set up his children for the long term. Arguably, his reluctance to pay them or pass on property too soon was an approach well suited to the emerging, competitive milieu which put a premium on economies of scale and reducing expenditures in order to save and invest. By 2006, other farmers like Amin were beginning to organize their household economies in the same unified way. But in 1998 Idin's approach still jangled awkwardly with the "normal" practice of rewarding individuals for their work, hence the sympathy for Nisa and the sense that Idin was accumulating at her expense.

Relations between highlanders and merchants could also be a site of class struggle, since merchants extracted profit from highlanders through adverse pricing and interest on debt. Hence we might expect to see this relationship as a site of covert protest action. Indeed, highlanders often attempted to evade the claims of merchants who had lent them money, but I couldn't provoke them into articulating a defense of the practice. They knew of several tactics highlanders used to avoid repayment: instructing the porters to name someone else as the owner when they carried down the cacao, or selling via a third party to avoid the agents sent by the merchants to line the route on market days, waiting to grab hold of the product that was due to them. But highlanders classified these strategies as theft, emphasizing that merchants lent money in good faith. When neighbors were cut off from lines of credit as a result of their dishonesty, no one was sympathetic. They understood full well why merchants had introduced the crop mortgage system, which didn't require so much surveillance.

In general, highlanders described the merchants who lent them money as helpers rather than exploiters. I often heard people in Sibogo describe their main merchant, Rilenti, as a kind man who was willing to help when needed. They emphasized their personal relationship with him and his kin-like practices of generosity and care. Indeed, some of them were related to him as he was originally from Sipil. He fled during the drought in 1977 and stayed in Sigenti, where he prospered. "We only need to send him word when we need rice," Amin observed, "and within a day or two the rice is there, ready for us to pick up." Note that Amin could afford to pay for the rice he ordered, if not immediately in cash then within a few weeks, making for an easy relationship. Despite his personal bonds with highlanders, Rilenti cut people off when they were chronically unable to pay their debts or cheated by selling cacao to someone else. He was a reliable patron only to his reliable clients, and highlanders found his approach reasonable. In his position, they would do the same.

Highlanders were quicker to attribute a protest motive in the case of arson. The usual target was the clove trees of the larger landowners that mysteriously burst into flames in the middle of the night. Neighbors' ungenerous reading of this action was the same one they proffered for a mysterious illness afflicting someone who had prospered: jealousy. Both actions signaled the frustration of people who watched others accumulate while their own condition deteriorated. But they weren't linked to an argument that rich people deserved to be made sick as punishment for their excessive accumulation. As I noted earlier, highlanders argued that jealousy was petty and unreasonable—it wasn't a sentiment they would publicly acknowledge. Nevertheless, the risk of incurring spirit or arson attacks did have a modest leveling effect, as it had in the shallot era. It encouraged some prosperous highlanders to maintain the goodwill of people around them by being generous and helpful. Amin and Hamdan certainly modified their conduct in view of these concerns and devised compromises. Amin would give away food, but he seldom hired workers and generally tried to keep to himself. Hamdan stopped lending money, relieving one set of tensions but provoking another. As both men withdrew from informal interactions with their neighbors, they took on prominent public roles. Hamdan became a prayer leader in the small Sibogo mosque. Amin became a ritual specialist, communicating with the spirits to bring his neighbors healing and good fortune. Both men continued to accumulate.

PELALANG: A SHARP DIVIDE

Comparing across conjunctures, it would actually be rather surprising if highlanders in Sibogo and Sipil understood class relations in terms of a sharp divide, for two reasons. First, the class division was very recent, and had emerged, idiosyncratically, in front of their eyes. The next generation born into a world already divided into haves and have-nots might well experience class divisions more sharply. Second, these highlanders were still linked by ties of kinship and common experience that cross-cut the emerging class divide.[8] A contrast with the conjuncture I encountered in Pelalang in 2006 will help to clarify the role these two elements played.

Pelalang was the site of the "people's garden project" I described in chapter 3. The project had provided a bridgehead that enabled Muslim Lauje from the coast to buy and grab land in the inner hills. Gilanan's cluster, the victims of this grab, were furious about it, and they had clear targets for their grievance: the headman, their kinsman the broker Katulu, and the newcomers themselves. But they were too intimidated to protest openly. Most of them retreated to the do'at frontier far inland, but Gilanan's brother Punat and a few others stayed in Pelalang, their homes wedged between the fields of cacao and clove belonging to the new landowners. The relations between the two groups were cool to hostile. The new landowners were aware that their disgruntled "bela" neighbors had the power to send their precious trees up in smoke, or to steal cacao pods from the trees before they could harvest them. In the absence of state-backed enforcement of their property right, they had to defend it indirectly by mounting guard, or defend it directly by enmeshing themselves in the neighborly relations that were the main guarantee of property and security in the highlands. But they didn't find it easy to establish neighborly relations. There were tensions over pigs that some "bela" were trying to raise as a source of income, causing affront to the Muslims who wanted the animals to be penned or banned. There were also tensions over work and pay.

Punat stubbornly insisted that Pelalang was the place of his ancestors, and he didn't plan to leave it. One afternoon, as we sat at the doorway of his house which overlooked the new road, a woman from the coast came by on her motorbike to drop off some cooked food. She explained to me that the food was left over from the work-party she held that day, as few people had attended due to a mix-up in the date. "These people are close to nature," she observed. "They don't understand about wages, they just work for free." After she left, Punat offered his account of what had happened that day. He and others had helped this woman with her work at first, as neighbors should, but no one went to her work-parties anymore because they were not reciprocal. She never offered to work for them in return, and even if she did, she wouldn't be any use as she had neither strength nor skill. They would have been willing to work for her in return for a proper wage, as the price of rice was very high and all of them needed cash. But this woman expected them to work for her for free.

Other coastal landowners in Pelalang did hire workers, but they did not hire their "bela" neighbors. Instead, they brought workers up from the coast on fleets of motorbikes. The ready supply of workers from the pool of un- and underemployed people on the coast enabled the landowners to bypass their highland neighbors entirely. In Sibogo, as I noted in chapter 4, Idin attempted to take advantage of his neighbors' need for work and the abundant labor pool to push down the wages of his porters, but they pushed back. He did not take the further step of importing workers from the coast. In Pelalang, the new landowners did not share kinship links with their "bela" neighbors and had no sense of obligation to them. Wage work was integral to production in both Pelalang and Sibogo, but the specific, concrete relations between owners and workers at each conjuncture were distinct. It was a consequential difference that shaped the way class relations were experienced, and the responses they provoked.

As the new landowners in Pelalang watched their "bela" neighbors sink into debt and disarray, they blamed their lack of work ethic and their desire to consume in ways they could not afford. The landowners reiterated, in short, the discourse that explains downward trajectories in terms of personal deficiencies, and upward trajectories—like their own—in terms of superior effort and initiative. They added references to the primitive nature of the "bela" which made it impossible for them to adapt to modern ways. They didn't discuss how their own practice of extending credit to "bela" neighbors and buying their land at low prices had contributed to their sorry state. Punat told me about his own very precarious situation as he was deeply in debt. But despite his difficulties, he announced his intention to stay and fight. He could see that land was coming to an end, and he wanted to hold on to his house, which was right by the road, in a prime location. Like Linajan above Sibogo, he wasn't only concerned about his own livelihood. He wanted to enforce a boundary that the "people from below"—Muslim Lauje from the coast and the middle hills—could not cross. But Punat was more isolated than Linajan, and less effective. Despite his bravado, he could not hold on. Swamped by debt, he sold his remaining land and pulled his children out of school to rejoin Gilanan and others who were clearing do'at far inland. He did not, or could not, mobilize with others to hold the line in Pelalang.

Voice

Highlanders did organize one collective, open protest during the period of my study. It was in Sibogo in 2006. Its focus wasn't impoverishment, debt, or loss of land. It was the failure of the government to deliver a promised road because "crocodiles in the path"—corrupt officials and desa headmen—were still preventing them from receiving their share of development benefits. The complaint was the same one I had heard in the early 1990s, but the conjuncture was different. In the repressive conditions of Suharto's New Order rule, social groups excluded from development benefits were too intimidated to protest overtly. The regime used state subsidies to sponsor the formation of a loyal elite that would help keep the rural poor in check.[9] Official development schemes in the Lauje area followed this pattern. Subsidies and valuable property such as land and houses in a settlement scheme about one hundred kilometers east of the Lauje area were given out in the name of the rural poor, but channeled mainly to members of the coastal elite. The only free inputs to reach the highlands—some cacao seedlings handed out in the early 1990s—fell into the hands of the group that was accumulating, strengthening their position. On the coast and in the highlands alike, poorer people were keen observers of the activities of the "crocodiles" but they had no means to stop them.

The period of reform that began in 1998 after President Suharto resigned was characterized by increased democracy, administrative decentralization, and open protests by aggrieved villagers who organized demonstrations that were reported in the press. The old districts were divided, creating smaller administrative units with some autonomy in budgeting and with an explicit mandate to improve services and promote "development" where it was lacking. In keeping with this trend, the Lauje area became part of a smaller district Parigi-Moutong (Parimo) with a new and more dynamic district head, who had previously worked in the department of community development.

When I visited the new district head in 2006, he showed me a map of his district, and commented on its strange shape: little more than a thin strip of mountains reaching down to the sea.[10] He had no land to allocate to big ventures like plantations so his only option was to try to improve the productivity of the highlands, mainly by encouraging farmers to plant more cacao, the main export from his district. His plan was to extend roads into the highlands, a measure he suggested would also end the shameful neglect that had left highlanders still living in a primitive state "just like in colonial times." Roads would increase highlanders' access to services such as health and education. He had even earmarked funds to build them free houses, to bring their living conditions closer to national standards. These plans were consistent with the desires of highlanders themselves, as I noted in chapter 1: they wanted to continue to live in the highlands and farm on their ancestral land, but they also wanted to be more fully included in national life, to live in decent houses, and send their children to school. So what could go wrong?

One problem concerned a process I have already described: new roads intensified the dispossession of highlanders, as they enabled coastal people with capital to buy or grab land. Recall Punat, swamped by debt, who was obliged to abandon his precious house by the road and pull his children out of school to move far inland. The district head wasn't interested in my account of this problem. If highlanders didn't benefit from new roads, he argued, the problem lay in their persistently primitive ways, which only more roads and education could solve. A second problem the district head failed to anticipate was the level of frustration among highlanders who had developed a new sense of entitlement and were no longer willing to follow the Suharto-era practice of holding their tongues and waiting patiently for development gifts to come their way.[11] It wasn't impoverishment, but rather high hopes and broken promises that stimulated the protest in Sibogo.

In 2006, the district head had announced a project to build a road along the Sipil ridge through Sibogo, past the school, and up to the church near Linajan's cluster. Keen to perform well in community development, he had adopted the process promoted by the World Bank through its subdistrict (*kecamatan*) development program (KDP), which emphasized participation and transparency in the planning of desa infrastructure. Information was key: desa residents were fully informed about the project budget, so they could monitor it to ensure the road was built as planned. The World Bank staff who devised this model expected it to empower villagers and "chip away at the fortress of monopoly power and impunity" that had characterized New Order rule.[12] Translated into Lauje idiom, the bank's project procedures aimed to stop rapacious crocodiles from grabbing resources, and highlanders were all in favor.

CROCODILES IN THE PATH

Construction of the road began shortly before my visit in 2006, but it stopped abruptly a few days later, having reached only halfway up the Sipil ridge. A group of angry highlanders met and delegated Hamdan and Hilo to ask the desa headman why the building had stopped. These were men whose new wealth and status entitled them to approach figures of authority to make claims, exercising "voice" in a direct way that poor highlanders still found difficult. The headman told them the funds allocated for the project were insufficient, and they would have to wait for further funds before the road could be completed. Because of the open budget, the Sibogo group knew this was not so. Armed in advance with crucial information, they had monitored the process closely. They had interviewed the driver of the bulldozer whom the headman hired to do the work. From the driver, they found out the cost per day to rent the machine and pay his wages. They calculated that the budget was more than sufficient for the road to reach Sibogo. Indeed, they knew precisely how much money had been stolen from them and they were furious. They mobilized to protest against corruption in just the way World Bank planners promoting village empowerment intended.

Learning that the district head was to visit the highlands, a group of about thirty people waited where the road ended to present their grievance. From the accounts I received, it was a diverse and quite remarkable group because it combined middle hill Muslims and a dozen people from Linajan's cluster, who arrived clutching their blowpipes. It also crossed class lines, as everyone wanted the road. Even desperately poor people like Adam, who would lose his job as a porter, thought the road was necessary—without it, his children wouldn't have the chance to attend a properly functioning school. The highlanders waited all day, but the district head did not arrive. Their protests to the desa headman and the subdistrict head fell on deaf ears, and they assumed these officials had been paid off. Hilo had an additional problem. The desa headman was the brother of Rilenti, the merchant who was supplying him with credit to expand his landholdings, hence someone he did not want to alienate. For both Hamdan and Hilo the matter was more delicate still as the person who had managed the road building contract, and was therefore implicated in the theft, was their brother-in-law. He was married to another daughter of the widow Samina, sister to their wives Sara and Dama. They were reluctant to confront him because they didn't want to damage valued family ties. If they could get the district head to solve the problem, they wouldn't have to point fingers directly. But their protest hadn't worked. The district head ignored them, leaving them searching for another means of redress.

When I arrived a few weeks after the ineffective protest, Hamdan, Hilo, and other highlanders pressed me for suggestions about where they could turn for help. Hours of brainstorming did not produce an answer. Indonesia has an activist movement dedicated to uncovering corruption, but the targets are usually high-level officials and politicians. Corruption among district, subdistrict, and desa-level administrators is so routine it barely merits note. I suggested seeking a politician who might support their cause, but they had no links with politicians or political parties. Since the end of the repressive New Order, a great number of new political parties had been founded, but highlanders shared the popular view that all of them were corrupt, they bought their votes, and after elections were over it was impossible to hold them to account.[13] None of them had a consistent focus on rural development. I suggested contacting journalists, but they did not think journalists would be interested in bringing their distress to public attention. Besides, they had heard that journalists must be paid to run a story, and in the case of a dispute, they would take the side of the highest bidder. In sum, neither the transparency rules attached to the road building project nor the "reform" movement that opened up apparently democratic spaces post-Suharto had empowered highlanders to obtain their fair share of "development" resources.

Although the highlanders' collective protest failed to get redress for the stolen funds and the unfinished road, it marked a significant shift. Highlanders exercised "voice," a big step from their previous tendency to remain silent. Their fury signaled the emergence of a new structure of feeling based in a sense of entitlement to fair treatment. This is the meaning of "moral economy" in the work of the British historian E. P. Thompson, who highlighted the "moral consensus" that there were "limits beyond which the Englishman was not prepared to be 'pushed around.'"[14] The consensus Thompson described had a particular history: it combined elements from the old agrarian order and the new industrial one, from religious organizations and protest traditions, and from an established legal regime that protected citizens from arbitrary power. His famous example was the bread riot, in which a crowd gathered to take sacks of grain from grain merchants with the aim of reinstating customary food prices after these had been artificially inflated by speculators "profiteering upon the necessities of the people."[15] The purpose of the riot was not to challenge the legitimacy of profit, only to curb monopoly and excess.

As in Sibogo's road protest, the English crowds involved in bread riots were drawn from across the class spectrum. Almost everyone suffered from the high price of grain, hence their willingness to participate in collective action to seek redress. In both cases, protesters were angry not just because they were hungry but because something that rightfully belonged to them had been stolen. Sadly in Sibogo, highlanders' voice fell on deaf ears: no one seemed to hear them. The officials to whom they addressed their complaints did not respond. Highlanders acting as a group could not make them listen. Nor were they able to connect up with allies who might have amplified their voices and compelled the authorities to take note.

More serious than the lack of a road was the deepening impoverishment of land-short highlanders, but the district head and other government officials did not attend to this problem, nor did highlanders mobilize around it, for reasons I have explained. From a government perspective, highlanders were still generally out of sight, and out of mind. Their impoverishment was grinding and banal. There was no emergency, no earthquake or famine to establish official lines of responsibility or relations of humanitarian care. Highlanders didn't protest effectively, nor did they die dramatically, rather one poorly nourished child at a time. Their suffering did not constitute an event.[16] It lacked traction. It enabled abandonment—the condition of Kasar, Punat, Adam, and so many others. But why were highlanders so isolated?

RECOGNITION

Voice isn't just a matter of speaking (or acting) up, but also a matter of making connections that amplify a protest, draw in allies, and create momentum.[17] Connection, in turn, requires recognition, a word that has three meanings, as anthropologist Johannes Fabian points out: fitting into an established category, being known through familiarity (as in re-cognized, seen again), and being acknowledged as someone competent to represent his or her own interest and participate in a debate (as in "the chair recognizes the speaker").[18] In each of these dimensions, the disruptive desires and practices of Lauje highlanders, and the consequences that followed from them, made recognition difficult. Indeed, a social movement activist who read a draft of this book told me explicitly he was puzzled by highlanders' isolation because he did not recognize it. It did not fit with his established categories or previous experience as an activist, which exposed him mainly to conjunctures at which oppressed villagers had activists on hand to help them in their struggle. He was often in places marked by eviction, violence, or arrest, but less often in places where villagers' main concern was to obtain a road to improve their access to schooling and reduce the cost of getting their cacao to market.

After the bloody elimination of the Indonesian communist party in 1965, until then the largest communist party outside China and the Soviet Union, social movements emerged to undertake important organizing and advocacy work, but their spatial and topical reach was limited. Their main focus circa 2000 was on environmental protection and defending villagers' land from seizure by state agencies or state-sponsored corporations. They also promoted "alternative" development, food sovereignty, and indigenous rights.[19] These platforms connected poorly with Lauje highlanders' predicament. Highlanders had switched from producing food to cacao, a move out of step with the "food sovereignty" campaign of Indonesian affiliates of the transnational peasant movement, La Via Campesina.[20] Moreover there was no agribusiness villain to blame: they had made the switch on their own initiative, because their old swidden system left them chronically vulnerable to drought. Lack of fit with the indigenous rights movement was equally severe. Lauje highlanders weren't dedicated to preserving their language, culture, and customary systems of land and forest management. They dismantled their own commons. They were eager to leave behind their condition of backwardness and acquire goods they associated with a modern life. Their impoverishment wasn't the result of a corporate land grab or misguided development scheme. It had emerged by stealth, leaving land-short highlanders more bewildered than angry and without a clear target for complaint. Social movement activists to whom I explained these processes were also bewildered. They saw no focus for mobilization, and no obvious point of connection with their own agendas. So long as the categories through which they came to know rural people and recognize them as proper objects of concern remained intact, it was difficult to bridge the gap.

The third sense of recognition, acknowledgment of a person's standing as a legitimate participant in a debate, is not something that can simply be granted. As Fabian stresses, it cannot be "doled out like political independence or development aid." It is the product of unsettling confrontations that challenge existing knowledge.[21] It requires setting aside familiar scripts and making space for new knowledge to emerge, an intrinsically political practice. In Indonesia, acknowledgment is impeded by government policies that position highlanders as backward primitives who need to be guided, or as isolated people who need more market access. It is also impeded by social movement expectations about indigenous frontiers as natural sites for "alternative" development. If my disruptive work in this book is effective, it could open a space for acknowledging highlanders as competent contemporaries caught up in complex problems of a wholly modern kind. But the challenges of acknowledgment are severe, and they are reciprocal. As I noted earlier, my attempts to disrupt Lauje highlanders' understanding of class formation as an outcome of individual merit were not successful, indeed they were politely rebuffed. Highlanders obliged me to reassess my categories and attend more closely to theirs. When it came to knowledge about their own lives, they questioned my competence. I know what I learned from these encounters, but I suspect the learning was one-sided.

Most outsiders who visit the Lauje highlands learn less than I did, because they aren't committed to the ethnographic art of observing and listening closely. I witnessed a complete failure of acknowledgment in 2006, when an NGO arrived in the Lauje highlands to deliver a government program that involved reforesting the highlands with teak. Sibogo folk who listened to the NGO's account of the program were bemused. If the land was covered with teak, where would they plant their cacao? And how would they live for the twenty years it takes the teak to grow to marketable size? These were sensible questions, but the NGO workers could not hear them. I spent a week discussing the problem with Hamdan, Hilo, Imsalin, and other informal leaders at Sibogo. Malia's younger brother asked me to coach him as he tried to pluck up courage to speak at an upcoming meeting the NGO had organized. He did speak, but the NGO workers brushed him off and they made a threat, New Order style, that uncooperative villagers might go to jail. When the attempt at verbal communication failed, I suggested to the NGO workers that they hike uphill for an hour or two, to see for themselves just how many people were living and farming on the slopes they intended for teak, but they didn't want to do this. They were delivering a national program based on the assumption that steep slopes should be forested, and villagers who cut forests to plant crops were making a mistake. This was not an assumption they were about to challenge. No new knowledge was generated by this encounter. Neither side acknowledged the other as competent to participate in a debate.

Exit?

In 2006, Lauje highlanders were profoundly isolated, and some of them were suffering acutely. At this point, the third pathway out of a tight spot—exit—might seem to beckon. Yet many desperately land-short and impoverished highlanders stayed in place. Why was that so? What was it that made land's end into a dead end, from which highlanders couldn't find a way out?

Exit is the standard remedy for impoverishment proposed by development planners. Planners know full well that increased efficiency in agriculture will squeeze out farmers who can't compete, but they argue the squeeze is necessary. It is the so-called creative destruction upon which increased productivity and economic growth depend. From this perspective, Lauje highlanders who planted cacao did the right thing by switching from their inefficient land use to a more productive one, and some of them achieved a much better standard of living as a result. In the view of experts from the World Bank, farmers who cannot compete should be encouraged to sell their land to people who can use it more productively. Land markets, like the one that emerged spontaneously in the Lauje highlands, enable the process of getting land into the most efficient hands, and Bank-sponsored land-titling schemes are intended to strengthen such markets and extend their reach.[22]

Contemporary development experts seldom specify where the people who exit agriculture should go, or what they should do, placing their trust in market processes to generate jobs and secure the optimal use of resources.[23] Indeed, many experts no longer think it worthwhile to engage in "development planning" of the type that was widely practiced in the period 1950–80, when national governments attempted to manage transitions out of agriculture and anticipate which sectors of the economy would grow to absorb ex-farmers or their children. Faith in market processes and worries over efficiency lead them to reject subsidies designed to help farmers stay on the land, weather the "simple reproduction squeeze," or survive competition with large plantations and agribusinesses. Planners justify the subsidies received by agribusiness corporations in the form of cheap credit and virtually free land and infrastructure as public investments necessary to generate jobs, although the empirical support for this is thin. The number of jobs agribusiness corporations generate in relation to the amount of land they occupy and the public funds they absorb is not impressive, and the opportunity cost of locking out small-scale farmers who might otherwise make use of these frontier spaces isn't taken into account.[24]

WHERE IS THE LAND?

Exit into jobs is the main strategy anticipated by development experts, but for Lauje highlanders accustomed to life on a land frontier, a more obvious response to the land squeeze was to search for suitable land to pioneer. Thousands of Lauje highlanders had migrated out in previous decades to escape the hardships caused by the collapse of the tobacco economy and the devastating effects of drought. They headed for desas like Sigenti that still had primary forest not too far from the coast. The Sigenti headman welcomed Lauje migrants because he had plenty of land, and increased population meant that more schools would be built and more funds would flow through the desa coffers. Conditions for pioneers in these forests were rugged, especially on the health front. Many migrants were overcome by malaria. Atar and Amin abandoned their pioneering efforts and returned to Sibogo in the early 1990s when their children died, two children in each family in rapid succession. Those who stayed away and prospered provided a bridgehead for their kin, especially young people who went off to visit their cousins and ended up finding marriage partners.

Lauje highlanders' opportunities for outmigration to a pioneer front closed down around 2000 for the same reason they closed down in their own desas: all over the province of Central Sulawesi, people with access to capital, force, or the powers associated with their position as government officials staked out the remaining primary forest land. They favored land alongside newly built roads, or land where a road was promised, where they hoped to profit from cacao, or from land speculation. The new landholders seldom had a legal basis for their claims, and some of them invested no capital at all. In much of the province, the new landholders filled "their" land with migrants from South Sulawesi and anyone else who was willing to work for free in return for half of the land and trees once they started to yield, unwritten agreements that sometimes ended with the workers being chased away empty-handed.[25] Tabang's brother Samir had a bitter experience of just this kind. He wasted five years on a pioneer front in another desa before he retreated back to Sibogo, with nothing to show for his efforts.

Whether they staked their own land, or worked on a share basis for someone else, Lauje highlanders and other would-be pioneers still had to solve the problem of how to survive before they could harvest their first crop of food. The lag was at least a year in primary forest where the trees must be cut, dried, and burned before anything can be planted. Often they needed daily wages to survive, slowing their progress and dooming many attempts to failure. In several cases I tracked, the people who finally succeeded in establishing tree crops on frontier land had significant capital and usually bought the land at third or fourth hand. The same was true of official resettlement schemes which were designed to support poor people by giving them land and a year's supply of free food while they established themselves, but in practice were often monopolized by government officials and people with capital.[26] Rina's brother spent ten years on such a scheme, but he was outmaneuvered and outcompeted, and ended up with just one hectare of coconut palms.

In addition to the piecemeal enclosures of one to fifty hectares initiated by farmers, or by officials and merchants seeking to profit from tree crops or land speculation, the provincial government also set aside large areas for use by plantation and mining corporations, and for forest conservation. In 2010 the official agricultural survey listed 12 percent of the provincial land base under rice and other food crops, 20 percent under tree crops (half in plantations, half managed by farmers), 47 percent as national forest, and the remaining 21 percent under settlement and other uses.[27]

Customary landholders were vulnerable to eviction whenever official license holders attempted to translate paper boundaries into real ones. Forest boundaries were being enforced more strongly by 2009, under pressure from transnational conservation agencies. More than two million hectares, or 30 percent of the provincial land area, was classified as protected forest or designated for conservation, and there were twenty-six separate named conservation areas covering more than a million hectares.[28] The conservation element intensified in 2010 when the United Nations declared Central Sulawesi a pilot province for a climate-change program called "Reducing Emissions from Deforestation and Degradation" (UN-REDD), and the other donors promised funds. These land uses competed with the push by district governments to allocate land to large mining and plantation corporations as a way to generate revenues. None of these contending land uses envisaged granting room for small-scale farmers to expand their enterprises on the land frontier. Taken together, they made it very difficult for would-be farmers to find new land. Not just in the Lauje highlands but across the province, access to land for smallholders—especially poor ones who lacked capital and connections—really had closed down.

WHERE ARE THE JOBS?

People who can no longer access sufficient land on which to support themselves need jobs, but none of the large land enclosures in the province generate much demand for workers. Conservation needs just a few forest guards. Mining requires many workers for construction but only a few highly skilled workers to man the machines thereafter. Oil palm, the main crop grown in the large plantations that are expanding in the province, needs only one worker per five hectares.[29] The character of the crop is relevant: if the plantation crop moving into the province was rubber, more people would find work, as rubber needs one worker per hectare.[30] Access to plantation jobs is also a problem. A survey I conducted with the Palu-based NGO Yayasan Tanah Merdeka in 2009 found that oil palm plantation managers were following the pattern established in colonial times: they favored migrant workers over "locals" because migrants were totally dependent on the plantation, and hence more easily disciplined.[31] The plantations met their core labor needs by hiring migrants from Java who entered the province through the transmigration program. They hired locals on a casual basis on wages well below the provincial minimum, taking advantage of the large pool of landless people in the surrounding desas.[32] They did not need to recruit workers from the Lauje area.

The dearth of jobs drawing people out from the Lauje area into the broader provincial labor force was confirmed by a survey I carried out in a coastal neighborhood called Tolia in 1990, and repeated in 2006. The neighborhood is a few kilometers from Tinombo town, the subdistrict capital. In my initial survey of twenty households, I recorded the names of all the children, so sixteen years later I was able to track what had become of them. Very few had moved away. Of the fifty-nine people who were aged zero to twenty at the time of my original survey, four siblings had moved to the provincial capital Palu, having been taken there by their Chinese "boss" when he opened a rattan factory. In another family, one sibling had moved to Palu and three were in other towns. All the others—fifty-one people—were still within the Lauje area, mostly in Tolia itself or in a neighboring desa where they had moved upon marriage.

Immobility among Lauje highlanders could be explained by their lack of language skills and education, combined with their relative isolation. But Tolia is located on the main coastal road, and all the children completed primary school so they could speak Indonesian. Tolia also had some powerful push factors: the land was barren, residents owned almost no coconut trees, and jobs loading copra onto ships at the Tinombo dock had dried up when the coastal road opened to truck traffic. Some young men worked loading trucks, and a few worked in Palu in construction, but they did not stay away.

Despite the dearth of wage work in Tolia during the 1990s, neither the nearest cities nor the regional agrarian economy presented them with better options. A century after ships first began to ply the Tomini coast to pick up rattan and damar, extraction of forest products was still the main source of employment. Lauje men from the coast had no choice but to join the highlanders who lived for weeks isolated in the forest collecting rattan to haul down on a piece rate, extremely strenuous work with very low return which often led to injury and sometimes to death from falls, infected wounds, and hernia.

If work within the province was so scarce, what of migration farther afield? In 1994, a Lauje labor broker recruited sixty-five young men from the coastal strip, including some from Tolia, to work in Kalimantan on an industrial tree-planting scheme. It was a disaster. Lacking experience, the broker and the workers had accepted the standard Central Sulawesi wage but arrived to find that the plantation on which they were to work was so isolated that prices for food and cigarettes were very high. They would need a wage 300 percent higher to make any money at all. With the broker's encouragement, the workers fled the contractor to whom their labor had been "sold" on the basis of false promises. They looked for work on other plantations and he lost track of them. They did not have enough money to return home. Two years later they had not come back, and the broker was trying to save money to go to search for them as he felt responsible to their parents, who were his neighbors. He feared they had fallen sick and died. As of 2009 no regular stream of migration from the Lauje area to other parts of Indonesia had been established. Labor recruiters who visited the area sought only short-term workers for occasional construction projects, like building roads.

A few Lauje men had attempted a more daring exit, going to work in Malaysia. This is a route many Indonesians have found to be profitable although it can also be high risk, especially for novices. In the case I tracked, the passports the workers were promised never materialized and they found themselves illegal in another country, vulnerable to all kinds of abuse.[33] Adin, the returned worker I interviewed, had not been recruited directly from his home on the Lauje coast. He had been working in a factory in Palu and was recruited together with seven of his co-workers. The young men were enticed by the adventure and the expectation of high wages in Malaysia. They thought they were going to work in a factory but found themselves on a plantation far in the interior. This wasn't rural to urban migration as transition models assume. It was urban to rural, or rural to rural: "It was OK for me and the other Lauje guys, three of us, because we are used to roughing it, but the guys from Palu had never been in the forest," Adin observed.

Adin and the others had left home without a written contract or even a verbal agreement about their wages. As a result they were entirely at the mercy of the local contractor. "We were sold," Adin admitted, "because we owed them money." They were tied by means of the debt they had incurred for their passage and expenses en route, though the sum was never made clear to them, nor was the cost of the food they bought on credit at the contractor's store. It was five months before the contractor gave them any cash at all. They had to run and hide in the forest every time the plantation was raided by the immigration police. "It felt like we were being hunted," commented Adin. "Only workers with proper documents didn't run." Every five months the contractor took them to his house in the local town for a few days' rest, but they dared not go outside for fear of being arrested. When they left after two years, he gave them a lump sum without furnishing any accounts. After they paid for their passage home, they were left with the equivalent of just $300 to show for their efforts. They had stories to tell, but mostly bitter ones.

Adin's job in a Palu factory was, in retrospect, a better deal than exit to Malaysia: he had decent pay, food, water, and a shared room in company barracks. It was a factory processing coconut oil. But two decades into the cacao boom there was no processing of cacao in the province, nor were there new jobs in assembly work of the kind that drew rural women into factories in Java in the 1970s and '80s.[34] As I noted earlier, in 2009 only 5 percent of the labor force in the province was employed in mining and manufacturing combined.[35] A few young women worked in Palu as housemaids for a year or so and benefited by becoming more fluent in Indonesian and expanding their horizons, but the pay was minimal and none of them stayed away for more than a year. They weren't able to move laterally into other service or manufacturing jobs, which were scarce and allocated according to social networks they couldn't enter.

There was, in sum, very little demand for the labor of the men and women of Central Sulawesi in 2009, leaving those who didn't have a livelihood as farmers stranded without a viable alternative. In a global regime of footloose capital, places like Central Sulawesi do not attract investors who need workers. They attract investors who want land for plantations and mines, neither of them labor intensive. As I mentioned at the outset, much of the growth in Indonesia and in other parts of Asia in the past few decades has been virtually jobless. Though it seems very distant, the rise of China's manufacturing sector in the period 1990–2010 which undermined manufacturing on Java and resonated across the archipelago was part of the conjuncture that left Lauje highlanders stranded. Shorn of teleological assumptions and optimistic win-win scenarios, land's end is a profoundly disturbing place.

After Cacao?

When I left the highlands in 2006, I thought I could predict how some of the processes I had tracked would unfold in the years ahead. The "bela" would continue to be displaced by coastal folk until they too were left to "hang from a tree" in Amisa's memorable image; and however fervent their hopes and plans, there was no way the land-short highlanders of middle hill neighborhoods like Sibogo and Sipil would be able to muster the capital and clout to acquire land in the face of competition from their prosperous neighbors, and coastal folk as well. As it turned out, one of the elements in the conjuncture shifted in a way I did not foresee, causing other elements to realign, although they didn't revert to the status quo ante.

Rather like my unplanned visit to the Lauje area in 1998, prodded by a news report about famine caused by a severe El Niño drought, I went back in 2009 due to news reports. The topic was the ecological collapse of cacao all over Central Sulawesi. In one report from a desa about a hundred kilometers away from the Lauje area, the headman stated that disease had made cacao unproductive, and thirty migrants from South Sulawesi who had moved into his desa to grow cacao had abandoned their farms and returned to their home province, or moved on to Kalimantan. He expected more to follow.[36] Another report stated that 60 percent of the cacao in Sulawesi was infected with a new disease, vascular streak dieback, that kills trees outright, and has no chemical cure. In a third report the Indonesian Cacao Association made small gestures toward assisting farmers by supplying more resilient seed stock, but simultaneously announced plans to move cacao production to Sumatra and West Papua.[37] From the perspective of national cacao production and export revenues, the interruption would be temporary. Sulawesi's cacao farmers, with their worn-out land and their old and diseased trees, would be replaced by different farmers on a different land frontier. They had become surplus to the industry's requirements. Industry officials quoted in these reports didn't seem interested in the hardships the end of cacao would cause to everyone in Central Sulawesi whose livelihoods had come to depend directly or indirectly on this crop, which contributed 80 percent of the U.S.

dollar value of the province's exports.[38] Nor were they concerned about the structural changes cacao had provoked in the countryside, which included the arrival of streams of migrants in some areas, and profound transformations among indigenous people as well.

As I read this news, I tried to imagine how livelihoods in the Lauje highlands would be reconfigured by the removal of cacao, an element that had played such a prominent role in the conjuncture I had studied. I could picture everyone cutting down the dead cacao in disgust. The land use would change, but what would be the effects on landownership? Was it possible that land could be de-commoditized and re-collectivized, reverting to its previous status as a "common" resource governed by rules for shared access? Could the capitalist relations that had formed over the past two decades unform as competitive pressures dissipated, together with profits? The end of cacao seemed to open up at least two possibilities:

1. *The intensification of land concentration.* The ecological collapse of cacao might have effects similar to the El Niño drought in 1997: it would provide an opportunity for owners of capital to strengthen their position by buying land from struggling farmers at low prices. The result would be to deepen the process of land concentration that was already under way. The landowners would replace the cacao with clove and other crops, hold it in speculation, or sell it to another party, further cementing its status as a full-fledged commodity and entrenching the exclusion of highlanders from access to their ancestral land.

2. *The withdrawal of capital.* Capital is mobile, and owners of capital are compelled by competition to seek at least average rates of profit. The collapse of cacao might cause merchants to cut off credit, write off un-payable debts, and put their money somewhere else. Landowners who couldn't sell their land might hold on to it as absentees, but they would take out any liquid capital they could muster and look around for more profitable investments. As capital withdrew, highlanders acting alone or collectively could make use of the vacuum to reassert their control over the land.

The conjuncture I encountered on my revisit in 2009 did not give a definitive answer to which scenario would unfold in the long term, but a version of the first—a sustained and deepened hold upon the land by the owners of capital—was under way. Alongside the roads that crisscrossed the province I noticed scores of empty houses that had been abandoned by migrant cacao farmers and field after field of dead cacao. But when I talked to the few migrants who were still in place, they confirmed that their neighbors had not sold their land. They were holding it as absentees, waiting to see if the cacao disease problem could be solved or another lucrative crop found to take its place.

In the Lauje highlands, vascular streak dieback had not yet arrived, but the decline in the productivity of the cacao was severe: the harvest was down by 70 percent over the previous year. Once again, however, the global price of cacao, acting like a wild card, had shaped the conjuncture: the reduced harvest was offset by a 130 percent increase in the price of cacao, which spiked during the 2008–9 financial crisis.[39] The effect was to stimulate successful cacao farmers from the middle hills like Hamdan and Hilo, as well as coastal people with capital, to push farther into the inner hills and acquire more land from the "bela." Hilo's tactics were shameless: he told me he deliberately cultivated friendships with "bela" elders and lent them money, especially near Christmas, then took repayment in land.

The preferred planting pattern among farmers who were in a position to expand their holdings was to combine cloves, which they saw as a source of income for the long term, with cacao that they brought into production as quickly as possible to take advantage of the high price. No one replanted the diseased cacao with new stock. As the cacao historian François Ruf has discovered through his comparative research, cacao farmers always find it more efficient to move off to pioneer new land, preferably in primary forest where rich soils and a disease-free environment produce high yields quickly without expensive chemical inputs.[40] The successful farmers at Sibogo and other middle hill neighborhoods I had tracked over the years left their old diseased trees behind. They also left their poor neighbors and kin behind, perched on their tiny barren plots. It was these left-behind people I encountered in 2009, nursing dying trees in the hope that they would yield a few last precious fruit, and stealing fruit from the trees of their prosperous neighbors who had moved away.

Land-short highlanders facing the end of cacao would have been ecstatic if a clever extension agent had offered them a very high value, very quick yielding crop that would enable them to make a living from their worked-out land, but no such miracle crop had presented itself. For people who were entirely landless, even new crops wouldn't help as they had no place to plant them. Perhaps they would act, covertly, to burn down some of the old diseased trees abandoned by their neighbors, creating a bit of space on which to plant some cassava. I really don't know what would happen if they tried to reclaim large fields, big enough for a crop of corn to feed a family. Would the owners reassert their rights as owners, which had become detached from the use they made of the land? Or would they give up their claims, and leave the land to people who could make some use of it, while they focused their attention on more lucrative prospects?

The conjuncture would shift after cacao, but it wouldn't revert to the one I had encountered in 1990 because it wasn't just cacao that had come and gone; it was entire sets of relations, meanings and practices. Conceivably, elements from the old repertoire that had receded in the cacao era could be recovered and dusted off: concepts like "we all borrow from each other," "it is all the land of the ancestors," and excluding people who want to work from accessing land isn't "the way we do things here." Highlanders might begin to assert collective claims to bounded territories that belong to particular, bounded groups, and become more effective in defending them, following the lead of Linajan who drew a line that "people from below" could not cross. They might invent rules to prevent land concentration, a move that would re-democratize land access but jangle awkwardly with their respect for a person's right to own the property created through his or her work. In short, the necessary elements for a new common property regime could be found from within highlanders' own, accumulated experiences, but assembling them would take a lot of work. Plus, the problem of how highlanders could secure a decent living from their rugged, drought prone terrain—the initial problem they had set out to solve in 1990—would still loom.

Conclusion

My exploration of politics in this chapter is necessarily open-ended, because my study covers only two decades, a mere snapshot in time, and it focuses on the generation that experienced land's end for the first time. In Sibogo and Sipil, land-short highlanders did not mobilize against landowners; they hoped to follow their example. In Pelalang where class relations weren't modified by kinship, the separation between haves and have-nots was stark, and it coincided with a divide between Muslims and Christians. It was softened, temporarily, by the ability of inner hill folk to withdraw deeper into the hills where they could still access some remaining do'at. Tensions can only increase as the inner hill land frontier closes down as well.

In the more democratic climate that began to emerge after 1998, highlanders did mobilize collectively to confront rapacious "crocodiles," corrupt officials who stole resources that were intended for their benefit, and they began in small ways to stake a claim to fair treatment as entitled citizens. Their demand was for access to the standard development package of roads, schools, and subsidized handouts. In this struggle, and in the increasingly acute crisis of social reproduction experienced by many highlanders, they had no allies. Government officials ignored them. There was no patron, political party, or transnational humanitarian agency ready to help them. Nor was their plight of much interest to Indonesian or transnational social movements promoting sustainable agriculture or indigenous rights, because its deviation from their standard script made it hard to recognize.

Development experts like the ones who write World Bank reports would readily recognize the process that divided highlanders into haves and have-nots—indeed they promote this process as necessary for increased productivity. They expect failed farmers to move along a transition path toward new work, somewhere else. But this expectation is challenged by the predicament of Lauje highlanders, and far too many others who find themselves at a dead end. Development planners have little to offer people who become landless in contexts where there aren't enough jobs that provide a living wage. Addressing the situation of highlanders who find themselves in this predicament—with no land, no work, no welfare, and no allies—is our shared political challenge.

Conclusion

This book has examined what happens when land is put to new ends and when farmers' access to land comes to an end as a result of enclosure. Lauje highlanders had an open land frontier until 1990 and could put themselves to work to produce food and build relations of care. Their labor and crops supplied coastal merchants with a source of profits, but they retained the capacity to withdraw from these relations, an autonomy coastal people read as a sign of backwardness. Highlanders were alert to the value of their work and guarded against its appropriation. When they began to enclose their land, they had no procedures to ensure its even distribution among neighbors and kin because the experience of land scarcity was new.

Highlanders did not anticipate the rapid emergence of inequality among them, as some farmers accumulated land while others lost their land through debt. Far from expanding their freedom and choice, as liberal theories propose, they were soon caught in capitalist relations governed by competition and profit. Land-short farmers could not afford to grow food. They had to plant their tiny plots with a high value crop and hope the revenue would be sufficient to buy food and inputs. Many succumbed to the "simple reproduction squeeze" and were left with only their labor to sell, *if* they could find a buyer. The process wasn't dramatic, and it can't be captured in a media sound bite or movement slogan. It emerged in a particular form in the conjuncture I have described, but it isn't unique to it. The "simple reproduction squeeze" among small-scale farmers has been widely reported, even though the elements contributing to it (e.g., climate, pests, prices) are diverse. The perilous condition of people who need to sell their labor but can't find a buyer for it is all too common. Land's end demands new knowledge, and a new politics.

The rapid emergence of capitalist relations among indigenous highlanders on a land frontier runs counter to the expectation of scholars and advocates who highlight the stability of common property arrangements and the staying power of "middle peasants." Advocates expect small-scale farmers, especially indigenous ones, to have strong institutions and habits of caution that enable them to engage with markets but protect themselves from the capitalist imperative of competition. To explain why capitalist relations emerged among these highlanders, I adopted an analytic of conjuncture that enabled me to explore how different elements had combined. I didn't seek a single cause, but a textured understanding capable of grasping how unruly pigs and wild prices, severe droughts and high hopes, could have formative effects. I focused on capitalist relations because they were so consequential: they didn't determine everything, but they set the conditions in which profound inequalities would emerge and become cumulative, leaving some people stranded.

Capitalist relations were not imposed upon rural people who were previously content in their subsistence ways. For centuries Lauje highlanders had lived in conditions of insecurity as their food production was vulnerable to catastrophic droughts and they struggled to earn enough cash to meet even the most basic needs—salt, kerosene, and clothing. In 1990 they lived in tiny, flimsy bamboo huts; they had little or no access to education; their diets were deficient, and one in three of the children born did not reach adulthood. Far from being romantic about life in the hills, highlanders considered themselves to be poor and they wanted to change their situation. They had good reason to switch to cacao and clove, productive crops, which they thought would offer them and their children a better life. Some of them achieved that goal, while for others the likelihood that they can follow suit is increasingly remote. Without access to land, they cannot put themselves to work, frontier style. Land's end is a devastating blow. Landless and land-short highlanders can no longer meet their own standards for what it means to be a whole person—someone who sustains a family, builds relations of care, and works hard to secure improvements in their material conditions.

Observing these processes, Amisa feared a future in which landless people would have to live suspended from a tree. Where I stressed capitalist relations, highlanders stressed land's end as the critical turning point that changed their world. I took highlanders' understandings seriously because they were formative elements in the conjuncture. No doubt they were positioned and partial, but they could not be dismissed as false. My struggle to make sense of the conjuncture was partial as well. Nevertheless, the productive disruptions of ethnographic engagement opened up a space in which I could produce new knowledge that was neither identical to theirs, nor was it limited by my initial categories and assumptions.

The stark and most intractable problem presented by my study concerns land's end as a dead end. Across Asia and much of Latin America and Africa as well, small-scale farmers who lose their existing land are increasingly locked out of the land frontier. Concerns about global warming and the search for sources of "renewable energy" are encouraging the allocation of massive areas of land to large-scale, mono-crop production of corn, sugar, and oil palm for use as biofuels. Climate concerns are also promoting renewed attention to forest conservation.[1] Neither of these land uses—large-scale farms and conservation—generate many jobs, yet they close the land frontier for smallholders who might otherwise use the land to generate jobs for themselves.

Agrarian transitions in which farmers displaced from the land become proletarians and rural economies become diverse sites of production and consumption fueled by remittances, pensions, and other state transfer schemes have occurred in some places. In Southeast Asia, Malaysia and Thailand are striking examples, and Vietnam seems to be heading in this direction.[2] But rural diversification fueled by remittances and state transfers wasn't happening in Central Sulawesi in 2009, or in many other parts of the world where rural areas have become slum lands, holding grounds for people whose sources of livelihood are radically insufficient, and insecure.[3] Their poverty isn't a residual problem to be solved by the march of progress, the extension of markets, or the promotion of economic growth. Too often, it is the *product* of the capitalist form taken by this "progress" that entrenches inequalities and fails to provide jobs. Poverty in these places isn't being reduced, as optimistic development narratives propose. It is expanding and intensifying, exacerbated by development policies that place their faith in markets to generate economic growth from which all are expected to benefit, as transition follows its "natural" course.

If transition isn't an inevitable unfolding, and if indeed it isn't happening or going to happen in the foreseeable future across large swathes of the globe, we need a different framework for understanding and responding to the predicament of hundreds of millions of people whose current and future livelihood needs are left out of account. In place of transition narratives that assume, too optimistically, that everyone will find a way forward, or a way out, we need to pay attention to the blocked paths and dead ends that go unnoticed in transition accounts and to the political challenges that emerge from such locations.

Too often, dead ends have been masked by expectations that deeply impoverished people will somehow sustain relations of care and be protected by their social institutions from the full blast of capitalist competition. The work of Karl Polanyi and related discussions of moral economy support this expectation. At some conjunctures, locally based protective regimes are indeed in place. Where they exist, they should be recognized and supported. But their existence, and their capacity, cannot be assumed.[4] In the Lauje highlands, existing institutions were not sufficient to prevent the emergence of inequalities because they were not designed for that purpose. Their situation was not unique. As I pointed out in the introduction, indigenous people living on land frontiers are especially unlikely to have protective institutions forbidding the enclosure of land because land is abundant. They tend to accept unequal reward as the natural result of unequal luck, effort, and skill. Hence Lauje highlanders did not mobilize collectively to protect themselves from the polarizing effects of capitalist competition. They let old practices erode and new ones emerge, spurred on by their search for a better life.

Rather than fault highlanders for what they did, and what they failed to do, my ethnographic approach enabled me to explore how they became subjects with particular hopes and plans. It also enabled me to explore how capitalist relations formed around competition could take hold in the highlands, as an unintended effect of mundane practices like planting cacao, borrowing a sack of rice, or seeking a loan in a moment of crisis. Once formed, these relations really were compulsory. They eroded choice. They couldn't be deselected, or wished away. Noncompetitive farmers lost their land and joined a class of non-owners. Even when they were kin, the interests of workers and landowners diverged because the practices they needed to engage in to sustain themselves were not the same. Put differently, followers of Polanyi who might have expected to find a locally generated countermovement that put social protection ahead of profit have to confront the processes identified by Marx.

For people who are left stranded by capitalist processes, protection is surely needed, but they can seldom generate it on their own. The highlanders in my study urgently need support through the distribution of land, access to jobs, or effective state-based transfer schemes. The obstacles concerning land and jobs are formidable. Much of the usable land in the province has already been allocated to other purposes. Even if some land was found, the record of state-sponsored resettlement schemes is not good: too often, elites find ways to grab land that is allocated in the name of the poor. Some Lauje highlanders had experience in such schemes, but they were outcompeted and eventually withdrew back to their highland homes. In relation to jobs, the province is currently heading in the wrong direction, notably through the promotion of oil palm. The justification for granting massive areas of land to oil palm plantations is that they generate jobs and economic growth. But as I noted, the actual jobs generated are few, and the opportunity cost of excluding smallholders is not taken into account. Growth can be helpful, but policies that promote growth need to anticipate the poverty that is generated—routinely and predictably—alongside growth. It is not enough to make economies grow and leave distribution to the market. Currently, direct cash transfers to the poor have the best prospect for helping impoverished highlanders. Indonesia's small, fragmented cash transfer scheme hasn't reached them. Crocodiles are still active, disrupting the flow of benefits to people who need them most. A monthly payment sufficient to provide nutritious food and to buy clothing and shoes for children so they could go to school without embarrassment would give them a better chance of surviving, and it would expand their possibilities for finding work.

There is no point in listing the good and helpful things that should be done, without a serious examination of the social forces that would be necessary to put such a distributive regime into place. Benign regimes of protection and distribution do not arise automatically, just because they are needed. Polanyi's discussion of countermovements does not provide much analysis of conjunctures at which such movements arise, nor of conjunctures at which they are crushingly absent. Global or national shame at a humanitarian disaster might be one prod to action, but humanitarian care, as I've noted, is usually triggered by a catastrophic event. The slow emergency of premature death in the Lauje highlands isn't on the humanitarian radar, although accurate reporting would help. Recall that government officials were embarrassed at the suggestion that highlanders had starved to death during the 1997 drought. Perhaps they could be embarrassed by statistics that show rates of mortality among highlanders that are far higher than the Indonesian average and recognize the consequences of their neglect. There are pockets of neglect in many parts of the archipelago, in cities as well as in rural areas that would benefit from this kind of critical attention. But we need to ask: why isn't this happening already? Why doesn't Indonesia have political parties, social movements, and journalists shaming the government by highlighting problems of impoverishment and neglect? Where are the social forces that could hold governments, corporations, and development planners to account for the fate of people neglected or impoverished by their plans? Why are thousands of Lauje highlanders still suffering in silence, with little sense of entitlement, and no way to claim the rights guaranteed to them as citizens of Indonesia? Why haven't more highlanders switched from desiring development to demanding it, like the road protesters in Sibogo? Why can't they find allies?

A comparison across conjunctures where distributive regimes have emerged indicates that shame plays a limited role. Distributive regimes emerge as the outcome of struggles in which social groups with different interests contend. These struggles hinge on the question of whose claims become recognized, amplified, and effective, and whose claims are ignored, misrecognized, or denied. During the Cold War rural people in many parts of the world were seen as potentially "dangerous classes" capable not just of launching protests, but of connecting up with allies and a global communist movement. Their struggles yielded different resolutions, as we can see from a brief comparison of Thailand and Indonesia. In Thailand, the Communist Party gradually lost its appeal as the ruling regime worked to spread prosperity in the Thai countryside. Rural people were able to leverage the regime's fear of "dangerous classes," backed by their own, impressive capacity for collective mobilization, to claim generous benefits and make demands for infrastructure and other forms of support that increased rural welfare and productivity. According to anthropologist Andrew Walker, poverty of the kind I have been describing no longer exists in Thailand.[5]

In Indonesia, in contrast, the military engineered the massacre of half a million alleged communists in 1965. Their tragic absence from the political scene continues to resonate in many forms, not least in the sad state of farmers' unions and the dearth of robust critical debate. Despite the opening of democratic space since 1998, no political parties have emerged to articulate the concerns of the rural poor or attach them to electoral politics. Rural social movements focused on land reform or indigenous rights play an important role in amplifying particular kinds of struggles, but rural peoples' rights continue to be trampled with impunity. Indonesia's Islamic movements and parties have not seriously addressed the problem of rising inequality. Nor have deeply impoverished Muslim masses been viewed as potential Islamic extremists who need to be reintegrated in the nation. Their suffering is not seen as dangerous. Maldistribution isn't prominent in public debate. How the conjuncture could be shifted to increase the capacity of impoverished Indonesians to claim a fair share of national wealth is the central political question.

In China, rural people have been mobilizing against land seizures and making demands for state welfare provision, although it is not clear that they have made themselves dangerous enough for more than token gestures.[6] In India, a "right to food" movement has drawn together an alliance between urban activists and the rural poor, supported by political parties seeking votes and officials with an eye on the Maoist insurgency, worried about rural unrest. The movement helped push for a rural income guarantee scheme that potentially offers some relief to landless workers whose incomes are seasonal and radically insecure.[7] But the income gap between India's rich and poor, already scandalous, doubled between 1990 and 2010, and four hundred million people still struggle to survive on less than $1.25 per day.[8] In Brazil, the Landless Peoples' Movement has mobilized to secure land and technical support for farmers, and the government has instituted a system of cash grants that take the edge off rural and urban poverty.[9] But since 2000, farms over one thousand hectares have absorbed an additional thirty million hectares of land, and rural workers continue to lose their jobs and migrate to the city in a pattern scholars in the region call "agriculture without farmers."[10] It is yet to be seen whether there will be sufficient jobs in other sectors of the economy to absorb them. In Bolivia and Ecuador, mobilizations have focused on the rights of indigenous highlanders who have entered electoral politics, but the problem of distribution still looms very large.[11] In parts of southern Africa, ex-farmers who were deliberately displaced from the land a century ago to take up proletarian roles in mines and white-owned farms are reclaiming land and also making demands for state support in the face of persistently high unemployment. Attempts to reserve distributive benefits to national citizens or favor clients of ruling regimes present massive challenges.[12]

These movements are significant, but there is no room for complacency, or for arguments that the way things are is as good as they can be.[13] Too often movements are derailed by restatements of the transition narrative that counts on growth to solve most of the problem and envisages distribution as a "safety net" reserved for residual cases. The hard realities of jobless growth, and the uneven distribution of the costs and rewards of growth, are left out of the account. As the Indian economist Prabhat Patnaik has argued, when growth is put first, the moment of distribution never comes, or not on a scale sufficient to compensate for the livelihoods lost and the damage done. Progressive settlements aren't tied to growth, but to a commitment to distribution fought for on political terrain.[14] This is what a *politics* of distribution entails. It cannot come soon enough for millions of people worldwide—young and old, rural and urban, north and south—who struggle to survive under conditions that are becoming more precarious.[15]

Appendix

Dramatis Personae

AMISA was an energetic woman who raised eleven children to adulthood, creating a large, cooperative sibling set that came to prominence in the middle hill neighborhood of Sibogo after she died in 1995. She hailed from a tobacco family on Sipil, and she moved with her family to Sibogo after they returned from Sigenti where they took refuge during the severe drought of 1983. Her older son ATAR married into a Sigenti family, enabling one of her sons HAMDAN to stay in Sigenti to go to school. When they returned to Sibogo around 1992 her sons prospered and Hamdan became a major landowner. NIJO became a carpenter and AMAL farmed. Their brother-in-law NATUN (whose wife had died), and another sister, ALIA, struggled to provision their families from one day to the next.

Amisa's brother NASIR on Sipil was a diligent farmer who felt pressured to give away food or sell it cheap to his food-short neighbors who mostly survived on wage work. Her uncle DEKON, who was in his seventies in 1992, struggled to support himself and his widowed daughter LEKA with her five children. DEKON and his son SAMPO sold much of their land to cover debts. Leka survived mainly on wage work, weeding farms in Sibogo until the work dried up.

MALIA also grew up planting tobacco on Sipil and was the oldest of a large sibling set, including a brother SIAM, who became a successful farmer on Sipil, and sisters with quite varied fates. She was married to TABANG, who stayed behind in the drought of 1983 and planted corn in the inner hills. Tabang's first crop helped to feed his own and Malia's parents and siblings when they came back from Sigenti, hungry and sick. Malia's mother, her sister **RAMLA**, and Tabang's mother and his brother **SAMIR** lived nearby. Tabang and Malia had nine children, of whom six survived to adulthood. In the shallot era of the 1980s, Malia was renowned for her hard work and skill. She could produce a ton of shallots in a single harvest, and had several women working for her to weed the gardens.

AMIN'S family were ex-tobacco farmers from Sipil who migrated out in the 1970s. In his twenties he worked in long-distance trade carrying shallots across the mountains to sell on the other coast. Despite his mobility he spoke no Indonesian. He was married to **RAMLA** (Malia's sister). In 1992 when I first met the couple they were just starting to establish themselves in Sibogo having fled Sigenti where two of their young children died within a week. Amin carried back loads of cassava and yam down to the market to sell each week, enough to buy minimal supplies of salt, sugar, and kerosene. He was often away hauling rattan. Amin was acutely conscious of the snubs of his better-off kin. By 2006 the couple had prospered and were among the richest people in Sibogo.

ALIP was a poor farmer, and his wife, another of Malia's sisters, struggled to feed her family. Some neighbors said he was lazy; others just said he was passive and physically weak. He was much affected by the death of one of his children and sat dazed in his house for a year, unable to farm. He came to prominence on Sibogo as a ritual specialist and healer. His economic situation improved when his teenage son gently took charge and moved the family to Sipil where they obtained land to work on a half-share basis.

IDIN's father grew tobacco in the Walu foothills but bought some land on the coast in the 1960s, so Idin had the chance to go to school. He prospered through shallot production. He moved into Sibogo after the drought of 1977 and began to buy up land. Neighbors often commented on the remarkable hard work and physical strength of Idin's wife **SINA**, equal to a man, pointing out that Idin never did any work. He farmed with capital, and the labor of others, including his daughter **NISA**.

ELOK was born around 1938. He moved into Sibogo before the drought of 1983 and survived by collecting rattan. Later as more people moved in, he made a name for bravery as he alone dared to cut down the last remaining pockets of primary forest, said to be inhabited by spirits. In the 1990s he was appointed chief of custom (*kepala adat*). He struggled economically, too old for hard work and reliant on the labor of his sons and neighbors. He was close to the inner hill folk and helped to mediate relations with them.

EMSALIN moved in to Sibogo at the same time as Elok and Idin. Like Idin, he was the son of tobacco farmers from Walu, but he spoke some Indonesian from his school days on the coast in the 1950s. He used to hike into the inner hills to buy garlic and acted as a broker helping highlanders sell their garlic on the coast. He worked to bring people together for collective projects such as holding rituals to keep dangerous spirits at bay. His oldest son **OSAN** married at sixteen, had many children, and was a notorious gambler, as was his wife (Malia's sister). Emsalin worried over the future of his children and grandchildren.

SAMINA was widowed young and raised eight children on Walu before moving into Sibogo with her second husband, who served as the Imam at the small neighborhood mosque built around 1987. She was known as a hardworking farmer, unlike her second husband who did not work at all. Commuting daily from the foothills of Walu to the coast, her children all went to school for a few years at least. The girls went out to work as maids for households in Palu and Gorontalo, an experience that gave them some fluency in Indonesian and city ways. **DAMA** married **HILO**, a successful farmer on Sipil; **SARA** married Hamdan.

AYUB on Walu was Samina's uncle. He became a major landowner, and his son became a teacher who aggressively expanded his landholdings. **RONI**, a coastal merchant, also had extensive landholdings on Walu and employed three landless couples as full-time workers. He traded in cacao and promoted use of agricultural chemicals to increase yields and manage pests and diseases. **RILENTI** was the main merchant for Sibogo. He grew up poor on Sipil and made his fortune while living in Sigenti where he built up trading capital based on the trust of his neighbors, who waited to receive payment until after he had sold their cacao.

KASAR on Walu, **ADAM** on Sibogo, and **TIMIT**, **FILIP**, and **NISRAN** on Sipil were among the younger generation of farmers who inherited little or no land. The first four struggled to feed their families from their wages while Nisran was able to save and invest.

LINAJAN and **TEMPO** were inner hill leaders or so-called bela who lived just above Sibogo and attempted to regulate access to forest land. Tempo was killed by his son-in-law **BANIO** and later was succeeded as leader by another son-in-law, **ANDI**. Linajan did not allow middle hill farmers access to forest land; Tempo allowed some access. **KATULU** in Pelalang mediated between the inner and middle hills and the coast, and brokered land to coastal people for cacao. **GILANAN** and his brother **PUNAT** were displaced from Pelalang when coastal people moved in. **MOPU** was a renowned leader in another part of the inner hills, at Gau'ma.

Notes

Introduction

1 One in three children born to highland women I interviewed did not survive into adulthood, a rate that was unchanged since colonial times. David Henley, *Fertility*, 261.
2 For critiques of teleological narratives and discussion of bypassed or "surplus" populations whose labor is not incorporated into capitalist circuits of production, see Henry Bernstein, "'Changing before Our Very Eyes'"; Jason Read, "Primitive Accumulation"; Gavin Smith, "Selective Hegemony"; Tania Murray Li, "To Make Live or Let Die?"
3 BPS, *Sulawesi Tengah Dalam Angka 2010*, 103.
4 Indonesia's cash transfer system is discussed in Juliette Koning and Frans Husken, eds., *Ropewalking*; Chris Manning and Sudarno Sumarto, eds., *Employment, Living Standards and Poverty*.
5 The role of nonfarm incomes in supporting "farmers" is discussed in D. Bryceson, C. Kay, and J. Mooij, eds., *Disappearing Peasantries?*; Benjamin White, Paul Alexander, and Peter Boomgaard, eds., *In the Shadow of Agriculture*; Jonathan Rigg, "Land, Farming, Livelihoods, and Poverty"; Henry Bernstein, *Class Dynamics*, 104–8.
6 John Markoff, "Skilled Work."
7 On jobless growth in Indonesia, see Gustav F. Papenek, "Indonesia's Hidden Problem." See also World Bank, *Indonesia Jobs Report*. On jobless growth in India, see C. P. Chandrasekhar, "India." On South Africa, see "Jobless Growth." For a global perspective, see ILO, *Global Employment Trends 2013*.
8 Graeme Hugo, "Indonesia's Labor." See also World Bank, *Indonesia Jobs Report*.
9 Karl Marx, *Capital Volume 1*, 667–85. See also Jim Glassman, "Primitive Accumulation"; David Harvey, *The New Imperialism*; Derek Hall, "Rethinking Primitive Accumulation"; Derek Hall, Philip Hirsch, and Tania Murray Li, *Powers of Exclusion*.
10 Terence J. Byres, "Neo-Classical Neo-Populism."

11 In *Social Facts*, Sally Falk Moore used a similar, revisiting approach. See also Jonathan Rigg and Peter Vandergeest, eds., *Revisiting Rural Places*. In "Problems in the Empirical Analysis of Agrarian Differentiation," Benjamin White stresses the need to track processes and mechanisms of change, not just outcomes.

12 See Raymond Williams, *Marxism and Literature*, 115–35, on selections from tradition. His use of the term selection emphasizes emergence rather than conscious choice. See also David Scott, *Conscripts of Modernity*, 115–19, and Moore, *Social Facts*, 318.

13 See discussions of politics and the work of the intellectual in Antonio Gramsci, *Selections from the Prison Notebooks*, 326–43. See also Gavin Smith, "Hegemony"; Kate Crehan, *Gramsci, Culture and Anthropology*; Williams, *Marxism and Literature*, 128–34.

14 Transition debates among Marxist scholars are reviewed in A. Haroon Akram-Lodhi and Cristobal Kay, "Surveying the Agarian Question" (Parts 1 and 2). On peasant-based mobilizations see Eric Wolf, *Peasant Wars*; Bernstein, *Class Dynamics*; James Scott, *The Moral Economy*.

15 Bernstein, *Class Dynamics*, 22–23.

16 Robert Brenner, "Agrarian Class Structure"; Ellen Meiksins Wood, *The Origin of Capitalism*.

17 The staying power of landholding middle peasants or "smallholders" is highlighted by Robert McC. Netting, *Smallholders, Householders*; Jan Douwe van der Ploeg, "The Peasantries of the Twenty-First Century."

18 William Roseberry, *Anthropologies and Histories*, 197–232.

19 Social reproduction is never fully commoditized, as it is underpinned by the unpaid work of women and inter-household transfers, and often by state transfers as well. See Olivia Harris and Kate Young, "Engendered Structures"; Gavin Smith, *Livelihood and Resistance*; Susana Narotzky and Gavin Smith, *Immediate Struggles*; Harriet Friedmann, "Household Production"; Gavin Smith, "Reflections."

20 Marx, *Capital Volume 1*, 689.

21 In "Approaching Moral Economy," 78, Andrew Sayer argues that all economies are "moral," that is, "influenced and structured by moral dispositions and norms" that are variously "compromised, overridden or reinforced by economic pressures."

22 World Bank, *Agriculture for Development*; World Bank, "Land Policies"; Carlos Oya, "The World Development Report 2008"; Ravi Kanbur, "Economic Policy, Distribution and Poverty."

23 Karl Polanyi, *The Great Transformation*.

24 James Scott, *The Art of Not Being Governed*.

25 David Henley, *Jealousy and Justice*.

26 Anna Lowenhaupt Tsing, *In the Realm of the Diamond Queen*, 29–31; Jane Atkinson, *The Art and Politics of Wana Shamanship*, 267–68.

27 Scott's discussion of swidden as a form of "escape agriculture" in *The Art of Not Being Governed*, 187–207, underestimates the problem of pests and the time it takes to cut, dry, and burn a field before it can be planted. Henley, *Fertility*, explores linked cycles of violence, flight, disease, and famine.

28 On frontier imaginaries in Southeast Asia, see Michael Eilenberg, *At the Edges of States*; Anna Lowenhaupt Tsing, *Friction*; Tania Murray Li, "Marginality, Power and Production"; Andrew Turton, ed., *Civility and Savagery*; Thomas Sikor et al., eds., *Upland Transformations in Vietnam*.

29 James C. Scott, *Seeing Like a State*; Benedict Anderson, *Imagined Communities*; Danilo Geiger, "Turner in the Tropics."

30 On frontier imaginaries in Amazonia, see Hugh Raffles, *In Amazonia*; William H. Fisher, "Native Amazonians." Bayo Holsey, *Routes of Remembrance*, examines discourses of the cosmopolitan coast versus "savage bush" in Ghana.

31 Desires for modernity are discussed in Robert Hefner, *The Political Economy of Mountain Java*; R. A. Cramb, *Land and Longhouse*; Andrew Walker, "'Now the Companies Have Come.'"

32 Richard Drayton, *Nature's Government*; Nicholas Blomley, "Law, Property, and the Geography of Violence."

33 See Klaus Deninger et al., *Rising Global Interest*.

34 Geiger, "Turner in the Tropics"; Rodolphe De Koninck, "On the Geopolitics of Land Colonization"; Hall, Hirsch, and Li, *Powers of Exclusion*; Derek Hall, "Land Grabs."

35 Tsing, *Friction*, 31, notes that indigenous people seldom have a word equivalent to "frontier" in their languages. Lauje highlanders' concept of a frontier was the primary forest into which they could expand indefinitely.

36 BPS, *Sulawesi Tengah Dalam Angka 1993*, 284; BPS, *Sulawesi Tengah Dalam Angka 2010*, 272.

37 John Villiers, "The Cash-Crop Economy."

38 On colonial concerns, see Robert Elson, *The End of the Peasantry*; Henley, *Fertility*, 357. On extractive booms, see Christine Padoch and Nancy Lee Peluso, "Borneo People"; Michael Dove, *The Banana Tree*.

39 See Tania Murray Li, "Indigeneity, Capitalism."

40 Clifford Geertz, *Agricultural Involution*. See also Elson, *The End of the Peasantry*; Netting, *Smallholders, Householders*, 230. As Netting also points out (298), abundant land with poor transportation gives farmers no incentive to produce more than they can consume.

41 Rodolphe De Koninck and Jean-François Rousseau, *Gambling with the Land*.

42 Joel Kahn, "Culturalizing the Indonesian Uplands"; Hall, Hirsch, and Li, *Powers of Exclusion*.

43 The concept of conjuncture I adopt differs fundamentally from Marshall Sahlins's concept of the "structure of a conjuncture" by which he means that historical events are always absorbed back into structure, which for Sahlins is a synonym for enduring cultural essence. See Marshall Sahlins, *Culture in Practice*, 293–304, and the lucid discussion of Sahlins's attempt to defend a concept of cultures as closed systems in Victor Li, "Marshall Sahlins and the Apotheosis of Culture."

44 Timothy Mitchell, *Rule of Experts*, explores the hybrid relations too often homogenized into the "development of capitalism" as a singular thing. Bruno Latour, *We Have Never Been Modern*, emphasizes the formative effects of things—soil, trees,

pests, climate, slope—on social relations. These authors describe sets of elements as assemblages, but I reserve the term "assemblage" for ensembles pulled together for a human purpose. See Tania Murray Li, "Practices of Assemblage." The concept of conjuncture does not entail agency of this kind.

45 See Don Kalb and Herman Tak, *Critical Junctions*. In "At Home," 665, Stuart Hall and Les Black discuss situated perspectives on conjunctural shifts. See also Donna Haraway, "Situated Knowledges."

46 Donald L. Donham, "History at One Point in Time." Donald L. Donham, *History, Power, Ideology*, 132–42, reviews epochal and historical analysis in the work of Marx, Raymond Williams, and E. P. Thompson. See also Roseberry, *Anthropologies and Histories*, 197–232.

47 See Karl Marx, *Economic and Philosophical Manuscripts of 1844*. Marx's approach treats abstract concepts (capital, labor) as placeholders that enable the analyst to advance toward an understanding of capital and labor in their concrete, historical forms. His approach is different from treating capital or labor as ideal types, of which particular expressions are variants. For discussions of Marx's method, see Stuart Hall, "Marx's Notes on Method"; Bernstein, *Class Dynamics*, 10; Gillian Hart, "Geography and Development," 97; Vinay Gidwani, *Capital, Interrupted*.

48 See, among others, David Nugent, ed., *Locating Capitalism*; Roseberry, *Anthropologies and Histories*; Smith, *Livelihood and Resistance*; Don Kalb, *Expanding Class*; Gerald Sider, *Culture and Class*.

49 See, among others, Ann Whitehead, "'I'm Hungry, Mum'"; Stuart Hall, "New Ethnicities"; Donald Moore, *Suffering for Territory*; Sylvia Junko Yanagisako, *Producing Culture and Capital*.

50 See Donald S. Moore, "Subaltern Struggles"; Gavin Smith, *Confronting the Present*; Narotzky and Smith, *Immediate Struggles*; William Roseberry, "Hegemony, Power"; Gerald Sider, "When Parrots Learn to Talk." In "At Home," 664–65, Hall and Black distinguish between understandings of conjuncture drawn from Marx and Gramsci.

51 Henri Lefebvre, *The Production of Space*.

52 Doreen Massey, "Power Geometry."

53 Allan Pred and Michael John Watts, *Reworking Modernity*, 11.

54 Hart, "Geography and Development," 98, 97. See also Gillian Hart, *Disabling Globalization*.

55 Max Gluckman, *Analysis of a Social Situation*. In "The Extended Case Method," Michael Burowoy reviews the Manchester School's attention to "cases" and events.

56 See, among others, Eric Wolf, *Europe*; Sidney Mintz, *Sweetness and Power*.

57 Wolf, *Europe*, 6.

58 Akhil Gupta and James Ferguson, "Beyond 'Culture'"; see also Gillian Hart's critique of impact models in *Disabling Globalization*, 13.

59 Hall, "Marx's Notes on Method," 115–17.

60 Pierre Bourdieu, *Outline of a Theory of Practice*.

61 Williams, *Marxism and Literature*, 129–30.

62 Michel Foucault, "Afterword." For a critique of spatialized binaries, see Moore, "Subaltern Struggles."

63 John Allen, *Lost Geographies*, 196. See also David Scott, *Conscripts of Modernity*, 115–19.
64 In "Flattening Ontologies," Sallie A. Marston, Keith Woodward, and John Paul Jones examine the hierarchy of scalar optics with their "small-large imaginaries." See also Allen, *Lost Geographies*; James Ferguson and Akhil Gupta, "Spatializing States."
65 See Akhil Gupta and James Ferguson, "Discipline and Practice."
66 Moore, *Suffering for Territory*, 24, discusses the "*consequential materiality* of milieu" (emphasis in original).
67 François Ruf, Pierre Ehret, and Yoddang, "Smallholder Cocoa"; François Ruf and Yoddang, "The Cocoa Marketing Sector"; Jeff Neilson, "Global Markets."
68 The difference between treating conjunctures as "case studies" that illustrate general processes, and comparing across conjunctures to identify the relations that form them is discussed in Hart, *Disabling Globalization*; Gillian Hart, "Denaturalizing Dispossession," 996.
69 B. Schrieke, *Indonesian Sociological Studies*, 95–130; Akira Oki, "The Dynamics of Subsistence Economy"; Geertz, *Agricultural Involution*.
70 Joel Kahn, "Peasant Political Consciousness."
71 Neighborhood names and all personal names are pseudonyms. For ease of recall I've given women names that end with "a" and prepared a list of dramatis personae (appendix 1). Desa names are real, and neighborhoods are accurately situated on the Lauje area map.
72 Lila Abu-Lughod, "Writing against Culture," 154.

Chapter 1: Positions

1 Scott, *The Art of Not Being Governed*.
2 Peter Bellwood, *Prehistory*.
3 Anthony Reid, "Inside Out." In *Fertility*, Henley examines the historical demography of central and northern Sulawesi from 1600 to 1930. Contrast highlanders in the Southeast Asian mainland who believe their ancestors were lowland people who fled to the highlands to escape coercive rule. See Scott, *The Art of Not Being Governed*.
4 See Michael Dove, "The Agroecological Mythology"; Jefferson Fox et al., "Policies"; Ole Mertz et al., "Swidden Change"; Henley, *Fertility*; and David Henley, "Swidden Farming."
5 Henley, *Fertility*, 63–65. The new world crops were introduced by Spaniards who brought them from Mexico to the Philippines, from where they spread across the Indonesian archipelago from east to west. See Peter Boomgaard, "Maize and Tobacco."
6 A Netherlands East Indies Company archive mentions a kingdom in the Lauje area around 1591 that had disappeared by 1672. It also mentions Lauje slaves in Gorontalo around 1678. Henley, *Fertility*, 197, 218.
7 This raiding/trading system is described in Esther J. Velthoen, "'Wanderers.'" See also James Frances Warren, "Trade, Slave Raiding"; Henley, *Fertility*, 66, 71, 77–78; Albert Schrauwers, "Houses, Hierarchy." In the Lauje area imported prestige

goods commonly used in marriage payments and fines were brass trays and porcelain plates.

8 Han Knapen, "Epidemics," argues that hinterland Dayak in Kalimantan continually assessed the benefits of trade against the risks of disease, violence, or entrapment.

9 Velthoen, "'Wanderers,'" stresses the coerced dimension of this trade. See also Peter Boomgaard, "Introducing Environmental Histories," 14; Henley, *Fertility*, 34–5, 76.

10 Henley, *Fertility*, 82–85, 92.

11 Velthoen, "'Wanderers,'" 372; Henley, *Fertility*, 76–78.

12 Velthoen, "'Wanderers,'" 370, notes that highlanders "could abandon their homes and disappear into the jungle."

13 G. W. W. C. Baron van Hoëvell, "Korte Beschrijving," 354. See also Henley, *Fertility*, 218–21. Thanks to Albert Schrauwers for tracking and translating this source. Tinombo tobacco was noted in colonial records from the 1820s and 1870s. Nourse, *Conceiving Spirits*, 95; Henley, *Fertility*, 82.

14 Nourse, *Conceiving Spirits*, 66.

15 Thanks to Gerry van Klinken for checking Dutch sources. The colonial government kept administrative records on site for fifty years before transferring them to an archive, so the records from 1892 to 1942 were lost when the Japanese invaded. See Henley, *Fertility*, 44. There is no missionary archive because missionaries only arrived in the Lauje area in 1975.

16 Nourse, *Conceiving Spirits*.

17 Nourse, *Conceiving Spirits*.

18 Nourse, *Conceiving Spirits*, 257n24, notes that "most" highlanders did not recognize the aristocrats' leadership.

19 Nourse, *Conceiving Spirits*, 230fn7.

20 Buffalo- and cattle-focused systems in the region are described in Henley, *Fertility, Food and Fever*, 536–46.

21 Tania Murray Li, ed., *Transforming the Indonesian Uplands*; Tsing, *In the Realm of the Diamond Queen*.

22 See also Nourse, *Conceiving Spirits*, 33, 40; Tania Murray Li, "Relational Histories."

23 In 2009 the Department of Social Affairs, which is responsible for resettling people labeled isolated, estranged, or "traditional," reported that seventeen thousand Lauje qualified for this designation, making them the largest group in the province (30 percent of the total). See BPS, *Sulawesi Tengah Dalam Angka 2010*, 205.

24 In the 1990s I hesitated to show pictures of the steep highland terrain to officials in Palu, for fear they would undertake coercive resettlement. I later realized that officials had no capacity to resettle twenty thousand people, so no harm would come, and possibly some benefit if officials started to think creatively about how they could deliver services to the highlanders in situ.

25 Gillian Hart, "Agrarian Change"; Tania Murray Li, *The Will to Improve*.

26 Nourse, *Conceiving Spirits*, 41, describes Muslim highlanders' fear of the "bela" and their claim that "bela" were lazy, dirty, and violent.

27 Lauje highlanders had stories about naked people (*dampelau* L) who were reputedly so remote they had no clothes, yet only a few hunters claimed to have actually seen them. It seems a visiting Dutch official was told a similar dampelau story a century ago. See Van Hoëvell, "Korte Beschrijving," 354.

28 See discussions in Glassman, "Primitive Accumulation"; Hall, "Rethinking Primitive Accumulation."

29 Nourse, *Conceiving Spirits*, 31, 64, reports that the Dutch-appointed raja in Tinombo town played a similar role in the 1920s, enticing highlanders to bring down trade goods. He also invited them to study the Koran on his veranda.

30 Henley, *Fertility*, 551.

31 Gambling has long been used as a labor-enticing strategy in the Southeast Asian region. It was a tool for enslavement in nineteenth-century Toraja where "Bugis moneylenders called in their loans without permitting Torajans to redeem their debts with forest products." See T. Bigalke, "Dynamics," 350. See also Filomeno V. Aguilar Jr., *Clash of Spirits*; Ann Laura Stoler, *Capitalism and Confrontation*; and Jan Breman, *Labour Migration*.

32 Similarly, Sider, *Culture and Class*, describes merchants in Newfoundland who abandoned fishing families to starve in the winter if their production wasn't profitable enough to merit ongoing support. Boomgaard, "Maize and Tobacco," notes tobacco farmers' heavy reliance on credit.

33 Henley, *Fertility*, 317–28, examines linked episodes of famine, disease, and violence in the Gulf of Tomini triggered by El Niño events. El Niño events in recent years were 1972–73,* 1976–78,* 1982–83,* 1986–88,* 1991–92, 1994–5, 1997–98,* 2002–3, 2004–5, 2006–7, 2009–10. The events marked with an asterisk figured prominently in highlanders' memories due to their severe heat or duration.

34 See Henley, *Fertility*, 348–52. In *The Moral Economy*, 3–10, Scott builds on Wolf's discussion in *Peasant Wars*, 279, to highlight peasant vulnerability to climatic and other disasters. He sees vulnerabilty as the motor of a "moral economy" in which patrons, landlords, and rulers were obliged to provide a subsistence guarantee in return for the profits they extracted.

35 In *The Banana Tree*, 87, Dove describes frequent swidden failure among Dayaks in Kalimantan. See also Michael Dove, "The Chayanov Slope."

36 Mike Davis, *Late Victorian Holocausts*; Henley, *Fertility*; Michael Watts, *Silent Violence*. In *Poverty and Famines*, Amartya Sen links famines to changing relations between social groups, each with distinct entitlements.

Chapter 2: Work and Care

1 For example, Buid couples in the Philippines highlands in the 1970s had separate farms and made no claims on the labor of their children. They diffused the work of raising children among many adults to avoid burdening their children with a debt they could not repay. See Thomas Gibson, "The Sharing of Substance," 393. See also works cited in Tania Murray Li, "Working Separately."

2 C. B. MacPherson, *The Political Theory of Possessive Individualism*, 200. Marx criticized the bourgeois concept of the individual that mistook its historically pro-

duced form for an ahistorical essence. See the summary in Hall, "Marx's Notes on Method," 115–17. In *Sovereign Individuals*, Nicholas Abercrombie, Stephen Hill, and Bryan S. Turner explore the emergence of discourses of the self-sovereign, possessing individual in Britain during the seventeenth century.

3 For critiques of evolutionary narratives see Adam Kuper, *The Invention of Primitive Society*; Nicholas Thomas, *Entangled Objects*; Roseberry, *Anthropologies and Histories*. For studies of the role of gifts in establishing social relations see Bourdieu, *Outline of a Theory of Practice*; Marcel Mauss, *The Gift*; James Carrier, *Gifts and Commodities*; Maurice Bloch and Jonathan Parry, "Introduction."

4 Whitehead, "'I'm Hungry, Mum.'"

5 Henley, *Fertility*, 349, found a reference to rice that was individually owned and stored in separate containers in Minahasa in 1858.

6 In "Recasting Sex, Gender and Power," Shelly Errington distinguishes between regions of the Indonesian archipelago with loosely structured, often bilateral kinship systems like the Lauje one and regions with patrilineal clans, rigid rules for marriage and inheritance, and ranked hierarchies including nobles and slaves.

7 A sibling set is referred to as *vuntu puse* L, "of one navel." Highlanders emphasized birth order, and expected older siblings to nurture younger ones, who should show respect in return. See Nourse, *Conceiving Spirits*, 62, and the extended discussion of siblingship in Roxana Waterson, *Paths and Rivers*.

8 In *Conceiving Spirits*, 64, Nourse notes that some highlanders stopped selling food for cash because of a smallpox epidemic in the 1950s which they attributed to the displeasure of the spirits. The problem wasn't caused by their own food selling but by a Lauje aristocrat on the coast who failed to use their food tribute to perform health-giving rituals and sold it instead.

9 Michael Perelman, *The Invention of Capitalism*, 16; Nicholas Abercrombie and Bryan S. Turner, "The Dominant Ideology Thesis."

10 Dove, "The Chayanov Slope," reports a daily wage rate of 3.7 kilograms of rice per day among Dayak in Kalimantan in the 1970s. This wage compared favorably to the 7 kilograms per day they could make from rice farming, given that the wage was immediate and risk-free.

11 See David Henley, "Credit and Debt"; Anthony Reid, ed., *Slavery*.

12 According to Gibson, "The Sharing of Substance," 397–98, Buid highlanders avoided dyadic ties between specific individuals which they feared would undermine each person's autonomy, preferring the diffused solidarity of "the community" as a whole, institutionalized through rituals, feasting, and the obligation to share meat.

13 According to Nourse, *Conceiving Spirits*, 51, 196, 200, Lauje often questioned a medium's claim to secret knowledge, making the reputation of people who tranced (*to mensio* L) or became healers a matter of persuasion and trust. She examines Lauje spirit beliefs concerning birth, illness, and curing, which carry traces of Sufi thought.

14 Anna Lowenhaupt Tsing, "Politics and Culture," 491. Tsing notes that Dayak rajaki resembles the Islamic notion of *rezeki*, a sign that Islam, present in coastal areas since the thirteenth century left traces in the "non-Muslim" hinterlands as well.

15 Although there were rumors, I didn't hear of any highlanders being openly accused. Colonial officials and missionaries working in other parts of Sulawesi noted the killing of witches and "werewolves" (humans who could take on animal form) who were believed to have harmed their neighbors. See Henley, *Fertility*, 256.

Chapter 3: Enclosure

1 Togu means owner and is applied to mundane objects like houses, axes, clothing, bundles of corn, and so forth. Someone who wants to borrow something must ask the owner's permission; so too with spirit owners of water and earth.
2 In some contexts individual ownership is recognized but sale is forbidden or restricted. See Netting, *Smallholders, Householders*; Thomas Sikor, "Conflicting Concepts"; Eric Wolf, "Types of Latin American Peasantry"; Franz von Benda-Beckmann and Keebet von Benda-Beckmann, "Myths and Stereotypes."
3 Property is usually defined as a social, legitimate, and enforceable "bundle of rights." See MacPherson, *The Political Theory of Possessive Individualism*; Ribot and Peluso, "A Theory of Access"; Thomas Sikor and Christian Lund, "Access and Property."
4 Hall, Hirsch, and Li, *Powers of Exclusion*.
5 Colonial and contemporary approaches to customary law are discussed in Franz von Benda-Beckmann, "Symbiosis"; Martin Chanock, *Law, Custom*; Jamie S. Davidson and David Henley, eds., *The Revival of Tradition*; Christian Lund, *Local Politics*.
6 Arun Agrawal, "Common Property Institutions," summarizes common property theory and the misnamed "tragedy of the commons."
7 For overviews of Indonesia's contested land regime, see Nancy Lee Peluso, "Whose Woods Are These?"; Anna Tsing, "Land as Law"; Carol Warren, "Mapping Common Futures"; Daniel Fitzpatrick, "Land, Custom and the State."
8 Scott, *Seeing Like a State*.
9 In "The Peripatetic Peasant," Paul H. Kratoska explains why land pioneers often prefer to realize the cash value of the work of land clearing rather than grow food or cash crops under uncertain conditions.
10 Compare the Iban of Sarawak whose group boundaries are defined by residence in a longhouse, an enduring structure with a fixed territory. See Cramb, *Land and Longhouse*. Minangkabau people in Sumatra also have a more tightly defined property regime. See Benda-Beckmann and Benda-Beckmann, "Myths and Stereotypes."
11 See Henley, *Fertility*, 499–508, 516–21; Henley, "Swidden Farming."
12 Compare Nancy Lee Peluso, "Fruit Trees"; Tsing, *Friction*; Amity A. Doolittle, *Property and Politics*.
13 Some highlanders in Central Sulawesi sharply distinguish the "founding" family from latecomers or borrowers. See Lorraine Aragon, *Fields of the Lord*. See also F. K. L Chit Hlaing Lehman, "The Relevance of the Founders' Cult."
14 The link between planting trees and enclosing land is widely reported. See Moore, *Social Facts*; Dianne Rocheleau and Laurie Ross, "Trees as Tools"; Richard Schroeder, "Community, Forestry and Conditionality"; Keijiro Otsuka and Agnes R. Quisumbing, "Land Rights."

15 Nicholas Blomley, "Making Private Property." See also Blomley, "Law, Property."
16 In *Social Facts*, 318, Moore observes that changes in land tenure on Kilimanjaro introduced by planting coffee were fundamental, yet they were scarcely acknowledged within the conventionally stated rules of allocation; they were "simply incorporated" into practice.
17 On the role of purchase in securing land rights, see Otsuka and Quisumbing, "Land Rights."
18 I discuss these gendered dynamics in Li, "Working Separately." For a comparable discussion in an African context that also involves cacao, see Sara Berry, *No Condition*.
19 Lorraine Aragon, "Communal Violence"; Li, *The Will to Improve*; HRW, "Breakdown."
20 The project seedlings were supposed to be of higher quality, but a decade later highlanders in Sibogo noticed no difference in their productivity or vulnerability to disease.
21 Nicholas Blomley points out that the role of inscription in enclosure is not to make a set of previously concrete relations abstract, but rather to change the form of inscription and its insertion into networks. The wielding of an axe in the do'at effectively inscribed property among highlanders, but its meaning didn't travel well. The meaning of maps and lists of names traveled further; formal land titles would travel further still. See Blomley, "Law, Property"; Mitchell, *Rule of Experts*.
22 The double edge of Locke's labor theory of property as source of rights and denial of rights is discussed in Wendy Wolford, "Land Reform"; Drayton, *Nature's Government*.
23 E. P. Thompson, *The Making*, 239–42. See also Blomley, "Making Private Property."

Chapter 4: Capitalist Relations

1 Henry Bernstein, "Concepts," 11.
2 Bernstein, *Class Dynamics*, calls this process the commoditization of subsistence. Noncommoditized relations that help sustain middle peasants in Latin American contexts are examined in Wolf, "Types of Latin American Peasantry"; Smith, *Livelihood and Resistance*; Roseberry, *Anthropologies and Histories*.
3 On erosion, see David Scott, *Conscripts of Modernity*, 115–119, which draws on the work of Talal Asad.
4 The Canadian project envisaged a mixed agroforestry system that integrated tree crops with food crops and other annuals. It did not anticipate that farmers with limited land would be compelled to maximize their earnings in order to buy food. Expert-designed agroforestry systems have suffered the same fate in other locations. See Patrice Levang, "From Rags to Riches."
5 The price of cacao in 2006 was Rp 8,000–9,000 per kilogram, roughly stable since 1999, but the price of rice had risen to Rp 5,000 per kilogram. The daily wage in 2006 was Rp 10,000. This was enough to meet the rice requirement of a family

of six (.3 kilograms per person per day), but left nothing over for other expenses (buying fish, paying school fees).

6 Andrew Turton, "Local Powers," notes the emergence of separate social circles as inequalities among villagers deepen.

7 Vladamir Ilich Lenin, *The Development of Capitalism*. These elements are reviewed in Akram-Lodhi and Kay, "Surveying the Agarian Question (Part 1)."

8 The crucial role played by off-farm earnings in farm investment is discussed in White, Alexander, and Boomgaard, eds., *In the Shadow of Agriculture*; Rigg, "Land, Farming"; Bernstein, *Class Dynamics*, 106–7.

9 Alternate forms of marriage—bride price assembled by a group of kin, bride service, and elopement or "kidnap marriage"—were reported in Minahasa in colonial times. See Henley, *Fertility*, 380. See also Schrauwers, "Houses"; Nourse, *Conceiving Spirits*, 46, 66–67. In 2006 highlanders who hosted wedding celebrations paid an average bride price of around Rp 3.5 million, the equivalent of 350 days of work hauling timber.

10 Cacao prices fell in 1999, but were still double the 1997 value. The price of rice doubled between 1997 and 1999, so by 1999 farmers were back to a ratio of one kilogram of cacao for two kilograms of rice. See François Ruf and Yoddang, "The Sulawesi Cocoa Boom," 248–50.

11 Agus Saifullah, "Indonesia's Rice Policy," 111.

12 Ruf, Ehret, and Yoddang, "Smallholder Cocoa."

13 Neilson, "Global Markets."

14 See Dove, *The Banana Tree*; Cramb, *Land and Longhouse*. On the impact of tree crops in diverse Indonesian locales, see Levang, "From Rags to Riches"; John McCarthy, *The Fourth Circle*; Krisnawati Suryanata, "From Home Gardens"; Genevieve Michon et al., "The Damar Agroforests." For a classic study of cacao farming on a migrant frontier in Ghana in the 1950s, see Polly Hill, *The Migrant Cocoa-Farmers*.

15 In the rural Philippines, gamblers attempt to intervene with the spirits to manipulate their quotient of luck. See Aguilar, *Clash of Spirits*.

16 Debt as a mechanism of land loss has a long history in Southeast Asia. See Elson, *The End of the Peasantry*, 131–34.

17 This form of extraction is sometimes labeled "rent capitalism," where rent is defined broadly to include "actual rent, taxes, interest on loans, forced presale of produce at less than market price, etc, i.e. *any extraction of surplus value not based on the sale of labor power*," William Roseberry, "Rent," 51 (emphasis in original). Rent capitalism is widespread in the rice-producing lowlands of Southeast Asia. See Brian Fegan, "The Philippines"; Frans Husken, "Cycles of Commercialization"; Breman, *Labour Migration*.

18 The significance of leaving a surplus in some farmers' hands is discussed in Roseberry, "Rent," 53–54.

19 Polanyi, *The Great Transformation*; Marx, *Economic and Philosophical Manuscripts of 1844*.

20 The introduction of combine harvesters enabled a similar bypass in the Malaysian village studied by James C. Scott, *Weapons of the Weak*.

Chapter 5: Politics, Revisited

1 Albert O. Hirschman, *Exit, Voice, and Loyalty*, and others have used this triad to explain individual responses to dissatisfaction in marriage, in employment, and as consumers.

2 Scott, *The Moral Economy*.

3 Netting, *Smallholders, Householders*; Scott, *The Moral Economy*; Geertz, *Agricultural Involution*; Dove, *The Banana Tree*; Cramb, *Land and Longhouse*.

4 Change not as rejection but as fading and loss of relevance is discussed in David Scott, *Conscripts of Modernity*, 115–19, drawing on the work of Talal Asad.

5 See Gidwani, *Capital, Interrupted*; Smith, *Livelihood and Resistance*; Terence Byres, *Capitalism from Above*; Lenin, *The Development of Capitalism*; Tom Brass, "The Journal of Peasant Studies"; Watts, *Silent Violence*; Michael Watts, "The Southern Question"; A. Haroon Akram-Lodhi and Cristobal Kay, "The Agrarian Question"; Bernstein, *Class Dynamics*.

6 See Elizabeth Povinelli, *Economies of Abandonment*.

7 Scott, *Weapons of the Weak*.

8 Class relations among kin are discussed in Mintz, "The Rural Proletariat," 305–6.

9 Hart, "Agrarian Change." In *Class Power*, 149–52, Jonathan Pincus notes that poor villagers in Java paid monthly interest rates 40–150 percent higher than large landowners who could access formal credit and government subsidy schemes.

10 Parimo's rugged topography meant that much of its land could not be cultivated, yet it had a population density of sixty-one per two kilometers in 2009, the highest of the province's rural regencies: BPS, *Sulawesi Tengah Dalam Angka 2010*, 96.

11 See Peter Vandergeest, "Gifts and Rights"; Andrew Walker, *Thailand's Political Peasants*. Development as a right has been less prominent in Indonesia where paternalism predominates. See Li, *The Will to Improve*.

12 World Bank, "Kecamatan Development," 54. See also Scott Guggenheim, "Crises and Contradictions," and the discussion of KDP in Li, *The Will to Improve*.

13 Edward Aspinall, "A Nation in Fragments."

14 Thompson, *The Making*, 87. Emphasis in original.

15 Thompson, *The Making*, 68, 67–73.

16 Povinelli, *Economies of Abandonment*, discusses suffering in the absence of an event.

17 This double meaning of articulation as making explicit and forming connections is explored by Hall, "On Postmodernism." See also Tania Murray Li, "Articulating Indigenous Identity."

18 Johannes Fabian, "Remembering the Other." See also Tania Murray Li, "Masyarakat Adat"; Li, "Articulating Indigenous Identity." Tsing, *Friction*, argues that category confusions and mismatched agendas can sometimes spark progressive alliances.

19 Li, *The Will to Improve*; Warren, "Mapping Common Futures"; Nancy Lee Peluso, Suraya Afiff, and Noer Fauzi Rachman, "Claiming."

20 Maria Elena Martinez-Torres and Peter M. Rosset, "La Via Campesina"; Saturnino Borras Jr., "The Politics of Transnational Agrarian Movements"; Marc Edelman, "Social Movements."

21 Fabian, "Remembering the Other," 66.

22 World Bank, "Land Policies."

23 See World Bank, *Agriculture for Development*; Tania Murray Li, "Exit from Agriculture."

24 On World Bank support for large-scale land acquisition for agriculture, see Deninger et al., *Rising Global Interest*. For critiques see Tania Murray Li, "Centering Labour"; Olivier De Schutter, "How Not to Think."

25 Credit and sharecropping systems among Bugis cacao farmers are described in François Ruf, Jamaluddin Yoddang, and Waris Ardhy, "The 'Spectacular' Efficiency."

26 Li, *The Will to Improve*; Tania Murray Li, "Compromising Power."

27 Government agencies using different criteria claim different land areas. When these are added the total can exceed the provincial land mass. See BPS, *Sulawesi Tengah Dalam Angka 2010*, 263–77.

28 BPS, *Sulawesi Tengah Dalam Angka 2010*, 279–80.

29 In 2009 oil palm was the main plantations crop (55,000 ha). Other commercial tree crops were grown mainly by smallholders. The most important were coconut (177,000 ha); clove (42,000 ha); and cacao (225,000 ha). BPS, *Sulawesi Tengah Dalam Angka 2010*, 267–75.

30 Li, "Centering Labour." Cacao needs around one worker per two hectares.

31 Breman, *Labour Migration*; Stoler, *Capitalism and Confrontation*.

32 Transmigration and Sulawesi oil palm plantations are discussed in Li, "Centering Labour"; Arianto Sangaji, "Transisi Kapital."

33 Jonathan Rigg, "Moving Lives"; Rachel Silvey and Rebecca Elmhirst, "Engendering Social Capital"; Johan Lindquist, *The Anxieties of Mobility*; Breman, *Labour Migration*, discuss the risks of border crossing and uneven access to jobs based on criteria of age, gender, ethnicity, location, and costs of transportation.

34 Diane Wolf, *Factory Daughters*.

35 The totals are 59 percent agriculture, 1 percent mining, 4 percent manufacture, 4 percent construction, and 32 percent in trade and services. See BPS, *Sulawesi Tengah Dalam Angka 2010*, 103.

36 "Petani Eksodus."

37 Reuters, "Indonesia's Sulawesi Cocoa Bean Exports Fall"; Reuters, "Indonesia Cocoa Output." By 2011, nearly every cacao field in the province had been struck by VSD and national production was down by 80 percent. See Ruslan Sangadji, "Crop Disease"; Riski Masuto and Suharto, "Reviving C. Sulawesi Cocoa's Glory"; "Indonesia Cocoa Exports."

38 In U.S. dollar values, copra, shrimp, nickel, and palm oil accounted for just 3 percent each, and wood products 1 percent. See BPS, *Sulawesi Tengah Dalam Angka 2010*, 325.

39 The price was 9,000/kg in 2006 and 21,000/kg in 2009. The clove price rose from Rp 37,000/kg in 2006 to Rp 47,000/kg in 2009. BPS, *Sulawesi Tengah Dalam Angka 2010*, 443–44.

40 Ruf, Ehret, and Yoddang, "Smallholder Cocoa," trace cacao's disease trajectory to explain why cacao declined in West Africa and boomed in Sulawesi after 1980. See

also François Ruf, "Current Cocoa Production," and Jessica Leeder, "Savour That Chocolate."

Conclusion

1. See special issues on land grabbing, green grabbing, biofuels, and frontiers of land control in *Journal of Peasant Studies* (volumes 37.4, 38.4, 39.2, 39.3–4). See also Hall, Hirsch, and Li, *Powers of Exclusion*; Ian G. Baird, "Land, Rubber"; Keith Barney, "Re-Encountering Resistance."
2. Rigg, "Land, Farming."
3. Jan Breman, "Slumlands"; Jan Breman, "Myth"; Jan Breman, *The Poverty Regime.*
4. David Harvey, *Justice, Nature,* discusses the limits of what he calls "militant particularism" in defense of locally defined places and the "global ambition" necessary to change the conditions that form these places.
5. Walker, *Thailand's Political Peasants.*
6. Michael Webber, "The Places of Accumulation"; Kathy Le Mons Walker, "From Covert to Overt."
7. Prabhat Patnaik, "A Left Approach"; Li, "To Make Live"; Partha Chatterjee, "Democracy." On the Maoist movement, see Alpa Shah, *In the Shadows of the State.*
8. "India Income Inequality."
9. Wendy Wolford, *This Land.*
10. Miguel Teubal, "Peasant Struggles," 157.
11. Nancy Postero, *Now We Are Citizens*; Sarah A. Radcliffe, "Development."
12. See Moore, *Suffering for Territory*; James Ferguson, "The Uses of Neoliberalism"; Ian Scoones et al., *Zimbabwe's Land Reform.*
13. Refusing complacency is the definition of "left" politics proposed by Zygmaunt Bauman, "Has the Future a Left?"
14. Patnaik, "A Left Approach."
15. Guy Standing, *The Precariat.*

Bibliography

Abercrombie, Nicholas, Stephen Hill, and Bryan S. Turner. *Sovereign Individuals of Capitalism*. London: Allen and Unwin, 1986.

Abercrombie, Nicholas, and Bryan S. Turner. "The Dominant Ideology Thesis." *British Journal of Sociology* 29, no. 2 (1978): 149–70.

Abu-Lughod, Lila. "Writing against Culture." In *Recapturing Anthropology: Working in the Present*, edited by Richard G. Fox, 137–62. Santa Fe, NM: School of American Research Press, 1991.

Agrawal, Arun. "Common Property Institutions and Sustainable Governance of Resources." *World Development* 29, no. 10 (2001): 1649–72.

Aguilar, Filomeno V. Jr. *Clash of Spirits: The History of Power and Sugar Planter Hegemony on a Visayan Island*. Honolulu: University of Hawai'i Press, 1998.

Akram-Lodhi, A. Haroon, and Cristobal Kay. "The Agrarian Question: Peasants and Rural Change." In *Peasants and Globalization: Political Economy, Rural Transformation, and the Agrarian Question*, edited by A. Haroon Akram-Lodhi and Cristobal Kay, 3–33. London: Routledge, 2009.

Akram-Lodhi, A. Haroon, and Cristobal Kay. "Surveying the Agarian Question (Part 1): Unearthing Foundations, Exploring Diversity." *Journal of Peasant Studies* 37, no. 1 (2010): 177–202.

Akram-Lodhi, A. Haroon, and Cristobal Kay. "Surveying the Agrarian Question (Part 2): Current Debates and Beyond." *Journal of Peasant Studies* 37, no. 2 (2010): 255–84.

Allen, John. *Lost Geographies of Power*. Oxford: Blackwell, 2003.

Anderson, Benedict. *Imagined Communities: Reflections on the Origin and Spread of Nationalism*. Revised and Extended Edition. London: Verso, 1991.

Aragon, Lorraine. "Communal Violence in Poso, Central Sulawesi: Where People Eat Fish and Fish Eat People." *Indonesia* 72 (2001): 45–80.

Aragon, Lorraine. *Fields of the Lord: Animism, Christian Minorities, and State Development in Indonesia*. Honolulu: University of Hawai'i Press, 2000.

Aspinall, Edward. "A Nation in Fragments." *Critical Asian Studies* 45, no. 1 (2013): 27–54.

Atkinson, Jane. *The Art and Politics of Wana Shamanship*. Berkeley: University of California Press, 1989.

Baird, Ian G. "Land, Rubber and People: Rapid Agrarian Changes and Responses in Southern Laos." *Journal of Lao Studies* 1, no. 1 (2010): 1–47.

Barney, Keith. "Re-Encountering Resistance: Plantation Activism and Smallholder Production in Thailand and Sarawak, Malaysia." *Asia Pacific Viewpoint* 45, no. 3 (2004): 325–39.

Bauman, Zygmaunt. "Has the Future a Left?" *Soundings* 35 (2007).

Bellwood, Peter. *Prehistory of the Indo-Malaysian Archipelago*. Revised Edition. Honolulu: University of Hawai'i Press, 1997.

Benda-Beckmann, Franz von. "Symbiosis of Indigenous and Western Law in Africa and Asia: An Essay in Legal Pluralism." In *European Expansion and Law: The Encounter of European and Indigenous Law in 19th and 20th Century Africa and Asia*, edited by W. J. Mommsen and J. A De Moor, 307–25. New York: Berg Publisher, 1992.

Benda-Beckmann, Franz von, and Keebet von Benda-Beckmann. "Myths and Stereotypes about Adat Law: A Reassessment of Van Vollenhoven in the Light of Current Struggles over Adat Law in Indonesia." *Bijdragen tot de Taal-, Land- en Volkenkunde* 167, no. 2–3 (2011): 167–95.

Bernstein, Henry. "'Changing before Our Very Eyes': Agrarian Questions and the Politics of Land in Capitalism Today." *Journal of Agrarian Change* 4, no. 1–2 (2004): 190–225.

Bernstein, Henry. *Class Dynamics of Agrarian Change*. Halifax, Nova Scotia, Canada: Fernwood Publishing, 2010.

Bernstein, Henry. "Concepts for the Analysis of Contemporary Peasantries." In *The Political Economy of Rural Development: Peasants, International Capital, and the State*, edited by Rosemary E. Galli, 3–24. Albany: State University of New York Press, 1981.

Berry, Sara. *No Condition Is Permanent: The Social Dynamics of Agrarian Change in Sub-Saharan Africa*. Madison: University of Wisconsin Press, 1993.

Bigalke, T. "Dynamics of the Torajan Slave Trade in South Sulawesi." In *Slavery, Bondage and Dependency in Southeast Asia*, edited by Anthony Reid, 341–63. St. Lucia: University of Queensland Press, 1983.

Bloch, Maurice, and Jonathan Parry. "Introduction: Money and the Morality of Exchange." In *Money and the Morality of Exchange*, edited by Maurice Bloch and Jonathan Parry, 1–32. Cambridge: Cambridge University Press, 1989.

Blomley, Nicholas. "Law, Property, and the Geography of Violence: The Frontier, the Survey, and the Grid." *Annals of the Association of American Geographers* 93, no. 1 (2003): 121–41.

Blomley, Nicholas. "Making Private Property: Enclosure, Common Right and the Work of Hedges." *Rural History* 18, no. 1 (2007): 1–21.

Boomgaard, Peter. "Introducing Environmental Histories of Indonesia." In *Paper Landscapes: Explorations in the Environmental History of Indonesia*, edited by Peter Boomgaard, Freek Colombijn, and David Henley, 1–26. Leiden, Netherlands: KITLV Press, 1997.

Boomgaard, Peter. "Maize and Tobacco in Upland Indonesia 1600–1940." In *Trans-*

forming the Indonesian Uplands: Marginality, Power and Production, edited by Tania Murray Li, 45–71. London: Routledge, 1999.
Borras, Saturnino Jr. "The Politics of Transnational Agrarian Movements." *Development and Change* 41, no. 5 (2010): 771–803.
Bourdieu, Pierre. *Outline of a Theory of Practice*. Translated by Richard Nice. Cambridge: Cambridge University Press, 1977.
BPS. *Sulawesi Tengah Dalam Angka 1993*. Palu: Badan Pusat Statistik, 1993.
BPS. *Sulawesi Tengah Dalam Angka 2010*. Palu: Badan Pusat Statistik, 2010.
Brass, Tom. "The Journal of Peasant Studies: The Third Decade." *Journal of Peasant Studies* 32, no. 1 (2005): 153–80.
Breman, Jan. *Labour Migration and Rural Transformation in Colonial Asia*. Amsterdam: Comparative Asian Studies, Free University Press, 1990.
Breman, Jan. "Myth of the Global Safety Net." *New Left Review* 59 (2009): 29–36.
Breman, Jan. *The Poverty Regime in Village India*. Oxford: Oxford University Press, 2007.
Breman, Jan. "Slumlands." *New Left Review* 40 (2006): 141–48.
Brenner, Robert. "Agrarian Class Structure and Economic Development in Pre-Industrial Europe." In *The Brenner Debate: Agrarian Class Structure and Economic Development in Pre-Industrial Europe*, edited by T. H. Alston and C. H. E. Philpin, 10–63. Cambridge: Cambridge University Press, 1985.
Bryceson, D., C. Kay, and J. Mooij, eds. *Disappearing Peasantries? Rural Labour in Africa, Asia and Latin America*. London: Intermediate Technologies Publications, 2000.
Burowoy, Michael. "The Extended Case Method." *Sociological Theory* 16, no. 1 (1998): 4–33.
Byres, Terence J. *Capitalism from above and Capitalism from Below: An Essay in Comparative Political Economy*. London: MacMillan Press, 1996.
Byres, Terence J. "Neo-Classical Neo-Populism 25 Years On: Déjà Vu and Déjà Passé. Towards a Critique." *Journal of Agrarian Change* 4, no. 1–2 (2004): 17–44.
Carrier, James. *Gifts and Commodities*. London: Routledge, 1995.
Chandrasekhar, C. P. "India: More Evidence of Jobless Growth." *Political Affairs*. July 30, 2011. http://politicalaffairs.net/india-more-evidence-of-jobless-growth/. Last accessed November 15, 2013.
Chanock, Martin. *Law, Custom and Social Order*. Cambridge: Cambridge University Press, 1985.
Chatterjee, Partha. "Democracy and Economic Transformation in India." *Economic and Political Weekly* (April 19, 2008): 53–62.
Cramb, R. A. *Land and Longhouse: Agrarian Transformation in the Uplands of Sarawak*. Copenhagen: NIAS Press, 2007.
Crehan, Kate. *Gramsci, Culture and Anthropolgy*. Berkeley: University of California, 2002.
Davidson, Jamie S., and David Henley, eds. *The Revival of Tradition in Indonesian Politics: The Deployment of Adat from Colonialism to Indigenism*. London: Routledge, 2012.
Davis, Mike. *Late Victorian Holocausts: El Niño Famines and the Making of the Third World*. London: Verso, 2002.
De Koninck, Rodolphe, and Jean-François Rousseau. *Gambling with the Land: The Contemporary Evolution of Southeast Asian Agriculture*. Singapore: National University of Singapore Press, 2012.

De Koninck, Rodolphe. "On the Geopolitics of Land Colonization: Order and Disorder on the Frontiers of Vietnam and Indonesia." *Mousson* 9–10 (2006): 33–59.

De Schutter, Olivier. "How Not to Think of Land-Grabbing: Three Critiques of Large-Scale Investments in Farmland." *Journal of Peasant Studies* 38, no. 2 (2011): 249–79.

Deninger, Klaus, Derek Byerlee, Jonathan Lindsay, Andrew Norton, Harris Selod, and Mercedes Stickler. *Rising Global Interest in Farmland: Can It Yield Sustainable and Equitable Benefits?* Washington, DC: The World Bank, 2011.

Donham, Donald L. "History at One Point in Time: 'Working Together' in Maale, 1975." *American Ethnologist* 12 (1985): 262–84.

Donham, Donald L. *History, Power, Ideology: Central Issues in Marxism and Anthropology.* New York: Cambridge University Press, 1990.

Doolittle, Amity A. *Property and Politics in Sabah, Malaysia: Native Struggles over Land Rights.* Seattle: University of Washington Press, 2005.

Dove, Michael. "The Agroecological Mythology of the Javanese and the Political Economy of Indonesia." *Indonesia*, no. 39 (1985): 1–35.

Dove, Michael. *The Banana Tree at the Gate.* New Haven, CT: Yale University Press, 2011.

Dove, Michael. "The Chayanov Slope in a Swidden Society." In *Chayanov, Peasants, and Economic Anthropology*, edited by E. P. Durrenberger, 97–132. New York: Academic Press, 1984.

Drayton, Richard. *Nature's Government: Science, Imperial Britain, and the "Improvement" of the World.* New Haven, CT: Yale University Press, 2000.

Edelman, Marc. "Social Movements: Changing Paradigms and Forms of Politics." *Annual Review of Anthropology* 30 (2001): 285–317.

Eilenberg, Michael. *At the Edges of States: Dynamics of State Formation in the Indonesian Borderlands.* Leiden, Netherlands: KITLV Press, 2012.

Elson, Robert. *The End of the Peasantry in Southeast Asia: A Social and Economic History of Peasant Livelihood.* London: MacMillan Press, 1997.

Errington, Shelly. "Recasting Sex, Gender and Power: A Theoretical and Regional Overview." In *Power and Difference: Gender in Island Southeast Asia*, edited by Jane Monnig Atkinson and Shelly Errington, 1–58. Stanford, CA: Stanford University Press, 1990.

Fabian, Johannes. "Remembering the Other: Knowledge and Recognition in the Exploration of Central Africa." *Critical Inquiry* 26 (1999): 49–69.

Fegan, Brian. "The Philippines: Agrarian Stagnation under a Decaying Regime." In *Agrarian Transformations: Local Processes and the State in Southeast Asia*, edited by Gillian Hart, Andrew Turton, and Benjamin White, 125–43. Berkeley: University of California Press, 1989.

Ferguson, James. "The Uses of Neoliberalism." *Antipode* 41, no. supplement 1 (2010): 166–84.

Ferguson, James, and Akhil Gupta. "Spatializing States: Towards an Ethnography of Neoliberal Governmentality." *American Ethnologist* 29, no. 4 (2002): 981–1002.

Fisher, William H. "Native Amazonians and the Making of the Amazon Wilderness: From Discourse of Riches and Sloth to Underdevelopment." In *Creating the Countryside: The Politics of Rural and Environmental Discourse*, edited by E. Melanie DuPuis and Peter Vandergeest, 166–203. Philadelphia: Temple University Press, 1996.

Fitzpatrick, Daniel. "Land, Custom and the State in Post-Suharto Indonesia: A Foreign Lawyer's Perspective." In *The Revival of Tradition in Indonesian Politics: The Deployment of Adat from Colonialism to Indigenism*, edited by Jamie S. Davidson and David Henley. London: Routledge, 2007.

Foucault, Michel. "Afterword: The Subject and Power." In *Michel Foucault: Beyond Structuralism and Hermeneutics*, edited by Hubert L Dreyfus and Paul Rabinow, 208–26. Brighton, UK: Harvester, 1982.

Fox, Jefferson, Yayoi Fujita, Dimbab Ngidang, Nancy Peluso, and Lesley Potter. "Policies, Political-Economy, and Swidden in Southeast Asia." *Human Ecology* 37, no. 3 (2009): 305–22.

Friedmann, Harriet. "Household Production and the National Economy: Concepts for the Analysis of Agrarian Formations." *Journal of Peasant Studies* 7, no. 2 (1980): 158–84.

Geertz, Clifford. *Agricultural Involution: The Processes of Ecological Change in Indonesia*. Berkeley: University of California Press, 1963.

Geiger, Danilo. "Turner in the Tropics: The Frontier Concept Revisited." In *Frontier Encounters: Indigenous Communities and Settlers in Asia and Latin America*, edited by Danilo Geiger, 75–216. Bern, Switzerland: Swiss National Centre of Competence in Research North-South, 2008.

Gibson, Thomas. "The Sharing of Substance Versus the Sharing of Activity among the Buid." *Man* 20, no. 3 (1985): 391–411.

Gidwani, Vinay. *Capital, Interrupted: Agrarian Development and the Politics of Work in India*. Minneapolis: University of Minnesota Press, 2008.

Glassman, Jim. "Primitive Accumulation, Accumulation by Dispossession, Accumulation by 'Extra-Economic' Means." *Progress in Human Geography* 30, no. 5 (2006): 608–25.

Gluckman, Max. *Analysis of a Social Situation in Modern Zululand*. Manchester, UK: Manchester University Press, 1958.

Gramsci, Antonio. *Selections from the Prison Notebooks of Antonio Gramsci*. Edited and translated by Quintin Hoare and Geoffrey Nowell Smith. London: Lawrence and Wishart, 1971.

Guggenheim, Scott. "Crises and Contradictions: Understanding the Origins of a Community Development Project in Indonesia." Jakarta: World Bank, 2004.

Gupta, Akhil, and James Ferguson. "Beyond 'Culture': Space, Identity, and the Politics of Difference." *Cultural Anthropology* 7, no. 1 (1992): 6–23.

Gupta, Akhil, and James Ferguson. "Discipline and Practice: 'The Field' as Site, Method, and Location in Anthropology." In *Anthropological Locations*, edited by Akhil Gupta and James Ferguson, 1–46. Berkeley: University of California Press, 1997.

Hall, Derek. "Land Grabs, Land Control, and Southeast Asian Crop Booms." *Journal of Peasant Studies* 38, no. 4 (2011): 811–31.

Hall, Derek. "Rethinking Primitive Accumulation: Theoretical Tensions and Rural Southeast Asian Complexities." *Antipode* 44, no. 4 (2012): 1188–208.

Hall, Derek, Philip Hirsch, and Tania Murray Li. *Powers of Exclusion: Land Dilemmas in Southeast Asia*. Honolulu: University of Hawai'i Press, 2011.

Hall, Stuart. "Marx's Notes on Method: A 'Reading' of the '1857 Introduction'." *Cultural Studies* 17, no. 2 (2003): 113–49.
Hall, Stuart. "New Ethnicities." In *Stuart Hall: Critical Dialogues in Cultural Studies*, edited by David Morley and Kuan-Hsing Chen, 441–49. London: Routledge, 1996.
Hall, Stuart. "On Postmodernism and Articulation: An Interview with Stuart Hall." In *Stuart Hall: Critical Dialogues in Cultural Studies*, edited by Lawrence Grossberg, David Morley, and Kuan-Hsing Chen, 131–50. London: Routledge, 1996.
Hall, Stuart, and Les Black. "At Home and Not at Home: Stuart Hall in Conversation with Les Black." *Cultural Studies* 23, no. 4 (2009): 658–87.
Haraway, Donna. "Situated Knowledges: The Science Question in Feminism and the Privilege of Partial Perspectives." *Feminist Studies* 14, no. 3 (1988): 575–99.
Harris, Olivia, and Kate Young. "Engendered Structures: Some Problems in the Analysis of Reproduction." In *The Anthropology of Pre-Capitalist Societies*, edited by Joel S. Kahn and Josep R. Llobera, 109–47. London: MacMillan Press, 1981.
Hart, Gillian. "Agrarian Change in the Context of State Patronage." In *Agrarian Transformations: Local Processes and the State in Southeast Asia*, edited by Gillian Hart, Andrew Turton, and Benjamin White, 31–49. Berkeley: University of California Press, 1989.
Hart, Gillian. "Denaturalizing Dispossession: Critical Ethnography in the Age of Resurgent Imperialism." *Antipode* 38, no. 5 (2006): 977–1004.
Hart, Gillian. *Disabling Globalization: Places of Power in Post-Apartheid South Africa*. Berkeley: University of California Press, 2002.
Hart, Gillian. "Geography and Development: Critical Ethnographies." *Progress in Human Geography* 28, no. 1 (2004): 91–100.
Harvey, David. *Justice, Nature and the Geography of Difference*. Cambridge: Blackwell Publishers, 1996.
Harvey, David. *The New Imperialism*. Oxford: Oxford University Press, 2003.
Hefner, Robert. *The Political Economy of Mountain Java: An Interpretive History*. Berkeley: University of California Press, 1990.
Henley, David. "Credit and Debt in Indonesian History: An Introduction." In *Credit and Debt in Indonesia, 860–1930*, edited by David Henley and Peter Boomgaard, 1–40. Singapore: ISEAS Publishing, 2009.
Henley, David. *Fertility, Food and Fever: Population, Economy and Environment in North and Central Sulawesi, 1600–1930*. Leiden, Netherlands: KITLV, 2005.
Henley, David. *Jealousy and Justice: The Indigenous Roots of Colonial Rule in Northern Sulawesi*. Amsterdam: VU University Press, 2002.
Henley, David. "Swidden Farming as an Agent of Environmental Change: Ecological Myth and Historical Reality in Indonesia." *Environment and History* 17 (2011): 525–54.
Hill, Polly. *The Migrant Cocoa-Farmers of Southern Ghana: A Study in Rural Capitalism*. Cambridge: Cambridge University Press, 1963.
Hirschman, Albert O. *Exit, Voice, and Loyalty: Responses to Decline in Firms, Organizations, and States*. Cambridge, MA: Harvard University Press, 1970.
Holsey, Bayo. *Routes of Remembrance: Refashioning the Slave Trade in Ghana*. Chicago: University of Chicago Press, 2008.

HRW. "Breakdown: Four Years of Communal Violence in Central Sulawesi." New York: Human Rights Watch, 2002.

Hugo, Graeme. "Indonesia's Labor Looks Abroad." *Migration Information Source*, April 2007. http://www.migrationinformation.org/feature/display.cfm?ID=594. Last accessed on November 15, 2013.

Husken, Frans. "Cycles of Commercialization and Accumulation in a Central Javanese Village." In *Agrarian Transformations: Local Processes and the State in Southeast Asia*, edited by Gillian Hart, Andrew Turton, and Benjamin White, 303–31. Berkeley: University of California Press, 1989.

ILO. *Global Employment Trends 2013: Recovering from a Second Jobs Dip*. Geneva: ILO, 2013.

"India income inequality doubles in twenty years, says OECD," July 12, 2011, http://www.bbc.co.uk/news/world-asia-india-16064321. Last accessed November 18, 2013.

"Indonesia Cocoa Exports Fall for 8th Month." *Jakarta Globe*, February 16, 2011. http://www.thejakartaglobe.com/archive/indonesia-cocoa-exports-fall-for-8th-month/. Last accessed November 15, 2013.

"Jobless Growth." *The Economist*, June 3, 2010.

Kahn, Joel. "Culturalizing the Indonesian Uplands." In *Transforming the Indonesian Uplands: Marginality, Power and Production*, edited by Tania Murray Li, 79–103. London: Routledge, 1999.

Kahn, Joel. "Peasant Political Consciousness in West Sumatra: A Reanalysis of the Communist Uprising of 1927." In *History and Peasant Consciousness in South East Asia*, edited by Andrew Turton and Shigeharu Tanabe, 293–326. Osaka: National Museum of Ethnology, 1984.

Kalb, Don. *Expanding Class: Power and Everyday Politics in Industrial Communities, the Netherlands, 1850–1950*. Durham, NC: Duke University Press, 1997.

Kalb, Don, and Herman Tak. *Critical Junctions: Anthropology and History Beyond the Cultural Turn*. Oxford: Berghahn Books, 2005.

Kanbur, Ravi. "Economic Policy, Distribution and Poverty: The Nature of Disagreements." *World Development* 29, no. 6 (2001): 1083–94.

Knapen, Han. "Epidemics, Drought and Other Uncertainties in Southeast Borneo During the Eighteenth and Nineteenth Centuries." In *Paper Landscapes: Explorations in the Environmental History of Indonesia*, edited by Peter Boomgaard, Freek Colombijn, and David Henley, 121–52. Leiden, Netherlands: KITLV Press, 1997.

Koning, Juliette, and Frans Husken, eds. *Ropewalking and Safety Nets: Local Ways of Managing Insecurities in Indonesia*. Leiden, Netherlands: Brill, 2006.

Kratoska, Paul H. "The Peripatetic Peasant and Land Tenure in British Malaya." *Journal of Southeast Asian Studies* 16, no. 1 (1985): 16–45.

Kuper, Adam. *The Invention of Primitive Society: Transformations of an Illusion*. London: Routledge, 1988.

Latour, Bruno. *We Have Never Been Modern*. Cambridge, MA: Harvard University Press, 1993.

Leeder, Jessica. "Savour That Chocolate While You Can Still Afford It." *Globe and Mail*, February 11, 2011.

Lefebvre, Henri. *The Production of Space*. Translated by Donald Nicholson-Smith. Oxford: Basil Blackwell, 1991 [1974].

Lehman, F. K. L Chit Hlaing. "The Relevance of the Founders' Cult for Understanding the Political Systems of the Peoples of Northern Southeast Asia and Its Chinese Borderlands." In *Founders' Cults in Southeast Asia: Ancestors, Polity, and Identity*, edited by Nicola Tannenbaum and Cornelia Ann Kammerer, 15–39. New Haven, CT: Yale University Press, 2003.

Lenin, Vladimir Ilich. *The Development of Capitalism in Russia*. Moscow: Progress Publishers, 1964 [1899].

Levang, Patrice. "From Rags to Riches in Sumatra: How Peasants Shifted from Food Self-Sufficiency to Market-Oriented Tree Crops in Six Years." *Bulletin of Concerned Asian Scholars* 29, no. 2 (1997): 18–30.

Li, Tania Murray. "Articulating Indigenous Identity in Indonesia: Resource Politics and the Tribal Slot." *Comparative Studies in Society and History* 42, no. 1 (2000): 149–79.

Li, Tania Murray. "Centering Labour in the Land Grab Debate." *Journal of Peasant Studies* 38, no. 2 (2011): 281–98.

Li, Tania Murray. "Compromising Power: Development, Culture and Rule in Indonesia." *Cultural Anthropology* 14, no. 3 (1999): 1–28.

Li, Tania Murray. "Exit from Agriculture: A Step Forward or a Step Backward for the Rural Poor?" *Journal of Peasant Studies* 36, no. 3 (2009): 629–36.

Li, Tania Murray. "Indigeneity, Capitalism, and the Management of Dispossession." *Current Anthropology* 51, no. 3 (2010): 385–414.

Li, Tania Murray. "Marginality, Power and Production: Analysing Upland Transformations." In *Transforming the Indonesian Uplands: Marginality, Power and Production*, edited by Tania Murray Li, 1–44. London: Routledge, 1999.

Li, Tania Murray. "Masyarakat Adat, Difference, and the Limits of Recognition in Indonesia's Forest Zone." *Modern Asian Studies* 35, no. 3 (2001): 645–76.

Li, Tania Murray. "Practices of Assemblage and Community Forest Management." *Economy and Society* 36, no. 2 (2007): 264–94.

Li, Tania Murray. "Relational Histories and the Production of Difference on Sulawesi's Upland Frontier." *Journal of Asian Studies* 60, no. 1 (2001): 41–66.

Li, Tania Murray. "To Make Live or Let Die? Rural Dispossession and the Protection of Surplus Populations." *Antipode* 41, no. s1 (2010): 63–93.

Li, Tania Murray, ed. *Transforming the Indonesian Uplands: Marginality, Power and Production*. London: Routledge, 1999.

Li, Tania Murray. *The Will to Improve: Governmentality, Development, and the Practice of Politics*. Durham, NC: Duke University Press, 2007.

Li, Tania Murray. "Working Separately but Eating Together: Personhood, Property, and Power in Conjugal Relations." *American Ethnologist* 25, no. 4 (1998): 675–94.

Li, Victor. "Marshall Sahlins and the Apotheosis of Culture." *CR: The New Centennial Review* 1, no. 3 (2001): 201–88.

Lindquist, Johan. *The Anxieties of Mobility: Development and Migration in the Indonesian Borderlands*. Honolulu: University of Hawai'i Press, 2009.

Lund, Christian. *Local Politics and the Dynamics of Property in Africa*. Cambridge: Cambridge University Press, 2008.

MacPherson, C. B. *The Political Theory of Possessive Individualism: Hobbes to Locke*. Oxford: Clarendon/Oxford University Press, 1962.

Manning, Chris, and Sudarno Sumarto, eds. *Employment, Living Standards and Poverty in Contemporary Indonesia*. Singapore: ISEAS, 2011.
Markoff, John. "Skilled Work, without the Worker: New Robots Change Industry." *New York Times*, August 26, 2012.
Marston, Sallie A., Keith Woodward, and John Paul Jones. "Flattening Ontologies of Globalization: The Nollywood Case." *Globalizations* 4, no. 1 (2007): 45–63.
Marsuto, Riski, and Suharto. "Reviving C. Sulawesi Cocoa's Glory." Antara News. February 12, 2012. http://www.antaranews.com/en/news/80125/reviving-c-sulawesi-cocoas-glory. Last accessed November 15, 2013.
Martinez-Torres, Maria Elena, and Peter M. Rosset. "La Via Campesina: The Birth and Evolution of a Transnational Social Movement." *Journal of Peasant Studies* 37, no. 1 (2010): 149–75.
Marx, Karl. *Capital: A Critique of Political Economy*. Vol. 1. Moscow: Progress Publishers, 1986 [1867].
Marx, Karl. *Economic and Philosophical Manuscripts of 1844*. Moscow: Progress Publishers, 1959.
Massey, Doreen. "Power Geometry and a Progressive Sense of Place." In *Mapping the Futures: Local Cultures, Global Change*, edited by J. Bird, B. Curtis, T. Putnam, G. Robertson and L. Tickner, 59–69. London: Routledge, 1993.
Mauss, Marcel. *The Gift*. London: Cohen and West, 1954 [1923].
McCarthy, John. *The Fourth Circle: A Political Ecology of Sumatra's Rainforest Frontier*. Stanford, CA: Stanford University Press, 2006.
Mertz, Ole, Christine Padoch, Jefferson Fox, R. A. Cramb, and Stephen J. Leisz. "Swidden Change in Southeast Asia: Understanding Causes and Consequences." *Human Ecology* 37, no. 3 (2009): 259–64.
Michon, Genevieve, Hubert de Foresta, Kusworo, and Patrice Levang. "The Damar Agroforests of Krui, Indonesia: Justice for Forest Farmers." In *People, Plants and Justice: The Politics of Nature Conservation*, edited by Charles Zerner, 159–203. New York: Columbia University Press, 2000.
Mintz, Sidney. "The Rural Proletariat and the Problem of Rural Proletarian Consciousness." *Journal of Peasant Studies* 1, no.3 (1974): 291–325.
Mintz, Sidney. *Sweetness and Power: The Place of Sugar in Modern History*. New York: Penguin Books, 1986.
Mitchell, Timothy. *Rule of Experts: Egypt, Technopolitics, Modernity*. Berkeley: University of California Press, 2002.
Moore, Donald S. "Subaltern Struggles and the Politics of Place: Remapping Resistance in Zimbabwe's Eastern Highlands." *Cultural Anthropology* 13, no. 3 (1998): 1–38.
Moore, Donald S. *Suffering for Territory: Race, Place, and Power in Zimbabwe*. Durham, NC: Duke University Press, 2005.
Moore, Sally Falk. *Social Facts and Fabrications: "Customary" Law on Kilimanjaro, 1880–1980*. Cambridge: Cambridge University Press, 1986.
Narotzky, Susana, and Gavin Smith. *Immediate Struggles: People, Power, and Place in Rural Spain*. Berkeley: University of California Press, 2006.
Neilson, Jeff. "Global Markets, Farmers and the State: Sustaining Profits in the In-

donesian Cocoa Sector." *Bulletin of Indonesian Economic Studies* 43, no. 2 (2007): 227–50.

Netting, Robert McC. *Smallholders, Householders: Farm Families and the Ecology of Intensive, Sustainable Agriculture*. Stanford, CA: Stanford University Press, 1993.

Nourse, Jennifer. *Conceiving Spirits: Birth Rituals and Contested Identities among Lauje of Indonesia*. Washington, DC: Smithsonian Institution Press, 1999.

Nugent, David, ed. *Locating Capitalism in Time and Space*. Stanford, CA: Stanford University Press, 2002.

Oki, Akira. "The Dynamics of Subsistence Economy in West Sumatra." In *History and Peasant Consciousness in South East Asia*, edited by Andrew Turton and Shigeharu Tanabe, 267–92. Osaka, Japan: National Museum of Ethnology, 1984.

Otsuka, Keijiro, and Agnes R. Quisumbing. "Land Rights and Natural Resource Management in the Transition to Individual Ownership: Case Studies from Ghana and Indonesia." In *Access to Land, Rural Poverty, and Public Action*, edited by Alain de Janvry, Jean-Philippe Platteau, Gustavo Gordillo, and Elisabeth Sadoulet, 97–128. Oxford: Oxford University Press, 2001.

Oya, Carlos. "The World Development Report 2008: Inconsistencies, Silences, and the Myth of 'Win-Win' Scenarios." *Journal of Peasant Studies* 36, no. 3 (2009): 593–601.

Padoch, Christine, and Nancy Lee Peluso. "Borneo People and Forests in Transition: An Introduction." In *Borneo in Transition: People, Forests, Conservation, and Development*, edited by Christine Padoch and Nancy Lee Peluso, 1–12. Kuala Lumpur: Oxford University Press, 1996.

Papenek, Gustav F. Indonesia's Hidden Problem: Jobless Growth. Lecture presented at the Bank of Indonesia, Jakarta, August 11, 2011. https://crawford.anu.edu.au/acde/ip/pdf/lpem/2011/Papanek_2011.pdf. Last accessed November 15, 2013.

Patnaik, Prabhat. "A Left Approach to Development." *Pragoti*, August 3, 2010, http://www.pragoti.in/node/4082. Last accessed on November 15, 2013.

Peluso, Nancy Lee. "Fruit Trees and Family Trees in an Anthropogenic Forest: Ethics of Access, Property Zones, and Environmental Change in Indonesia." *Comparative Studies in Society and History* 38, no. 3 (1996): 510–48.

Peluso, Nancy Lee. "Whose Woods Are These? Counter-Mapping Forest Territories in Kalimantan, Indonesia." *Antipode* 27, no. 4 (1995): 383–406.

Peluso, Nancy Lee, Suraya Afiff, and Noer Fauzi Rachman. "Claiming the Grounds for Reform: Agrarian and Environmental Movements in Indonesia." *Journal of Agrarian Change* 8, no. 2 (2008): 377–408.

Perelman, Michael. *The Invention of Capitalism: Classical Political Economy and the Secret History of Primitive Accumulation*. Durham, NC: Duke University Press, 2000.

"Petani Eksodus Karena Produksi Kakao Anjlok." *Media Alchairat*, November 11, 2008. Last accessed November 18, 2013.

Pincus, Jonathan. *Class Power and Agrarian Change: Land and Labour in Rural West Java*. London: MacMillan Press, 1996.

Ploeg, Jan Douwe van der. "The Peasantries of the Twenty-First Century: The Commoditisation Debate Revisited." *Journal of Peasant Studies* 37, no. 1 (2010): 1–30.

Polanyi, Karl. *The Great Transformation*. Boston: Beacon Press, 1957 [1944].

Postero, Nancy. *Now We Are Citizens: Indigenous Politics in Postmulticultural Bolivia*. Stanford, CA: Stanford University Press, 2006.

Povinelli, Elizabeth. *Economies of Abandonment: Social Belonging and Endurance in Late Liberalism*. Durham, NC: Duke University Press, 2011.

Pred, Allan, and Michael John Watts. *Reworking Modernity: Capitalism and Symbolic Discontent*. New Brunswick, NJ: Rutgers University Press, 1992.

Radcliffe, Sarah A. "Development for a Postneoliberal Era? Sumak Kawsay, Living Well and the Limits to Decolonization in Ecuador." *Geoforum* 43, no. 2 (2012): 240–49.

Raffles, Hugh. *In Amazonia: A Natural History*. Princeton, NJ: Princeton University Press, 2002.

Read, Jason. "Primitive Accumulation: The Aleatory Foundations of Capitalism." *Rethinking Marxism* 14, no. 2 (2002): 24–49.

Reid, Anthony. "Inside Out: The Colonial Displacement of Sumatra's Population." In *Paper Landscapes: Explorations in the Environmental History of Indonesia*, edited by Peter Boomgaard, Freek Colombijn, and David Henley, 61–89. Leiden, Netherlands: KITLV Press, 1997.

Reid, Anthony, ed. *Slavery, Bondage, and Dependency in Southeast Asia*. New York: University of Queensland Press, 1983.

Reuters. "Indonesia Cocoa Output May Drop to 'Critical Level.'" September 15, 2008. http://www.flex-news-food.com/console/PageViewer.aspx?page=19082&print=yes.

Reuters. "Indonesia's Sulawesi Cocoa Ben Exports Fall 10 Pct in 2008." January 1, 2009. http://www.flex-news-food.com/console/PageViewer.aspx?page=21389&print=yes.

Ribot, Jesse C., and Nancy Lee Peluso. "A Theory of Access." *Rural Sociology* 68, no. 2 (2003): 153–81.

Rigg, Jonathan. "Land, Farming, Livelihoods, and Poverty: Rethinking the Links in the Rural South." *World Development* 34, no. 1 (2006): 180–202.

Rigg, Jonathan. "Moving Lives: Migration and Livelihoods in the Lao PDR." *Population, Space and Place* 13 (2007): 163–78.

Rigg, Jonathan, and Peter Vandergeest, eds. *Revisiting Rural Places: Pathways to Poverty and Prosperity in Southeast Asia*. Honolulu: University of Hawai'i Press, 2012.

Rocheleau, Dianne, and Laurie Ross. "Trees as Tools, Trees as Text: Struggles over Resources in Zambrana-Chacuey, Dominican Republic." *Antipode* 24, no. 4 (1995): 407–28.

Roseberry, William. *Anthropologies and Histories: Essays in Culture, History, and Political Economy*. New Brunswick, NJ: Rutgers University Press, 1989.

Roseberry, William. "Hegemony, Power, and Languages of Contention." In *The Politics of Difference: Ethnic Premises in a World of Power*, edited by Edwin N. Wilmsen and Patrick McAllister, 71–84. Chicago: University of Chicago Press, 1996.

Roseberry, William. "Rent, Differentiation, and the Development of Capitalism among Peasants." *American Anthropologist* 78, no. 1 (1976): 45–58.

Ruf, François. "Current Cocoa Production and Opportunities for Re-Investment in the Rural Sector, Côte D'ivoire, Ghana and Indonesia." Paper presented at *World Cocoa Foundation Meeting*, Amsterdam, May 23–24, 2007. Washington: World Cocoa.

Ruf, François, Pierre Ehret, and Yoddang. "Smallholder Cocoa in Indonesia: Why a Cocoa Boom in Sulawesi?" In *Cocoa Pioneer Fronts since 1800: The Role of Smallholders, Planters and Merchants*, edited by William Gervase Clarence-Smith, 212–31. London: MacMillan, 1996.

Ruf, François, and Yoddang. "The Cocoa Marketing Sector in Sulawesi: A Free Market and 'Almost Perfect' Competition." *Plantations, Recherche, Developpement* (1998): 170–75.

Ruf, François, and Yoddang. "The Sulawesi Cocoa Boom and Its Crises." *Plantations, Recherche, Developpement* (July–August 1999): 248–53.

Ruf, François, Jamaluddin Yoddang, and Waris Ardhy. "The 'Spectacular' Efficiency of Cocoa Smallholders in Sulawesi: Why? Until When?" In *Cocoa Cycles: The Economics of Cocoa Supply*, edited by François Ruf and P. S. Siswoputranto, 339–74. Cambridge, UK: Woodhead Publishing, 1995.

Sahlins, Marshall. *Culture in Practice*. New York: Zone Books, 2000.

Saifullah, Agus. "Indonesia's Rice Policy and Price Stabilization Programme: Managing Domestic Prices During the 2008 Crisis." In *The Rice Crisis: Markets, Policies and Food Security*, edited by David Dawe, 109–22. London: FAO/Earthscan, 2010.

Sangadji, Ruslan. "Crop Disease Devastates Cacao Farms in Central Sulawesi." *Jakarta Post*, February 2, 2011.

Sangaji, Arianto. "Transisi Kapital Di Sulawesi Tengah: Pengalaman Industri Perkebunan Sawit." *Kertas Posisi* 08 (2009), Yayasan Tanah Merdeka, Palu, Central Sulawesi.

Sayer, Andrew. "Approaching Moral Economy." In *The Moralization of the Markets*, edited by Christoph Henning, Nico Stehr, and Bernd Weiler, 77–98. New Brunswick, NJ: Transaction Books, 2006.

Schrauwers, Albert. "Houses, Hierarchy, Headhunting and Exchange: Rethinking Political Relations in the Southeast Asian Realm of Luwu." *Bijdragen tot de Taal-, Land- en Volkenkunde* 153, no. 3 (1997): 311–35.

Schrieke, B. *Indonesian Sociological Studies*. Vol. 1. The Hague, Netherlands: W. van Hoeve, 1955.

Schroeder, Richard. "Community, Forestry and Conditionality in the Gambia." *Africa* 69, no. 1 (1999): 1–22.

Scoones, Ian et al. *Zimbabwe's Land Reform: Myths and Realities*. London: James Currey, 2010.

Scott, David. *Conscripts of Modernity: The Tragedy of Colonial Enlightenment*. Durham, NC: Duke University Press, 2004.

Scott, James C. *The Art of Not Being Governed: An Anarchist History of Upland Southeast Asia*. New Haven, CT: Yale University Press, 2009.

Scott, James C. *The Moral Economy of the Peasant*. New Haven, CT: Yale University Press, 1976.

Scott, James C. *Seeing Like a State: How Certain Schemes to Improve the Human Condition Have Failed*. New Haven, CT: Yale University Press, 1998.

Scott, James C. *Weapons of the Weak: Everyday Forms of Peasant Resistance*. New Haven, CT: Yale University Press, 1985.

Sen, Amartya. *Poverty and Famines: An Essay on Entitlement and Deprivation*. Oxford: Oxford University Press, 1981.

Shah, Alpa. *In the Shadows of the State: Indigenous Politics, Environmentalism, and Insurgency in Jharkhand, India*. Durham, NC: Duke University Press, 2010.

Sider, Gerald. *Culture and Class in Anthropology and History*. Cambridge: Cambridge University Press, 1986.

Sider, Gerald. "When Parrots Learn to Talk, and Why They Can't: Domination, Deception, and Self-Deception in Indian-White Relations." *Comparative Studies in Society and History* 29 (1987): 3–23.

Sikor, Thomas. "Conflicting Concepts: Contested Land Relations in North-Western Vietnam." *Conservation and Society* 2, no. 1 (2004): 75–96.

Sikor, Thomas, and Christian Lund. "Access and Property: A Question of Power and Authority." In *Politics of Possession: Property, Authority, and Access to Natural Resources*, edited by Thomas Sikor and Christian Lund, 1–22. London: Blackwell, 2010.

Sikor, Thomas, Nghiem Phuong Tuyen, Jennifer Sowerwine, and Jeff Romm, eds. *Upland Transformations in Vietnam*. Singapore: National University of Singapore, 2011.

Silvey, Rachel, and Rebecca Elmhirst. "Engendering Social Capital: Women Workers and Rural-Urban Networks in Indonesia's Crisis." *World Development* 31, no. 5 (2003): 865–81.

Smith, Gavin. *Confronting the Present: Towards a Politically Engaged Anthropology*. Oxford, UK: Berg, 1999.

Smith, Gavin. "Hegemony: Critical Interpretations in Anthropology and Beyond." *Focaal* 43, no. 2004 (2004): 99–120.

Smith, Gavin. *Livelihood and Resistance: Peasants and the Politics of Land in Peru*. Berkeley: University of California Press, 1989.

Smith, Gavin. "Reflections on the Social Relations of Simple Commodity Production." *Journal of Peasant Studies* 13, no. 1 (1985): 99–108.

Smith, Gavin. "Selective Hegemony and Beyond-Populations with 'No Productive Function': A Framework for Enquiry." *Identities* 18, no. 1 (2011): 2–38.

Standing, Guy. *The Precariat: The New Dangerous Class*. London: Bloomsbury Academic, 2011.

Stoler, Ann Laura. *Capitalism and Confrontation in Sumatra's Plantation Belt, 1870–1979*. Second edition with a new preface. Ann Arbor: University of Michigan Press, 1995.

Suryanata, Krisnawati. "From Home Gardens to Fruit Gardens: Resource Stabilization and Rural Differentiation in Upland Java." In *Transforming the Indonesian Uplands: Marginality, Power and Production*, edited by Tania Murray Li, 257–78. London: Routledge, 1999.

Teubal, Miguel. "Peasant Struggles for Land and Agrarian Reform in Latin America." In *Peasants and Globalization: Political Economy, Rural Transformation, and the Agrarian Question*, edited by A. Haroon Akram-Lodhi and Cristobal Kay, 148–66. London: Routledge, 2009.

Thomas, Nicholas. *Entangled Objects*: Cambridge, MA: Harvard University Press, 1991.

Thompson, E. P. *The Making of the English Working Class*. Harmondsworth, UK: Penguin Books, 1982.

Tsing, Anna Lowenhaupt. *Friction: An Ethnography of Global Connection*. Princeton, NJ: Princeton University Press, 2005.

Tsing, Anna Lowenhaupt. *In the Realm of the Diamond Queen: Marginality in an Out-of-the-Way Place*. Princeton, NJ: Princeton University Press, 1993.

Tsing, Anna Lowenhaupt. "Land as Law: Negotiating the Meaning of Property in Indonesia." In *Land, Property, and the Environment*, edited by F. Richards, 94–137. Berkeley: University of California Press, 2002.

Tsing, Anna Lowenhaupt. "Politics and Culture in the Meratus Mountains." Doctoral Dissertation, Stanford University, 1984.

Turton, Andrew, ed. *Civility and Savagery: Social Identity in Tai States*. Richmond, UK: Curzon, 2000.

Turton, Andrew. "Local Powers and Rural Differentiation." In *Agrarian Transformations: Local Processes and the State in Southeast Asia*, edited by Gillian Hart, Andrew Turton, and Benjamin White, 70–97. Berkeley: University of California Press, 1989.

van Hoëvell, G. W. W. C. Baron. "Korte Beschrijving Van Het Rijke Mooeton [Bocht Van Tomini] (A Short Description of the Kingdom of Mouton [Bay of Tomini]." *Tijdscrift van het Koninklijk Nederlandsch Aardrijkskundig Genootschaap* (Second series) 9 (1892): 349–60.

Vandergeest, Peter. "Gifts and Rights: Cautionary Notes on Community Self-Help in Thailand." *Development and Change* 22 (1991): 421–43.

Velthoen, Esther J. "'Wanderers, Robbers and Bad Folk': The Politics of Violence, Protection and Trade in Eastern Sulawesi 1750–1850." In *The Last Stand of Asian Autonomies: Responses to Modernity in the Diverse States of Southeast Asia and Korea, 1750–1900*, edited by Anthony Reid, 367–88. New York: St. Martin's Press, 1997.

Villiers, John. "The Cash-Crop Economy and State Formation in the Spice Islands in the Fifteenth and Sixteenth Centuries." In *The Southeast Asian Port and Polity: Rise and Demise*, edited by J. Kathirithamby-Wells and John Villiers, 83–105. Singapore: Singapore University Press, 1990.

Walker, Andrew. "'Now the Companies Have Come': Local Values and Contract Farming in Northern Thailand." In *Agrarian Angst and Rural Resistance in Contemporary Southeast Asia*, edited by Dominique Caoutte and Sarah Turner, 61–82. Abingdon, UK: Routledge, 2009.

Walker, Andrew. *Thailand's Political Peasants: Power in the Modern Rural Economy*. Madison: University of Wisconsin Press, 2012.

Walker, Kathy Le Mons. "From Covert to Overt: Everyday Peasant Politics in China and the Implications for Transnational Agrarian Movements." *Journal of Agrarian Change* 8, no. 2–3 (2008): 462–88.

Warren, Carol. "Mapping Common Futures: Customary Communities, NGOs and the State in Indonesia's Reform Era." *Development and Change* 36, no. 1 (2005): 49–73.

Warren, James Frances. "Trade, Slave Raiding and State Formation in the Sulu Sultanate in the Nineteenth Century." In *The Southeast Asian Port and Polity: Rise and Demise*, edited by J. Kathirithamby-Wells and John Villiers, 187–212. Singapore: Singapore University Press, 1990.

Waterson, Roxana. *Paths and Rivers: Sa'adan Toraja Society in Transformation*. Leiden, Netherlands: KITLV Press, 2009.

Watts, Michael. *Silent Violence: Food, Famine, and Peasantry in Northern Nigeria*. Berkeley: University of California Press, 1983.

Watts, Michael. "The Southern Question: Agrarian Questions of Labour and Capital." In *Peasants and Globalization: Political Economy, Rural Transformation, and the Agrarian Question*, edited by A. Haroon Akram-Lodhi and Cristobal Kay, 262–87. London: Routledge, 2009.

Webber, Michael. "The Places of Accumulation in Rural China." *Economic Geography* 84, no. 4 (2008): 395–421.

White, Benjamin. "'Agricultural Involution' and Its Critics: Twenty Years After." *Bulletin of Concerned Asian Scholars* 15, no. 2 (1983): 18–31.

White, Benjamin. "Problems in the Empirical Analysis of Agrarian Differentiation." In *Agrarian Transformations: Local Processes and the State in Southeast Asia*, edited by Gillian Hart, Andrew Turton, and Benjamin White, 15–30. Berkeley: University of California Press, 1989.

White, Benjamin Paul Alexander, and Peter Boomgaard, eds. *In the Shadow of Agriculture: Non-Farm Activities in the Javanese Economy, Past and Present*. Amsterdam: Rural Tropical Insitute, 1991.

Whitehead, Ann. "'I'm Hungry, Mum': The Politics of Domestic Budgeting." In *Of Marriage and the Market*, edited by Kate Young, Carol Wolkowitz, and Roslyn McCullough, 93–115. London: Routledge and Kegan Paul, 1981.

Williams, Raymond. *Marxism and Literature*. Oxford: Oxford University Press, 1977.

Wolf, Diane. *Factory Daughters: Gender, Household Dynamics, and Rural Industrialization in Java*. Berkeley: University of California Press, 1994.

Wolf, Eric. *Europe and the People without History*. Berkeley: University of California Press, 1997 [1982].

Wolf, Eric. *Peasant Wars of the Twentieth Century*. New York: Harper and Row, 1969.

Wolf, Eric. "Types of Latin American Peasantry: A Preliminary Discussion." *American Anthropologist* 57 (1955): 452–71.

Wolford, Wendy. "Land Reform in the Time of Neoliberalism: A Many-Splendored Thing." *Antipode* 39, no. 3 (2007): 570–90.

Wolford, Wendy. *This Land Is Ours Now: Social Mobilization and the Meanings of Land in Brazil*. Durham, NC: Duke University Press, 2010.

Wood, Ellen Meiksins. *The Origin of Capitalism: A Longer View*. London: Verso, 2002.

World Bank. *Agriculture for Development: World Development Report*. Washington, DC: World Bank, 2008.

World Bank. *Indonesia Jobs Report: Towards Better Jobs and Security for All*. Jakarta: World Bank, 2010.

World Bank. "Kecamatan Development Program Phase One: Final Report 1998–2002." Jakarta: Ministry of Home Affairs and World Bank, 2002.

World Bank. "Land Policies for Growth and Poverty Reduction." Washington, DC: World Bank, 2003.

Yanagisako, Sylvia Junko. *Producing Culture and Capital: Family Firms in Italy*. Princeton, NJ: Princeton University Press, 2002.

Index